FLAWLESS

FLAWLESS

INSIDE THE LARGEST DIAMOND HEIST IN HISTORY

SCOTT ANDREW SELBY
and GREG CAMPBELL

UNION SQUARE PRESS
An imprint of Sterling Publishing Co., Inc.

New York / London
www.sterlingpublishing.com

STERLING and the distinctive Sterling logo are registered trademarks of Sterling Publishing Co., Inc.

Library of Congress Cataloging-in-Publication Data

Selby, Scott Andrew.
Flawless : inside the largest diamond heist in history / by Scott Andrew Selby and Greg Campbell.
p. cm.
Includes bibliographical references and index.
ISBN 978-1-4027-6651-0
1. Robbery–Belgium–Antwerp–Case studies. 2. Jewelry theft–Belgium–Antwerp–Case studies. 3. Diamond industry and trade–Belgium–Antwerp. I. Campbell, Greg. II. Title.
HV6665.B422003 S45 2010
364.16'287362309493222–dc22

2009040766

2 4 6 8 10 9 7 5 3 1

Published by Sterling Publishing Co., Inc.
387 Park Avenue South, New York, NY 10016

Distributed in Canada by Sterling Publishing
c/o Canadian Manda Group, 165 Dufferin Street
Toronto, Ontario, Canada M6K 3H6
Distributed in the United Kingdom by GMC Distribution Services
Castle Place, 166 High Street, Lewes, East Sussex, England BN7 1XU
Distributed in Australia by Capricorn Link (Australia) Pty. Ltd.
P.O. Box 704, Windsor, NSW 2756, Australia

Manufactured in the United States of America

Sterling ISBN 978-1-4027-6651-0

For information about custom editions, special sales, premium and corporate purchases, please contact Sterling Special Sales Department at 800-805-5489 or specialsales@sterlingpublishing.com.

For Sweden:

The Land of Wild Strawberries and Dalahästar

—Scott Andrew Selby

For Rebecca and Turner

—Greg Campbell

Map of the Diamond District

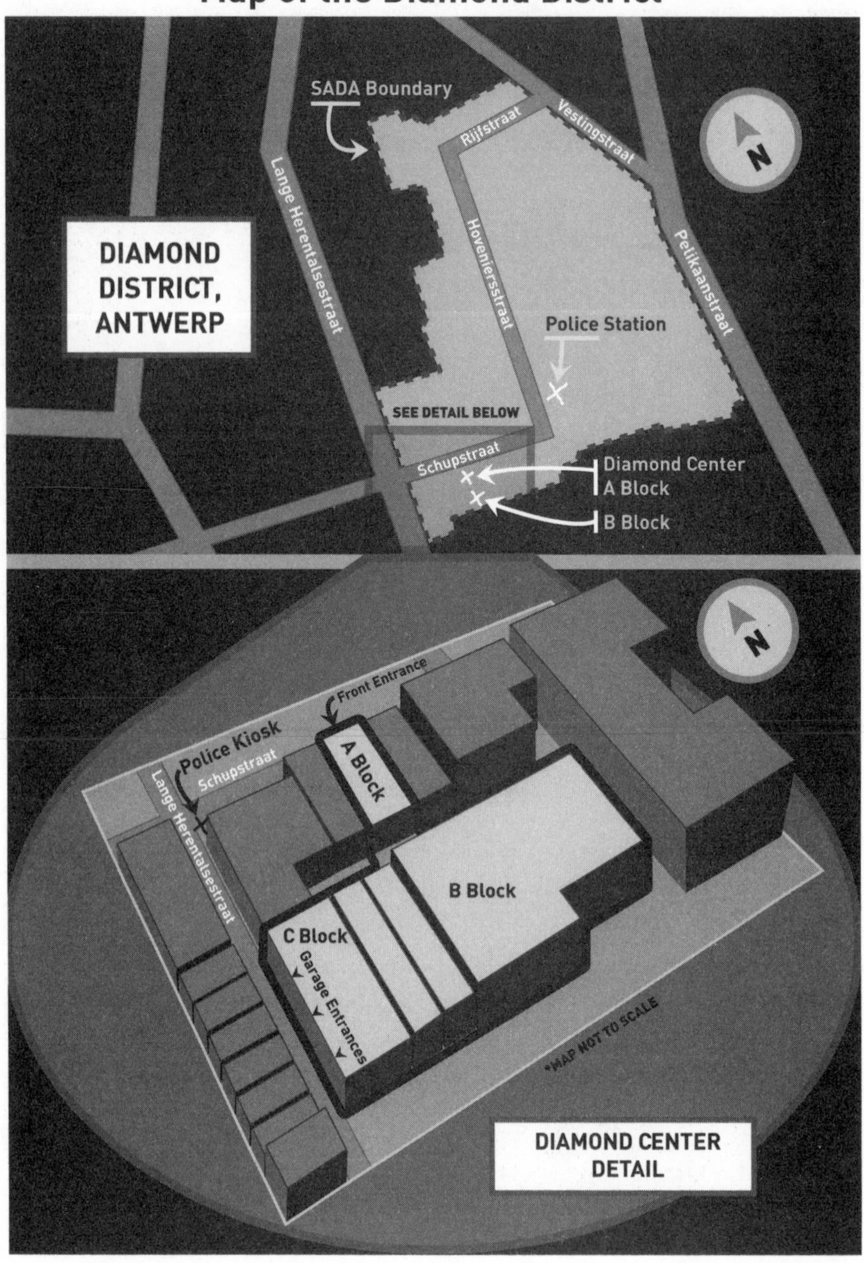

Map of the Vault

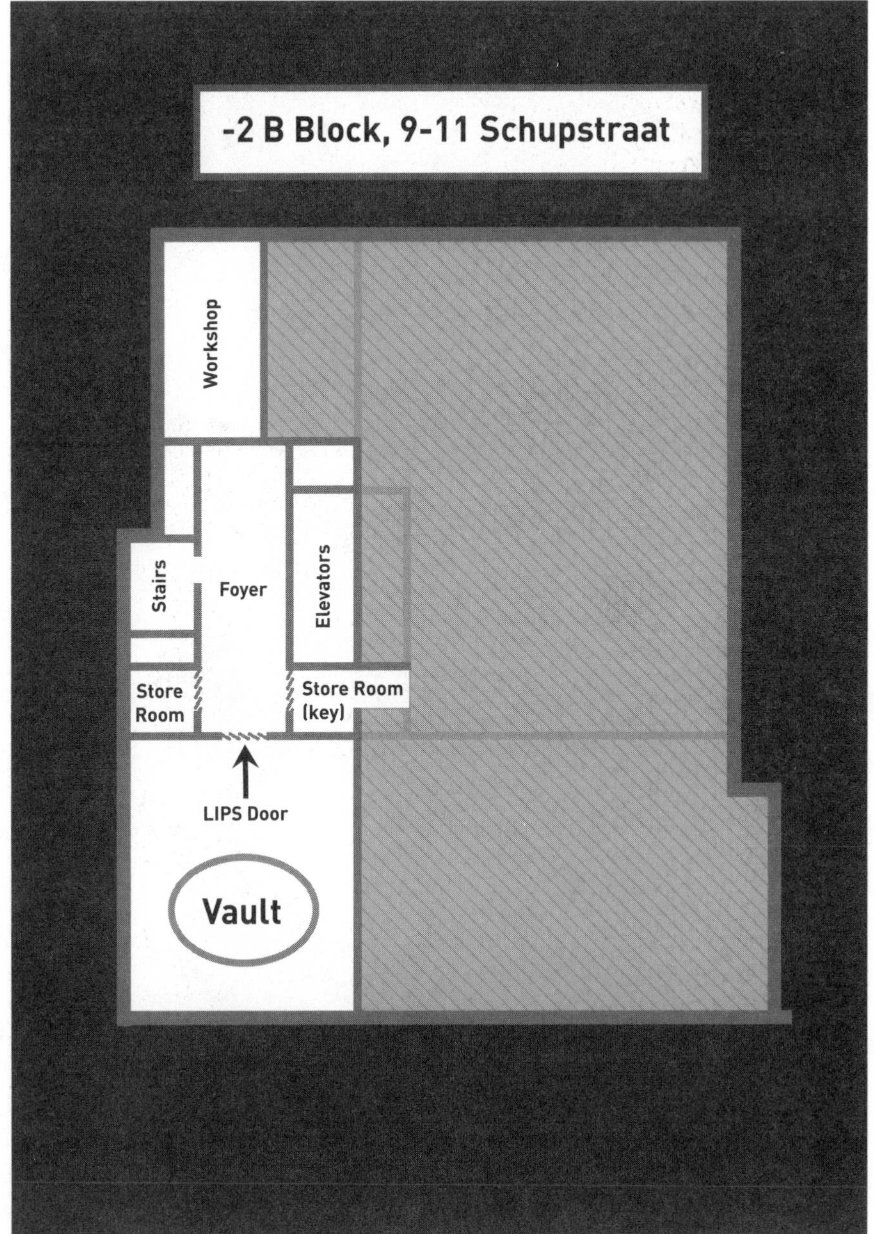

"Let us not be too particular. It is better to have old second-hand diamonds than none at all."

—Mark Twain

CONTENTS

A NOTE FROM THE AUTHORS

Researching and reporting on the 2003 Antwerp Diamond Center heist presented unique challenges. Most significantly, Belgium's justice system is not tilted in favor of public disclosure. Court records, police reports, and other documents are not readily available in most instances, and it is illegal for police detectives to discuss their investigations with journalists. This is the only criminal case in which detectives were permitted to break with that protocol.

The story in these pages was assembled from many sources in several countries. Key documents were discovered in a variety of places, as if collected during a scavenger hunt, and interviews with important characters took place in locales ranging from seedy public parks and taverns to ultramodern prisons and ritzy diamond offices. Assembling this book has been much like assembling a puzzle, the pieces of which were found throughout Europe, sometimes in unlikely places. What emerged was not only a spectacular story about the heist of the century, but also a wide array of conflicting details, divergent opinions, and incongruous theories.

Most facts about the diamond heist are clear and indisputable. Others are less so. Even some detectives disagree about the precise course of events. We strove to present the most accurate representation of the crime as possible through deduction, logic, common sense, and triangulation of facts from reliable sources. Where there is a dispute as to what happened, it is noted in the text or in the endnotes.

With a crime such as this—one that produced equal parts awe and conjecture to the degree that it has achieved mythical proportions—it's fitting that there remains some mystery as to precisely how it was pulled off. Only a small group of men know for sure, and to date not one of them has provided a full and credible explanation, if they've spoken about it at all.

Scott Andrew Selby and Greg Campbell
October 2009

PROLOGUE

Ali Baba expected to find only a dark and obscure cave; and was much astonished at seeing a large, spacious, well-lighted and vaulted room . . . He observed in it a large quantity of provisions, numerous bales of rich merchandise, piled up, silk stuffs and brocades, rich and valuable carpets, and besides all this, great quantities of money, both silver and gold, some in heaps and some in large leather bags . . . He took up at several times as much as he could carry, and when he had got together what he thought sufficient for loading his three asses, he went.

—*The Arabian Nights*

The white-tiled floor of the vault was littered with diamonds, pearls, emeralds, rubies, gold, and silver. Empty velvet-lined jewelry cases, cardboard cigar boxes, and tin-clasped metal containers lay amid sparkling gemstones of every imaginable cut, color, clarity, and carat. There were ancient heirlooms, gilded bond notes, a Rolex watch, and a brick of solid gold heavy enough to stub toes. Loose stones rolled and bounced like marbles as the detectives picked through the debris, their low gasps and whistles of amazement echoing softly in the bright underground chamber. Detective Patrick Peys thought that if he were to shovel it all up, pour it into any one of the empty and discarded containers scattered about, he would have enough wealth to finance a decadent retirement not only for himself but also for the five other detectives in his unit of specialized diamond-crime investigators.

Like everyone else who descended to the bottom floor of the Antwerp Diamond Center that day—Monday, February 17, 2003—Peys needed some time to process the enormity of what he saw. He was no stranger to audacious crimes committed—or at least attempted—in Antwerp's high-security Diamond District, but he'd never seen anything like this.

By almost any measure, the safe room two floors underground was as impenetrable a fortress as any to be found in the tightly protected Diamond

District. Its walls of brushed-metal safe deposit boxes, which stood pillaged of an amount of treasure yet to be calculated, were inside a room equipped with a light sensor, a motion detector, and an infrared heat detector. Each of the safe deposit boxes had been locked with a key and a three-letter combination known only to its owner, yet more than half of them now stood open and empty. The room itself was secured with a foot-thick, double-locked, bombproof steel door armed with a magnetic alarm, as well as a locked, gated inner door that could only be opened with a buzzer from the control booth on the main floor. Both of those doors stood wide open that morning, undamaged.

These physical barriers were only the capstone of the vault's security. Over the weekend, when the crime occurred, the building had been sealed with heavy, rolling metal barriers that covered locked plate glass doors at the main entrance and heavy mechanical vehicle arms at the garage entrance. Closed-circuit television cameras monitored the building's entrances, corridors, and elevators as well as the antechamber to the vault, the small foyer that the elevators opened into. The building itself was situated in the heart of one of the most secure square miles on Earth, within what insurance investigators called the Secure Antwerp Diamond Area, a three-block canyon of gray glass-and-concrete buildings as well defended against thieves as Fort Knox. The district was protected with retractable vehicle barriers at either end to prevent cars from entering—or leaving—and was blanketed from every possible angle by a multitude of video cameras. Those cameras were monitored around the clock by a dedicated, heavily armed police force whose sole job was to prevent theft. In fact, there was a police security booth only forty yards from the Diamond Center's front entrance and, in the other direction, a full-service police station just around the corner.

In the Diamond Center's main corridor two stories above the vault, panic gripped tenants who enumerated the contents of their safe deposit boxes to police officers and insurance investigators. One dealer lost a million dollars in cash alone. A woman who had inherited her husband's box and its contents upon his death found herself suddenly destitute; the large gemstones and irreplaceable heirlooms left to her by her husband were meant to finance her remaining years, and now they were gone.

Peys looked down at the piles of wealth and debris scattered across the floor. What was rolling under his feet—those gems and jewels, those scattered and discarded riches, the individual treasures of the building's tenants who had stored them in the vault under the reasonable assumption that they would be safer here than in any bank—were the items the thieves had left behind. They had robbed and ransacked more than they could carry.

The detective was momentarily overwhelmed by the scale of the heist. Someone had overcome all of these security measures and made off with an untold fortune of diamonds, jewelry, precious metals, and cash without tripping a single alarm or injuring anyone. Peys didn't say it out loud—not at the moment, anyway—but he couldn't help but be awed by the skill required for such a heist.

That thought was quickly followed by another, darker realization: whoever had pulled off this seemingly perfect crime would be impossible to find.

Chapter One

THE TROJAN HORSE

Money isn't everything. There's also diamonds.

—Proverb

Leonardo Notarbartolo set the world's greatest diamond heist into motion on a cold gray autumn day in 2000 with a smile and a polite "merci beaucoup," as building manager Julie Boost granted him free reign of the place he planned to rob.

As far as she knew, Boost had simply signed a new tenant and filled another vacancy in the tower of offices at the Diamond Center, the largest office building inside Antwerp's storied Diamond Square Mile. The blue-eyed Italian was disarmingly charming. He said he was a diamond merchant interested in renting an office in the diamond capital of the world to supply his local retail stores in Turin, Italy, and his jewelry design business in Valenza. From what Boost could see, he'd be a perfectly adequate tenant.

In fact, Notarbartolo didn't plan to buy a single stone in Antwerp; he hoped to steal as many as he could carry.

Notarbartolo was prepared for whatever interrogation the building's manager might have prepared for him. He was armed with official-looking documents and glossy brochures describing his modest chain of jewelry stores in Turin. In his attaché case, he carried examples of his handcrafted jewelry manufactured in Valenza—shiny bracelets, necklaces, and diamond rings that he'd designed himself. He was prepared to explain that his business was going so well, particularly on the manufacturing side, that it made sense to open an office in Antwerp, where 80 percent of all diamonds bought and sold throughout the world changed hands. Anyone who was serious about trading in diamonds did business in Antwerp—and, by extension, so too did anyone who was serious about stealing them.

If Notarbartolo aroused any suspicions during Boost's first meeting with him, he allayed them by employing the most effective tools at his disposal: charm and good looks. At forty-eight, Notarbartolo was handsome, although he carried a few extra pounds and his dark hair was thinning. With his open and expressive face, he could evoke in complete strangers a warm feeling of brotherhood and kinship the moment the tiny lines around his mouth crinkled into a captivating smile. He acted as if everyone around him was an old and treasured friend. He had perfected the ability to melt defenses and subvert suspicion. And just as important, he had the skill to make you forget him within minutes—he was engaging, but only exactly as engaging as he needed to be for the task at hand. He didn't want to create a lasting impression; for his purposes, it was better to be quickly forgotten. This was precisely why he had been chosen for this part of the job.

After Boost and Notarbartolo concluded their introductions, they embarked on a tour of the facility. As they strolled through the halls, Boost pitched the office building as a smart choice for a merchant like Notarbartolo. At the equivalent of about $500 a month, the rent was competitive. Smack in the heart of the Diamond District, the building was conveniently located within steps of any business or service one might require, including three diamond quality–certification businesses, an array of cutters and polishers, supply stores that sold everything from loupes to grinding wheels, the country's import/export agency, and, of course, the wholesalers themselves. Belgium recorded tens of billions of dollars of transactions for both rough and polished diamonds every year; in the course of just an average day, some 200,000 carats were traded, representing a value of about $200 million. Practically every decent-sized stone ever mined made its way at some point through the Diamond District's three city streets. Many of those diamonds—hundreds of millions of dollars' worth—circulated among the offices at the Diamond Center.

Boost was a prim and petite woman, her short blonde hair done in an almost retro-looking no-nonsense poodle cut. She toyed with the eyeglasses hanging around her neck on a long gold chain as she recited the building's amenities. None of it was news to Notarbartolo; he already knew everything she was selling him on, and he didn't care at all about such details as the affordable rent. While he was in fact an Italian jeweler, it was cover for his true vocation: Notarbartolo was a renowned thief in Italy embarking on the most daring scam of his colorful career. As the tour wound through the building's hallways, he was far more interested in the building's security measures than its proximity to the conveniences of the diamond industry. He'd already started compiling a mental list of the things he observed long before Boost pointed them out.

The most obvious antitheft measure was the building's video surveillance system. There had been no attempt to conceal the cameras positioned in the hallways; quite the opposite, they were made as obvious as possible to relay the message to anyone walking around that they were being watched. Notarbartolo had already seen the security control room filled with monitors displaying images of tenants coming and going—he and Boost passed it in the main corridor as they began their tour—but he couldn't tell with a passing glance what sort of system it was. Did the cameras record digital images on a computer hard drive or onto videotape? The difference was critical, and it was just one of the many things he planned on learning with his newly acquired inside access.

They took the elevator to the fifth floor, Boost jingling a set of keys in her hand. They turned onto a narrow hallway with doors on both sides; these were private offices. Since each tenant had his own preference of video surveillance, the walls were festooned with different models of cameras that craned overhead like huge insects, each aimed at a doorway. These weren't so much antitheft measures as they were a means for the office occupant to see who was knocking at the door before deciding to let them in or not.

Boost unlocked door number 516, one of the few that didn't have a camera, and motioned Notarbartolo inside. The office was quite plain, furnished with just a desk, a worktable, some cabinets, and a few chairs. Fluorescent light tubes flickered overhead, just like in the hallways, and the floor was covered with flat gray industrial carpeting. A bank of windows overlooked a gravel alleyway and some overgrown vacant lots behind the building. Tenants on the other side of the hallway enjoyed the better view of the Diamond District and Antwerp's famous skyline, dominated by the gothic cathedral that lorded over the sixteenth-century market square. But Notarbartolo didn't mind his subpar view. The office was just part of the ruse, a place to kill time between reconnaissance missions to the vault, the heart of the building where its tenants stored hundreds of millions of dollars' worth of diamonds, gold, cash, and jewels.

Finding the office more than satisfactory for his purpose, Notarbartolo was led back to the elevator, where Boost pushed the button for floor -2, two levels underground. When the doors slid open, Notarbartolo was struck by how bright the vault foyer was. Fluorescent bulbs lit the white walls and white tile floor, lending the space the appearance of an antiseptic operating room. A large white Siemens video camera was slung from the ceiling; the lighting in the foyer provided it with a television-studio-quality image of the small room.

They exited the elevator and turned left. At the end of the small room, a heavy vault door stood open into the foyer. Unlike in the movies, where vault doors are the color of handsome brushed chrome, this was painted a flat rust-colored maroon and it stood out under the stark lighting. A secondary steel-gated door barred entry to the safe room itself.

Boost rattled off the vault's security features as they walked to the gate and peered through the bars into the safe room, but she wasn't telling Notarbartolo anything he couldn't see for himself with his specially attuned eyes. He saw that vault door was made by the Dutch company LIPS, and was among the sturdiest ever constructed. It was at least a foot thick and made of iron and steel.

The big vault door was open during business hours, Boost explained, but the day gate was always closed and locked. In order to get inside the vault, one had to buzz the control room on the main floor by using the intercom on the right side of the doorway. A guard would check the video monitor and, when he recognized the tenant, he would press a button that unlocked the gate. Boost demonstrated how it worked as she and Notarbartolo turned and stared into the shark's eye of the video camera. There was a loud click from the gate. She pushed it open, and they stepped inside.

The low-ceilinged safe room was an almost perfect square about three times the size of the foyer, and just as brightly lit with rows of overhead fluorescent tubes. It looked deceptively empty, but Notarbartolo knew that the honeycomb of 189 brushed-steel safe deposit boxes covering the walls from floor to ceiling was filled with immense wealth. Each safe deposit box had a keyhole and three golden dials; tenants needed both a metal key and an alphabetic combination of their choosing to access their treasures.

Notarbartolo noted that the safe room was equipped with a combination motion detector/infrared sensor and a light detector, all of which were in plain sight. Even if thieves could get through the vault door, they wouldn't be able to move, emit body heat, or turn on the lights—much less crack almost two hundred safes inside the room—without setting off alarms.

Every night at 7:00 p.m., the tenants' treasures were sealed inside when one of the building's two caretakers locked the LIPS door. The door stayed locked until 7:00 a.m. the following morning. On weekends, the vault remained closed from Friday night to Monday morning. There were no exceptions.

There were more than locks keeping this room safe. The vault door was armed with a magnetic alarm that, like the other sensors inside the room, was connected to an offsite security company. A magnet the size of a brick was bolted to the door itself. When the door was closed, it connected magnetically with another that was bolted to the doorjamb. Opening the door would separate the magnets and break the magnetic field, triggering the alarm; the security company would immediately notify the police that a break-in was in progress.

There were human defenses to be avoided as well. One of the two caretakers, known as concierges, was always on duty around the clock. Both lived in private apartments in the office towers. Their presence and their work schedules weren't so much security measures—they also acted as twenty-four-hour-per-day assistants who opened garage doors for tenants needing to get into the building at odd hours. The diamond industry is international, after all, and there are times when a dealer has to do business with Hong Kong even when it's the middle of the night in Europe. Even though little more than glorified after-hours doormen, the concierges nevertheless had important responsibilities: They were the ones who locked and unlocked the vault door every weekday. They both knew the combination; they both had access to the key.

◆ ◆ ◆

And so, with a flourish of pen strokes, Notarbartolo infiltrated the Diamond Center. As the police would later say, he became officially "operational" the moment he signed his real name on a lease agreement and a safe deposit box rental form. He signed as the proprietor of Damoros Preziosi, a front company that would never conduct a single legitimate diamond transaction. He sealed the deal with a three-month cash advance payment for both. Boost handed Notarbartolo three keys: one to his new office, one to his safe deposit box, and a microchipped badge-card to get through the turnstiles at the front entrance.

The Diamond Center hadn't required a reference check, a criminal background check, or proof that his company was registered with the Belgian government to export commercial goods. It was stunningly easy for Notarbartolo to insinuate himself where he didn't belong using just his charm and a few brochures. Still, walking out the front door with the keys in his pocket, he was aware that he couldn't yet let his guard down. Exiting the building didn't end his security concerns; if anything, it heightened them.

While the Diamond Center's 24/7 surveillance and antitheft measures were impressive, what made the building practically impenetrable was its location within the secure zone of the Antwerp Diamond District. This area, also known as the Diamond Square Mile, left nothing to chance when it came to securing its diamonds and the merchants who traded them. If a person had any doubts about the area's level of security, they would likely be dissolved in one visit, as its security precautions were both extensive and obvious.

The district itself was composed of three short streets connected end-to-end at 90-degree angles creating the shape of a stiff S. The streets dated back centuries. They were old and narrow, a hard-angled ravine of steep concrete and glass office buildings. These three blocks were home to thousands of businesses that served the diamond industry in some way—banks, currency exchanges, supply stores, and four members-only bourses, which served as private diamond-trading cooperatives responsible for most of the diamond transactions that occurred throughout the world.

The Antwerp diamond industry's headquarters, which at the time was called the Diamond High Council (the Hoge Raad voor Diamant, known as the HRD), was located here, as was the Belgian government's diamond import/export agency. Brinks, the American armored car company, had a building here. The value of the diamonds in the pocket of a single person walking by was often enough to comfortably equip anyone for a life of luxury.

As a result of this concentrated wealth, the area's obsession with security bordered on paranoia. The three streets—Schupstraat, Hoveniersstraat, and Rijfstraat—were closed to almost all vehicle traffic. Each end of the district, at the tips of Schupstraat and Rijfstraat, was protected with a space-age anti-vehicle system composed of fourteen knee-high, foot-wide, steel cylinders that sprouted from the streets to form a wide oval, like a modern interpretation of Stonehenge. It was impossible to ram through this barricade with anything less than a military tank.

Only approved vehicles could get through, and arduously at that. Police officers at the Schupstraat entrance triggered a mechanism that caused the outside of the oval to retract into the ground, the great cylinders sliding down like pins inside a lock when a key is inserted. As the vehicle moved forward, the cylinders reemerged, trapping it for a moment inside the oval. Then the cylinders composing the inside arc of the oval slid down and the vehicle could drive into the Diamond District.

This anti-vehicle system had been implemented after Palestinian terrorists detonated a car bomb outside the ancient Portuguese synagogue on Hoveniersstraat in 1981, killing three and injuring more than a hundred. Since then, the barricades had served the dual purpose of protecting the district's substantial Jewish population and, as an added benefit, causing any gangs of thieves to scrap plans that involved driving up to their target in the hope of making a quick getaway.

Equally daunting, if not more so, was the district's aggressive use of closed-circuit television cameras (CCTVs) to provide round-the-clock eye-in-the-sky surveillance of every inch of the Diamond Square Mile. Dozens of shoebox-shaped cameras surveyed the area with their wide black eyes shrouded by metal hoods. They perched on the street corners, on overhangs, and on windowsills like sentinel gargoyles, sprouting cables, high-wattage floodlights, and stout brackets anchoring them to the walls. Some cameras were mounted ten stories high for global overviews, while others were positioned just ten feet off the ground for close-ups of everyone coming and going though doors that opened onto the Diamond District.

The majority of the cameras were privately owned and operated by building and business owners. In scores of security control rooms throughout the district, guards watched monitors that broadcast footage from every conceivable angle. As with the cameras inside the Diamond Center, the placement of these cameras was overt, to serve as a reminder to anyone coming or going that they were being filmed, watched, and recorded by someone. The white plastic casings of many cameras were smeared with pigeon droppings, but that didn't dampen the impact they had on visitors.

Video was also fed to the district's dedicated platoon of specialized diamond police, who had their own cameras connected to joysticks and zoom lenses to follow the trail of anyone who raised their suspicion. The police also provided a physical presence by patrolling the streets in teams of two, and at two stations: one on Schupstraat next to the vehicle barrier and the other on Hoveniersstraat, a few paces from the synagogue. Uniformed officers were supplemented by colleagues in plain clothes who could easily be overlooked amid the throng of diamond traders circulating through the streets.

The overall effect of these security measures was an in-your-face display of armed, protected, and monitored fortifications that, over the years, had disheartened some of the world's most infamous criminals. No less notorious a crook than Richard "The Iceman" Kuklinski, Mafia boss John Gotti's personal hit man, had passed on a plot to pull a job in the Diamond District. He needed only one look around to see that security was simply too daunting.

"Tight as a nun's ass," he told his associates.

♦ ♦ ♦

Notarbartolo might well have been thinking the same thing. But when he awoke on the day he was first going to use his new keys, he must have been buoyed by the knowledge that the initial part of the complicated—and, at that stage, still nebulous—plot to rob the Diamond Center had gone off exceptionally well. He had nearly unrestricted access to the building he planned to rob, as Julie Boost hadn't batted an eye at anything he'd told her. If she had any lingering doubts after he'd left her office, he was confident his story would hold up if she decided to check it out. He did, in fact, own three small jewelry stores in Turin, each of which did legitimate by-the-books business. Additionally, a call to Valenza, where his manufacturing business was located, would confirm he was well known among jewelers there. Notarbartolo was actually quite proud of his jewelry designs.

The only hitch would be if Boost called the police and mentioned his name. His track record with law enforcement in Turin wasn't so clean; among the detectives who investigated organized crime in the city he called home, his name was synonymous with theft. Considering the ease with which the transaction for his new office had been conducted, however, it was hard to imagine Boost would bother.

Notarbartolo's day began a few blocks from the Diamond Square Mile, in a small and dingy one-bedroom apartment that was, compared to his stately home near Turin, woefully second-rate. The walls were peach-colored and grimy, like a kindergarten classroom gone to seed. The floors, originally tiled with white laminate squares, were now so well trod that they appeared gray. The apartment came furnished with a mishmash of outdated black vinyl couches, painted plywood tables, a faded reddish rug, and a sagging mattress on a single bed. Like many of his countrymen, Notarbartolo treasured his meals, and it's not hard to imagine his disappointment in the cramped and Spartan kitchen. There was only enough room for a college dormitory-sized refrigerator and a tiny microwave that bore the scars of heavy use by the previous tenants. The stove and the dishwasher looked as if they'd been salvaged from a soup kitchen. It was fortunate he didn't plan on doing much entertaining.

The apartment on the seventh floor of Charlottalei 33 did have its advantages. There was a nice view onto the broad street out front that, in warmer months, was shaded with the leaves of maple trees planted in long rows in its green medians. The half mile to the Diamond Center took only about ten minutes to walk. The apartment's main draw, though, was its anonymity: Notarbartolo paid his rent in cash and his agreement with the landlord involved only a handshake, no paperwork. Part of his assignment was keeping as low a profile as possible; the tiny one-bedroom with its scuffed tiles and drippy faucets served that purpose perfectly.

While getting ready, Notarbartolo considered his wardrobe. Again, balance was key. Everything about his appearance needed to be both appropriate and forgettable. A stroll through the Diamond District showed a wide diversity of styles, from crisply attired Indians wearing sharp Armani suits with shiny leather shoes to Hasidic Jews in long black jackets, dark pants, white shirts, and old fashioned brimmed hats. There were also dreadlocked messengers in T-shirts and jeans, as well as a smattering of badly dressed tourists gawking at all the security cameras and police. In the end, Notarbartolo sought the middle ground, completing his ensemble with an overcoat and his attaché case.

The elevator in the apartment building was ridiculously small. Notarbartolo's bulky 5-foot-11-inch frame nearly filled the car. After it discharged him into a tiny lobby, Notarbartolo walked through the security door, past a bank of post boxes, and exited into the brisk air on Charlottalei. He was in character from the moment he stepped outside, a humble Italian jeweler on his way to work, just a tiny cog in the machinery of the multibillion dollar international diamond industry, a simple merchant among the hundreds who bought and sold diamonds in Antwerp.

Though he would soon become an expert in the little universe between his apartment and his office at the Diamond Center, Notarbartolo was still a stranger to the city during this morning walk on his first official day. Turning right outside the building, he strolled to the end of the street, where its neighborhood charm was left at the curb of a busy intersection. If he were to turn right from here, it was a short walk on Plantin en Moretuslei to the Delhaize grocery store, which was blessed with a decent selection of Italian meats, cheeses, and wine. If he turned left, he could stroll through Stadspark and admire its small groves of trees and its little manmade pond. Instead of turning, he walked straight ahead, past an old brick building across the intersection which was fitted with a modern blue and white illuminated sign that read *Politie*, which meant "police." Notarbartolo must have enjoyed the subversive thrill that came from walking by the local police station on his way to the Diamond District.

Beyond the police station hung a business sign with a familiar name: Fichet, the famous British safe manufacturer. Among locksmiths and safecrackers, the brand held an esteemed reputation, one Notarbartolo knew well. If you wanted to keep your valuables safe, Fichet was a godsend; if you were trying to steal those valuables, it was a curse. If there was any silver lining to the obstacles he faced, it was that the vault door in the Diamond Center wasn't a Fichet, although it was small consolation. LIPS vaults were among the best in the world, up there with other well-respected manufacturers like Tann and Sargent & Greenleaf. The Fichet store displayed vault doors, safes, and examples of bulletproof glass in its window, a signal to pedestrians that they were close to the Diamond District. It was also a sign for Notarbartolo to turn right on the next avenue.

The moment he turned the corner onto the narrow boulevard, Notarbartolo appeared on the Diamond Square Mile's CCTV network, albeit as a dot in the background. If he were in a car, he could only go another block before being stopped by the security cylinders blocking Schupstraat that prevented unauthorized vehicles from continuing straight ahead. On foot, Notarbartolo simply walked through the barriers and past the police substation, a small enclosed booth filled with video monitors and, presumably, a small arsenal of weapons and ammunition.

In passing the security cylinders, Notarbartolo had entered an invisible shell of safety and security. Insurance investigators had a name for it, the Secure Antwerp Diamond Area, or SADA. The SADA was defined by a hard line drawn around all the buildings facing Schupstraat, Hoveniersstraat, and Rijfstraat. Diamond businesses outside that boundary on adjacent streets comprised what was known in insurance lingo as the ADA, the Antwerp Diamond Area. This area included a long row of glittering retail diamond shops for tourists on Pelikaanstraat, which abutted the SADA. There were still plenty of cameras in the ADA, but there were more cars and fewer cops; therefore, insurance premiums were generally higher for diamond businesses in the ADA than in the SADA.

As a rule, diamond dealers kept their goods inside the SADA, the three-block bubble of electronic surveillance and crack-proof vault doors. There was no hesitation when they needed to carry diamonds across the streets of the SADA to have them evaluated, polished, or sold. The merchants simply put them in their pocket and walked out the door. Or, if they wanted a little extra reassurance, they carried their goods in briefcases handcuffed to their wrists with high-tensile-strength steel chains. It was astounding to consider the wealth being toted from building to building in passing backpacks, attaché cases, and courier bags.

Considering the staggering value of the diamonds people carried—a small handful can be worth tens of millions of dollars—it was easy to conclude that diamonds were handled casually, almost recklessly, on the streets of the district. While most transactions took place indoors behind several layers of security, the streets were important meeting places for spontaneous wheeling and dealing; it was a testament to the diamond brokers' confidence in the Big Brother surveillance of a myriad of CCTV cameras and a squad of cops to discourage theft attempts. It provided them with the sort of psychic comfort needed to be able to produce from a coat pocket a paper parcel filled with millions of dollars' worth of diamonds while chatting with a colleague during a cigarette break.

Even on days when the Belgian sky was overcast, some of the diamonds being admired on the district's street corners were large enough to sparkle like miniature flashbulbs from twenty yards away. What was most amazing was not their beauty or their jaw-dropping value, but how unceremoniously they were unwrapped and passed from one unarmed merchant to another, right there in broad daylight in the middle of a busy street filled with strangers. The diamond dealers may have been offering each other sticks of gum for all the drama these displays seemed to generate.

A few paces beyond the security bubble, though, out into the ADA, this laissez-faire attitude evaporated. The feeling of exposure—to thieves, muggers, con artists, even to the possibility of getting hit by a car while carrying millions of dollars' worth of diamonds—could be chokingly claustrophobic. That was why whenever diamonds left the secure zone in any notable volume, they did so in armored Brinks trucks or customized bulletproof personal cars filled with private security guards. Diamond dealers might have chanced crossing out of the Diamond District's borders with a small cache of stones in a locked briefcase, but only if they were going just around the corner to a cutter and polisher. No one left with any sizable stash on his person. Not only was it too dangerous, but there was simply no practical reason to do it.

Dramatic heist tales circulated among diamond dealers like folklore, serving as a reminder of the dangerous world beyond the range of the CCTV cameras. One gold dealer's experience was particularly cautionary, proving that there was no such thing as over-preparation. This man had a small fleet of unmarked armored BMW sedans with reinforced suspension that made regular runs to deliver solid gold ingots from the airport in Amsterdam, one hundred miles away, to the Diamond District in Antwerp. The cars were equipped with GPS systems and panic buttons that would broadcast their positions to a security company in the event of trouble. They would leave

Antwerp empty and return positively gravid with solid gold bars filling the trunks. As a precautionary measure, the merchant frequently changed the days and times for his gold runs, in the hope of thwarting holdup attempts.

As one of these convoys was approaching the Belgian border from Amsterdam, a motorcycle cop, lights and sirens blaring, swooped in front of the lead BMW. At the same time, a dark SUV boxed it in from behind. The BMW's suspicious passengers hit the panic button, but it was of no use; the signal worked only in Belgium and didn't connect to anyone in the Netherlands. Instead of flooring it and risking running down what may or may not have been a cop on the motorcycle, the driver allowed himself to be led off the highway and under a bridge. As masked men surrounded the car brandishing weapons, the couriers locked themselves inside the vehicle, assuming the car's armored windows and reinforced trunk would be enough to keep the thieves out. The thieves, of course, were prepared: they used a modified club that was capable, after many blows, of smashing in one of the car's windows. Once a pistol was waved through the window, the passengers wisely decided to surrender and pop the trunk. Millions of dollars in gold were transferred to the SUV, the BMW was set on fire, and the driver and passengers were left hog-tied under the bridge. None of the gold was recovered.

Stories like this were sobering to diamond merchants because they served as reminders that sophisticated bands of criminals were spending a lot of time plotting to rob them. The smart merchants lived as if the next big heist was being planned against them personally. In the case of those renting offices at the Diamond Center, that was certainly true, even though the man doing the plotting walked past them as a peer while they stood under the building's awning smoking cigarettes.

♦ ♦ ♦

The Diamond District wasn't originally planned as a fortress. Its streets were on the fringe of the city center that dated back to the 1200s, and, even though the diamond industry established its permanent hold in Antwerp in the 1400s, the three-block area was considered a slum until as late as the turn of the twentieth century. Modernity, in the form of CCTV cameras, vehicle barriers, and bulletproof plate glass façades, was superimposed upon the area gradually.

If old buildings couldn't be retrofitted to accommodate impact-resistant glass and ducts for high-speed coaxial video and Internet cables, they were razed and replaced with modern structures. The result was a mishmash of new buildings alternating with old ones.

An example of this architectural schizophrenia was the archaic home of I. David, a diamond-business supply company that looked more like the den of a chronic hoarder. It was one story high and wedged between the modern brick Bank of India building and the Kneller building, home to many more modern supply houses, diamond dealers, and currency exchange offices. I. David looked like a bad tooth in an otherwise flawless set of dentistry. In contrast, just around the corner, the headquarters of the Diamond High Council was a sleek and modern glass-fronted affair.

Antwerp was filled with such architectural contradictions. Broad, stately boulevards smartly appointed with green medians and tall oaks and maples interlaced with crooked, narrow streets that were little more than glorified alleyways. The center of the city was the impressive Grote Markt, Antwerp's cultural and aesthetic hub about a mile from the Diamond District. Around it, the wider streets and the narrow arteries connected in twisting, haphazard patterns and were crowded with pedestrian plazas, one-way streets, tramlines, and outdoor cafés that threatened to overflow the sidewalks.

Just blocks away from the city center, the seaports on the Scheldt River provided the city a rich heritage as one of Europe's most impressive art and culture capitals. The cobbled plazas were home to ancient guild houses with their intricate stone embroidery and gilded rooftop filigree. The gothic Cathedral of Our Lady displayed paintings by Flemish master Peter Paul Rubens just a few steps away from the city's oldest pub, which had been serving Belgium's famous beer since the 1200s.

Across from the cathedral was the city's iconic fountain by Jef Lambeaux, which depicted Roman soldier Silvius Brabo preparing to hurtle the amputated hand of a giant into the river. The fountain paid homage to the legend of the city's founding, wherein the giant extorted tolls from passing ships. The captains who refused lost their hands until the giant lost his; *Antwerp* is an outgrowth of the old Flemish words for "hand throw."

The Grote Markt and its cathedral were among the few places in Antwerp where the city's history had been preserved for its own sake;

elsewhere, old buildings remained standing only if they could be put to use as apartment buildings, banks, bus stations, or private businesses. If not, they were destroyed with wrecking balls and dynamite to make room for more practical structures. This was evident everywhere, but particularly near the Diamond District.

Only a block from the CCTV cameras and vehicle barricades was the city's central train station, a unique melding of modern and ancient building styles that still served as the main point of arrival for most visitors. The train platforms were covered by an avant-garde glass and steel structure more evocative of an airport than a train station, but passengers were immediately faced with the old station's original ornately carved stone edifice featuring a grand old clock that was more impressive, and just as useful for those waiting for the train, than any digital display could be.

In the 1800s, the city's diamond industry initially located itself outside the train station, on Pelikaanstraat. Now the street was strewn with strip clubs alongside quaint cafés, and the only reminders of that former time were a slew of retail storefronts advertising their diamond jewelry with glaring neon signs. Though many tourists fell prey to the siren song, savvy visitors avoided the trap, knowing that these retailers were as much about the Diamond District as the strip clubs were about finding true love.

The Diamond Center was itself the result of old abutting new. In 1931, two buildings, numbers 9 and 11 Schupstraat, were combined into one. This structure was destroyed in 1969 by its new owner, diamond dealer Marcel Grünberger, to accommodate the Diamond Center, which became the largest office building in the district.

The new structure was more than just the storefronts facing Schupstraat. The complex comprised three interconnected buildings: blocks A, B, and C. A Block, a nine-story edifice facing Schupstraat, might have looked impressive when it was completed in 1972, but in 2000, when Notarbartolo first walked through its doors, it seemed dated and old fashioned. It was a narrow building barely forty paces wide, recognizable by its long, heavy-looking concrete awning that jutted onto Schupstraat over the front doors.

The rest of the building loomed into the sky, its face a reflection of the opposing structures in its plate glass windows. The address, 9–11 Diamond Center, was fixed to the front granite-work with plastic Helvetica letters, slightly askew and just below a large CCTV camera that recorded people coming and going through the front entrance.

B Block, the largest of the three, was situated directly behind A Block. This building was a staggered wedding-cake design, with thirteen floors above ground and two below. It was connected to A Block by a broad marble-walled corridor that ran from the elevators to the front doors which opened onto Schupstraat. Most tenants had their offices in B Block; some companies rented entire floors.

The least impressive building in the complex was C Block, a broad but low four-story structure accessible by taking a sharp right turn in the marble corridor just before the elevators for B Block. One could also enter C Block from the street that ran perpendicular to Schupstraat, Lange Herentalsestraat, through the garage doors. C Block might have been the ugly stepchild of the already less-than-stunning Diamond Center complex—several offices that faced Lange Herentalsestraat had cracked and smudged windows—but it served an important purpose for the tenants: it bypassed the vehicle barriers just a few yards away on Schupstraat, allowing tenants to park in the Diamond Center's underground parking lot without having to hassle with retractable cylinders and police officers.

During business hours and for a few hours during the weekends, three large corrugated garage doors facing Lange Herentalsestraat were rolled up and opened. The first, the closest to the police substation on Schupstraat, opened to give security guards in a glass-walled control room a view of the street. It also allowed pedestrian traffic to enter the Diamond Center. As with the main entrance, tenants needed to badge in for the inner doors to open; visitors would have to check in with the guard if they had an appointment with a tenant. The other two garage doors were for vehicles: the middle door accessed the main parking level on the ground floor under B Block, and the third door accessed the underground lot on the -1 level below B Block. Both of the vehicle entrances had striped yellow-and-white metal arms that rose when a button was pushed by a guard in the booth. Only tenants who'd paid to rent a parking spot would have the bars raised for them.

In all, the Diamond Center was home to approximately 250 offices where diamond companies—and, to a lesser extent, gold and jewelry companies—did business. It was by far the largest office building in the

Diamond District. From an aerial view, its footprint formed a backward L that hugged the Lens Building next door and the Andimo Building, outside of which the police substation was located, on the corner of Schupstraat and Lange Herentalsestraat.

If one could ignore the fact that the Diamond Center was completely tone-deaf to the architectural standards of Antwerp's historical buildings showcased within just a few blocks, it was easy to be impressed with the building—not because of its looks, but because of its sheer size and, of course, by the volume of diamonds that coursed through its threadbare hallways.

♦ ♦ ♦

Notarbartolo didn't pay much attention to the building's aesthetic deficiencies as he approached it that first morning. He wasn't there to critique the place, but to steal from it. His attention was on more practical matters, such as counting cameras as he approached the main entrance on Schupstraat.

One camera, on the corner of the awning, looked toward the vehicle barriers. There was a cluster of three across the street from the front doors covering a 180-degree arc. Two more cameras were positioned farther down where Schupstraat intersected with Hoveniersstraat looking toward the Diamond Center. Another was placed to the right of the doors and trained directly on them. Under the crooked address sign was a small fish-eye–lens camera embedded in an after-hours intercom equipped with a keypad for buzzing the concierges. Notarbartolo would have assumed there were more cameras that he couldn't see.

Notarbartolo pushed open the plate glass doors and entered the building. Inside the glass-walled booth on the right beyond the foyer, the guard, in civilian clothes, didn't seem to be paying particular attention to the foot traffic outside his booth. On the right side of the foyer was a bank of mailboxes. Straight ahead were the waist-high turnstiles, each with an electronic card reader for the badges. Tenants had to badge through the turnstiles both coming and going.

Notarbartolo swiped his badge-card through an electronic reader that unlocked the turnstile arm so he could enter the building. Every time he badged in or out of the building like that, an electronic record was made.

As he entered, he noted the security control room on the left. It was fronted with a huge glass window, allowing tenants a glance inside at the monitors displaying images from twenty-four internal cameras watching practically every corner of the building. Notarbartolo counted two more cameras as he walked to the elevators along the broad main hallway. This corridor was the nicest in the building, with dark marbled walls, a tiled floor, and smart cherrywood slats overhead with wide Art Deco circles cut out to accommodate recessed lighting. The hall dead-ended at a bank of elevators. Notarbartolo stepped inside and pressed the button for the fifth floor.

When the doors slid open on the fifth-floor landing, the view was as low-rent as Notarbartolo's apartment. The main corridor, badly in need of a fresh coat of paint, was grimy off-white with a dismal gray trim on the door frames. The walls were scuffed and dinged from years of careless movers wrestling tables and desks into the offices.

Only once he was inside office number 516 did Notarbartolo allow himself to relax. This was his sanctuary; there would be no cameras here unless he installed them himself.

Notarbartolo's Diamond Center hideout offered precious few distractions. There was no reason, he figured, to waste time or money furnishing it or decorating it with fake documents on the walls. He never planned to have anyone visit, at least not anyone who would expect to see the regular trappings of a diamond merchant. This was practical, perhaps, but it also created an obstacle he might not have anticipated: tedium.

Notarbartolo knew he must spend several hours in the office during each of his visits to give the illusion that he was working. It would surely arouse suspicion if his computerized badge traffic showed he spent only a half hour at a time in the building. Since his real work needed to take place outside the office, he made sure to bring with him several Italian-language newspapers and magazines to kill time. He was fortunate that the newspaper vendor across Schupstraat from the Diamond Center carried several Italian publications, lifesavers that kept him from pacing a hole in the carpet for hours on end. He also brought with him a pad of paper and some pencils. Pulling up a chair, he settled behind the desk and took notes on what he'd seen so far, drew a few preliminary sketches, and created the first of many to-do lists. The office was very quiet except for the sound of his pencil scratching on the notepad.

After an appropriate amount of time passed, he took his briefcase to the elevator and hit the button for floor -2, the vault level. When the doors slid open, he was again finely tuned to note and record to memory as much detail as possible. He noticed, for example, that although there were three elevators that served the upper floors of B Block, only two came to the bottom floor. He saw that the only decoration on the walls of the vault foyer was a framed diagram of the fire escape route, which conveniently showed which of the four doors in the foyer opened into the stairwell. He heard how the whole floor echoed, the tile amplifying every small cough and footstep. He made a mental note to wear sneakers when the time came.

He walked to the day gate that provided entry to the safe room, immediately memorizing the brand name printed on both the intercom keypad and the keypad connected to the magnetic alarm. He noted the manual fire alarm lever, a small camera in a smoked glass dome over the door and the flexible steel pipe containing the magnetic alarm's bundle of cables that vanished into the ceiling overhead.

Notarbartolo pressed the intercom buzzer and waited. As a new tenant, he was prepared to announce his name through the squawk box, so the guard on the main floor could confirm him as one of the safe deposit box renters. When the door clicked, Notarbartolo casually examined the jamb as he pushed it open. He didn't notice any overt signs that the day gate was alarmed; he made a mental note to keep checking this on subsequent visits. When he stepped inside and let go of the door, he heard the muted hiss of pneumatic hinges slowly closing the gate behind him.

Entering the vault, Notarbartolo stepped directly to his safe deposit box, number 149. When he'd rented the box, Boost had given him a small metal key with an oval handle and a two-inch-long round pipe. The end of the pipe was fitted with over-and-under metal flanges. Known as the "stamp," this was the part of the key that operated the lock. The silver-colored key fit into a horizontal slot in a round brass plug on the left side of the door. Three golden knobs adorned with all twenty-six letters of the alphabet around their circumference lined up horizontally to the right of the keyhole.

Once alone in the vault, Notarbartolo could finally begin the exploration he'd been itching to do. He dialed in his three-letter code on the worn golden dials, inserted the key, and twisted it clockwise. As he did so, a brass deadbolt inside the lock retracted from its slot in the doorjamb and the door swung smoothly open on its hidden internal hinges. With the box's door open, he twisted the key to the locked position and watched the deadbolt extend from the lock. He guessed it was an inch long, two inches tall, and a quarter of an inch thick. He would make precise measurements later—repeatedly. His first visit to the vault was just for the sake of walking around, opening his box, and getting the lay of the land.

Returning to his office, Notarbartolo transcribed his mental notes. Although his safe deposit box had been empty, it did contain one thing of immense value: a clue as to how it might be opened without a key or a combination. Notarbartolo hurriedly worked to capture everything while it was fresh in his mind. After he'd emptied his brain, he shuffled again through the pages and considered his mission. It was daunting.

Among the long list of security measures he would have to overcome, there was one glimmer of good news. Despite fortifications that would have made most thieves give up before they even began, the Diamond Center had a glaring weakness that a criminal as experienced as Notarbartolo would most certainly have noticed right away. Though most of the building was within the SADA, surrounded by the cocoon of cameras, cops, and ram-proof vehicle barriers, not all of it was.

The garage doors of C Block opened directly onto Lange Herentalsestraat, outside the security zone. There were cameras on that street, of course, and the police substation was close to the garage doors. The thieves would still have to dodge video surveillance; sidestep police patrols; enter the locked building without being detected; somehow penetrate the LIPS door without setting off the alarm; bypass motion detectors, infrared detectors, and light detectors; crack nearly two hundred locked safes and make off with as much loot as could be carried, all without alerting the onsite caretakers or being given away by a battery of closed-circuit TV cameras. But this major security hole might just be the key to pulling off the heist.

With the first stage of his reconnaissance mission complete, it was time for Notarbartolo to return to Italy, where his team of expert lock pickers, safecrackers, and alarm specialists awaited their briefing.

Chapter Two

THE SCHOOL OF TURIN

"This is the city of Turin, the industrial capital of Italy. The most modern in Europe, famed for its architecture and soon, I trust, for the greatest robbery of the twentieth century."

—*The Italian Job* (1969)

If anyone at the Diamond Center had called the Italian police to check on their new tenant, they would have eventually been transferred to Marco Martino. And if they'd ask him if he'd ever heard of a Turin resident named Leonardo Notarbartolo, it would have been like asking the Catholic police commander if he attended Mass regularly.

"Of course," Martino would have said, followed quickly by, "Why do you ask?"

Such a phone call never happened, but if it had, it may well have stopped the plot to rob the Diamond Center in its tracks. Martino would have pulled out the thick salmon-colored file folder with Notarbartolo's name emblazoned on it that he kept near at hand. The file was filled with details of the jeweler's criminal life that would have been more than the Diamond Center needed to know.

Martino's official title was Lieutenant Colonel Adjutant of the Questora di Torino, Squadra Mobile. In short, he was the commander of the police department's Mobile Squadron, a specially trained unit of police detectives who tackled vice, corruption, and organized crime in Turin.

The names of Notarbartolo and his associates were well known on the third floor of the medieval-looking police department. The dense and bustling city of Turin was known for many things—its world-class art and architecture, the holy shroud believed by many to be Christ's burial cloth, the area's checkered history as an automotive manufacturing center—but Martino and his team focused on an aspect of the city that rarely made the tourist guidebooks: its unique criminal element.

In terms of its underworld, Turin had two major distinctions: it was an organized-crime stronghold bitterly fought over in the 1980s and 1990s by warring Mafia clans and it was also home to the most successful band of jewelry thieves in the world. Because Mafia crimes dominated the detectives' time as they struggled to ensure Turin never got as bad a reputation as Naples or Palermo, the gang of jewel thieves was able to operate just outside of the police's grasp. And so, for over a decade, the bandits looted Turin's jewelry stores in a citywide spree that the cops seemed powerless to stop.

It was a particularly frustrating crime wave because the thieves were unusually clever and elusive. Martino knew who most of them were, but due to their singular skill in pulling off the heists, they got away with their crimes more often than they were caught and punished for them. Those arrested were usually out on the streets within a few years at most. Smart criminals employed smart lawyers.

Martino was a very disciplined detective, and he knew that patience was his ally in building a case against the likes of Notarbartolo and his associates. The more they operated, the more likely they were to slip up and get caught with their hands in a big enough cookie jar that they would do real time. But Martino was also human, and it frustrated him that the criminals' time had not yet come.

The jewelry heists had tapered off in the late 1990s. Martino knew the thieves' modus operandi well enough that this hiatus didn't signal retirement. It just meant that they were onto another score and were busy plotting its details. If anyone at the Diamond Center had called as he was turning these thoughts over in his mind, Martino would have seen the picture immediately.

But no one did.

◆ ◆ ◆

To understand how Turin produced thieves of Notarbartolo's caliber, it is important first to understand the city itself.

Turin is ancient, dating back to before the time of Hannibal, the Carthaginian general who marched his army over the French Alps from Iberia at the beginning of the Second Punic War in the third century BCE. Descending from the Alpine foothills leading from France into Italy, Hannibal discovered the Taurini tribe living in a valley formed by four rivers: the Po, Dora Riparia, Stura di Lanzo, and Sangone. The people who then lived in the area that would be Turin did not survive their encounter with the famous general.

The conquerors settled into the verdant and temperate northwestern Italian Piedmont, a natural gateway between the larger European continent and the Mediterranean Italian peninsula. The area's strategic importance to invading armies was such that military leaders were compelled to stop and pay proper homage to Turin's rulers. To pass through the city en route to battlefields in France, Switzerland, or elsewhere in Italy required the permission of local leaders.

In the first century BCE, Julius Caesar established a fort near the Po River and granted Roman citizenship to those living nearby. Portions of the ancient twenty-four-foot-high brick walls Caesar erected around the small city still stand. So too does the Roman Quarter, the Quadrilatero Romano, where the ancient Roman buildings now house trendy restaurants, cafés, and fashion retailers.

The Savoy dynasty left its own impact on the city when it ruled a shifting area that included parts of present-day Italy and France from palaces in Turin. As the center of its empire, Turin enjoyed lavish architectural and cultural attention from the Savoys, whose artists filled its streets with stunning Baroque buildings, *piazze* as wide as airport runways, and public works of art. The grand and opulent royal palaces, residences, churches, and government buildings survived invasion by the French, occupation by Napoleon, and Allied bombing strikes during World War II.

Most of those structures also survived the rise and fall of industrialization. Turin's claim to economic fame was the Fiat automobile company, which was founded in 1899. It provided Turin with its economic heart, attracting waves of poor and largely uneducated Italians who migrated north in search of a better life. In Turin, industries like Fiat promised work and stability. By 1951, some four hundred thousand people had migrated to northern Italy, primarily to Milan and Turin—two hours apart by car—and to smaller villages on their outskirts.

The southerners brought friction to their new home. To the more prosperous Turinese, their southern countrymen were illiterate embarrassments, crude and uncouth. Many of them came from Sicily, Calabria, and Naples, the home of Cosa Nostra and 'Ndrangheta mobsters since the 1800s. Indeed, by 1971, nearly 13 percent of Turin's population hailed from Calabria, Sicily, and Campania, areas notoriously dense with Mafia.

Such migration continued well into the twentieth century, as northern Italy continued to offer more economic opportunities and prosperity than the south. Notarbartolo was part of this migration; he was born in 1952 in Palermo, the capital of Sicily, and later moved with his family to Turin when his father sought work there as a truck driver.

Of course Turin had been no stranger to crime prior to the influx of Mob families and their associates. But these newcomers brought with them a sophistication that the police were ill equipped to handle. Drug trafficking, illegal gambling, and prostitution bloomed to new proportions in the postwar years and took root, quietly but firmly. Mafia activity from the 1950s through the 1980s was so prominent in places like Naples, Palermo, Moscow, New York, and New Jersey that the organization's expansion to northern Italy, especially Turin and Milan, went largely unnoticed except for those Italian anti-Mafia crusaders who spent their careers tracking the Mob's movements.

The Mob had a hand in everything from money laundering and real estate to politics and the administrations of Turin's local football teams, Juventus FC and Torino FC. Another notorious mainstay of Mafia business—extortion—was also among their rackets. It was fundamentally simple: a business owner would receive a phone call or a visit from strangers demanding payments that could reach as high as $200,000. They usually got paid, though it sometimes took a few firebombs or pistol shots fired through windows to encourage the payments. In Turin, a tire factory was set on fire, along with its stock of

30,000 tires, when the owner refused to pay. Knowing the possible outcomes, most owners ended up making some arrangement. In the early nineties, it was estimated that 60 percent of all businesses in Palermo paid the Mob *il pizzo*, the term for this protection fee. In Catania, an estimated 90 percent of business owners paid up, so much that the local chamber of commerce proposed making *il pizzo* tax deductible.

From the 1970s through the 1990s, detectives like Martino were inordinately busy trying to keep a lid on crime sprees that ended with bodies found in parks, in cars, and even on the sides of highways. Victims included not only casualties of rival factions' turf wars, but also businessmen who refused to pay *il pizzo*, the occasional innocent bystander caught in the crossfire, and the police themselves. Detectives, politicians, and judges were often whacked in particularly dramatic fashions; one judge was blown to bits by a powerful bomb that detonated as he drove down a highway near Palermo. Throughout Italy, it was nothing short of war between those who upheld the law, or tried to, and those who profited from breaking it. Turin was no exception.

Against this backdrop, attention to more pedestrian crimes like burglary all but evaporated. It was, in other words, a good time to be a crook in Turin. So long as they took care not to hurt anyone or display overt ties to the Mob, and as long as they covered their tracks well, chances were high that thieves would face at most a perfunctory investigation. The police were burdened by more pressing matters.

There was one other aspect about the city that may have been a factor in the thieves' long successful campaign in Turin, although it's one that Martino may have thought wise to keep to himself if he considered it at all. Turin has a somewhat hazy, but nevertheless enduring, reputation as a haven for magic. As the rumor goes, it is an intersection between the forces of white and black magic, of good and evil. Pagans attribute it to a so-called triangle of white magic formed by Turin with the cities of Lyon, France, and Prague, Czech Republic. It is said to overlap with a triangle of black magic Turin forms with San Francisco and London. Though these days the whole matter is considered by most to be an absurd superstition or an invention of the tourist industry, it wasn't long ago when Turin's supposedly mystical nature was accepted with less skepticism. After all, where else in the world can as miraculous an unsolved mystery as the Shroud of Turin share equal billing with the gates of hell, which are supposedly located beneath the Piazza Statuto? Even though cops look for hard clues when trying to explain the unexplainable, more than once "magic" seemed as plausible an explanation as any when trying to figure out how millions of dollars' worth of diamonds and jewels seemed to vanish into thin air.

♦ ♦ ♦

Considering that the main industry in Turin was an incubator for some of the most famous names in sports cars—including Ferrari, Maserati, Alfa Romeo, Pirelli, and Pininfarina—it was perhaps appropriate that a young Leonardo Notarbartolo first ran afoul of the law by stealing an Alfa Romeo 2000 Spider, a limited edition convertible hot rod manufactured between 1958 and 1961. He was nineteen when he was caught in Paris in 1971, sitting in its bordeaux leather interior listening to the AutoVox Melody stereo.

Arrested and sent back to Italy, Notarbartolo officially launched his criminal career. Over the course of the following decade, he generated a lot of paper in police stations from Genoa on the Mediterranean coast to Macerata on the Adriatic coast, on charges from speeding to auto theft. According to newspaper reports, he even had a record in Switzerland. Short stints in jail had little effect on his determination to find himself behind the wheel of yet another sports car, and even the temporary revocation of his driver's license in 1976 didn't deter his need for speed. He seemed intent on living up to his boyhood nickname, *Testa di Legno*, or Wooden Head. He earned it due to his tendency to head-butt people during arguments as a child, but it could just as well have applied to the stubbornness he displayed by continually breaking the law.

Notarbartolo carved out a racket for himself as a small-time hustler, a chronic and unrepentant thief who was immune to any potential rehabilitative influence of incarceration. The time he spent in jail, a few months here and there, instead provided an ideal education, as there is no better place to learn the skills of theft and burglary than in jail surrounded by thieves and burglars. As Notarbartolo's knowledge grew, so did his confidence as a criminal.

One of the many police officers who took his mug shot back in those days caught his arrogance on film perfectly: in the picture, Notarbartolo looks like a candidate for student-body president at the local university, a cocky and handsome fellow who knows the election is already in the bag. He has a thick shock of wavy jet-black hair and his expression seems both amused and irritated at the inconvenience of being sent to jail. His left eyebrow is arched almost imperceptibly, and his lips are curled into what could either be a sneer or a smile.

While his love of fast cars never waned, in the late seventies Notarbartolo graduated into the more sophisticated realm of jewelry, specifically diamonds. More than just an intelligent career move (as jewelry is much easier to steal and sell than automobiles), it was a shift that landed him in a field in which he had a genuine interest. In particular, he had an aptitude for designing his own pieces. He was good at sketching and considered himself something of an artist; when he was bored, he could often be found doodling out ideas for necklaces, bracelets, and rings.

By the time he decided to open a jewelry store, Notarbartolo had been married for eight years to Adriana Crudo, a woman who would later be described by police as smart to the point of cunning. With curly dark hair and a slightly olive Mediterranean complexion, Crudo, who kept her maiden name in accordance with Italian tradition, looked like the actress Karen Allen from *Raiders of the Lost Ark*. As his partner in both life and business—and, as some would allege, crime—she was fiercely dedicated to her husband. After suffering through Notarbartolo's frequent brushes with the law as an overt criminal, Crudo was happy to help him open a business that provided a veneer of respectability, a jewelry store on Corso Sebastopoli. It was a busy avenue with a popular outdoor market that operated on the weekends on its broad treelined median. It was a prime location for a retail store, not far from the Juventus football stadium and city sports complex where, decades later, Turin would host the 2006 Winter Olympics.

To the outside world, Notarbartolo had finally turned a corner and become a respectable member of society. Those who worked in the stores and cafés nearby knew him as the polite and gentlemanly neighborhood jeweler, always ready with a smile and some friendly banter about soccer. If there was anything an acquaintance could complain about, it was that Notarbartolo preferred to cheer for AC Milan over Juventus, the local heroes.

By all impressions that of an ordinary upstanding citizen, Notarbartolo's new life was simply an outgrowth of the ultimate lesson learned in prison: the value of keeping a low profile.

◆ ◆ ◆

When Notarbartolo and Crudo opened their first store, it was a risky time to be in the jewelry business in Turin. It had nothing to do with uncertainty in the luxury markets; it was because jewelry stores in Turin tended to get robbed on a fairly frequent basis. The rash of crimes was committed by men who were very smart, very careful, and very good at what they did. The crimes were remarkably sophisticated, not brash or brutish like a holdup or an even less graceful smash-and-grab. Instead, they took place after hours, usually in the middle of the night.

Despite precautions like alarms, sturdy locks, safe boxes, and motion detectors, the thieves cleaned their targets out, leaving few clues in their wake. Over the years, these seemingly perfect crimes netted their perpetrators an untold amount of precious stones and jewelry. In the larger stores, the value of the pilfered goods from a single heist could easily surpass a million dollars.

Here's how it usually happened for the unlucky jeweler: On a day that he assumed would be business as usual, he would arrive at his neighborhood jewelry store, unlock the door, and shuffle inside. The store would be dark save for the blinking red lights on video cameras and alarm system control panels, just the way he remembered it when he left the previous evening. He'd flick on the recessed overhead lighting and the LED lights for the window display, shrug out of an overcoat, and start wondering how soon he could escape to the corner café for an espresso and a cigarette—but then he'd stop in his tracks as if he had been slapped.

The counters would be empty. The window display would be barren. All that was left would be the velvet pillows and mirrored panels designed to maximize the effect of diamonds, sapphires, emeralds, and rubies. He'd find cardboard wrists and necklines used to showcase solid gold bracelets, pearl necklaces, and Rolex watches standing naked in the harsh light. It's easy to imagine any business owner in that situation immobilized for several long moments as he or she runs through the mental ticker tape of improbable explanations: *Did I enter the wrong store? Did I put everything in the safe for some reason? Am I dreaming?* Finally, the only explanation that's even remotely plausible would bubble to the surface: *I've been robbed.*

The police were left as confounded as the store owners at these break-ins: at first glance, there didn't seem to be any breaking at all. Although the details varied from crime to crime, the detectives would usually find that the locks often worked perfectly, the video cameras still functioned, the alarms were still armed, and the windows were intact. And yet, the merchandise had vanished. Aside from the obvious tasks like dusting for fingerprints and questioning the staff, there was little more they could do. The thieves rarely left any evidence or at least not enough to identify suspects. But the lack of clues was a clue in itself; it pointed to a level of expertise that is rare among criminals. It's harder to rob a jewelry store than other businesses; the whole building is sealed tight with special locks, the doors and windows are alarmed, video cameras monitor everything, and motion detectors can be calibrated to be so sensitive that they'll signal for help if a mouse wanders in front of them. The goods are always under extra locks in their cases—which themselves have alarms—or they're stored in bombproof safes in the back office, which of course is also locked.

In the absence of evidence, the first necessary assumption was that these were inside jobs. But that avenue never panned out. The only other possibility was that a gang of extraordinarily smart, very careful thieves was running an organized jewelry theft ring in Turin.

Because the heists were never committed using violence, intimidation, or other strong-arm tactics—and because the losses were usually mitigated by a jeweler's insurance coverage—their investigation fell to a lower priority than most police detectives would have liked to admit. High-profile matters like Mafia-backed drug running, arms trafficking, and murder took precedence.

That's not to say the string of burglaries was forgotten or that detectives quickly gave up trying to solve them. Law enforcement agencies around the world are skilled at investigating crimes with precious few leads, using scientific methods to gain insight into the criminals they track.

The police in Turin, however, didn't need science to suggest where they should start looking for their jewelry thieves. It would not have taken much gumshoe work to learn that one of the most unrepentant car thieves in the city had recently gotten into the jewelry business. According to one newspaper report, Notarbartolo didn't seem surprised by a visit from police officers curious to know how he managed to fill his store's display cases with rings, bracelets, watches, and necklaces when just a few years before he'd written them a letter begging for his driver's license to be reinstated so that he could get a job delivering paper for a local company. He'd come a long way, the police observed with suspicion, from scraping for low-paying jobs as a delivery boy to being his own boss at a high-end jewelry store.

In 1981, detectives searched Notarbartolo's house looking for evidence of stolen goods in connection with a robbery the year before. They found none, but they discovered and confiscated a Beretta .22-caliber pistol with the serial number filed off. Notarbartolo said that he kept it for protection from the gang of robbers plaguing his industry. It was harder to explain the ten blasting caps for C-4, the extremely powerful plastic explosive, that the police also found.

Notarbartolo was arrested in connection with the robbery and although he was acquitted, he fell permanently in the sights of Martino's Mobile Squad, if not as a prime suspect in the robbery spree then at least as a person of interest. His name was added to a special watch list, and, in 1987, he was given a red booklet that cops called a "preceptive document" but which criminals called a joke.

The size and shape of a passport, the document was required as part of Notarbartolo's identification papers and could be demanded by police at routine traffic stops. Listed within the booklet was a set of rules that red-book holders had to comply with, including "do not drink," "do not go to bars of ill fame," and "work honestly." In practice, it fell short of its intended effectiveness, and the red-booklet program was dropped not long after Notarbartolo was required to carry one.

Knowing that the police were actively watching him had an effect on Notarbartolo. He was careful about where he went and he made sure to arrive home well before nightfall, another red-book rule, when he'd be less likely to encounter police between Turin and his home in Trana, a rural community about forty minutes away.

Generally, he managed to stay clear of the police, with one notable exception in the autumn of 1990. In an incident that would have done nothing to convince the police that they were looking at the wrong man, Notarbartolo was questioned after he was caught following a diamond sales representative through the streets of Turin.

Although the practice has since faded away, at the time it wasn't unusual for diamond salesmen to make door-to-door sales calls to retailers. Notarbartolo employed one of these fellows himself. It was a dangerous assignment, to say the least, because they toted with them bags crammed full of diamonds and jewels. Unlike the merchants in the Diamond District in Antwerp, though, they didn't secure them with flashy handcuffs and chains. The logic was that such a precaution would only draw attention to the fact that there was something valuable enough inside the case to justify a chain. The men who took these assignments dressed down for the occasion, sometimes in jeans and T-shirts, with the goods in a rucksack, just for the sake of looking unworthy of a robbery attempt.

But in September 1990, whatever measures at subtlety this particular salesman had employed hadn't fooled Notarbartolo. Trained to recognize when he was being followed, the salesman noticed a metallic blue sports car—an Alfa Romeo—on his tail. He pulled over and parked, strolled to a phone booth, and called the emergency police number. He played it cool enough that Notarbartolo wasn't spooked into leaving. Though the event was noted in his record, Notarbartolo was able to charm his way out of this compromising situation once the police arrived.

Run-ins with the police were the exceptions, however, not the rule. While Crudo ran the chain of stores that eventually included three locations, Notarbartolo was usually far from the eyes and ears of the police, sometimes in the nearby city of Valenza, which had a thriving jewelry manufacturing and design industry. Just as frequently, Notarbartolo spent his time in smoke-filled cafés and taverns throughout Turin.

These places were in out-of-the-way locales, far from the downtown tourist traps and the main boulevards that could have been easily observed by curious cops. One of the hangouts Notarbartolo used to frequent was at the intersection of a few narrow residential streets lorded over by towering apartment blocks. The sidewalks were cracked and weedy and filled with older men nursing espresso at cheap plastic patio tables. Inside, the walls were old and worn, the wood paneling warping from the fumes of millions of cigarettes over the years. Men sipped thimbles of brandy while killing time waiting to see who came through the doors. Places like this were undoubtedly shady, but Notarbartolo made sure they were free of at least overt criminal activity that would threaten to attract the attention of the police. If standards slipped to the degree that the place became a magnet for drug addicts or hookers, he'd find another espresso joint. There was little point in pressing his luck out of loyalty to a bar stool; drug trafficking and other Mob activities were high on the list of crimes the police were resolved to abolish.

These places were important to Notarbartolo, but not for social reasons. In fact, he had a notorious hatred of smoke, and it must have been intolerable for him to sit amid the cigarette exhaust. But it was in the smoky back rooms of cafés like this that he conducted his off-the-books business. Though gambling in such places was illegal, it took place behind doors that were labeled "private," over velvet-topped tables scarred with cigarette burns. Those playing cards were always men; if there was a woman, she was bringing the drinks and emptying the ashtrays. Strangers stumbling through looking for the bathroom were sized up from every corner of the room; it was clear from the noticeable lull in the conversation that they weren't welcome to stay and play a few hands.

As with smoking, Notarbartolo didn't believe in gambling. He believed in the sure thing. He used these rooms to hold conversations that weren't meant to be overheard. He traded jewels and cash beneath the tables to stock his showroom windows. He also used these little espresso dens, which were scattered throughout Turin, for covert meetings with his more nefarious associates.

It would be a few years more before the thieves' activities were well known enough to earn them the moniker "the School of Turin." At the time, plotting intricately detailed jewelry heists in dimly lit back rooms, they were nothing more than a band of shadows.

◆ ◆ ◆

Those whom the police considered members of the School of Turin would have most likely never counted themselves as part of it. Mainly that's because "it" didn't exist, not really. There were no official meetings, no roster of members, no roll calls, no secret handshakes, and not even a name. They understood that to name a thing is the first step in controlling it. As long as they remained under the general public's radar, the better off they were.

The name School of Turin was coined in the late 1990s by a newspaper reporter who needed a handy way of referring to the group of men responsible for the wave of jewelry heists. Eventually, even the cops started using the term too. It made sense, as the group had evolved into something of an institution of higher learning. These men had taken the crime of theft and turned it into an academic pursuit. They were masters of their craft.

The School of Turin was not technically a gang, at least not in the way that term usually applies to organized crime syndicates. Even referring to it as "organized crime" is a stretch. It wasn't all that organized in the conventional sense. There was no structure, no hierarchy, and no real leadership. Instead, it was a loose affiliation of men who shared some common traits: They were smart, patient, and greedy. They each had specialized skills that complemented the others'.

What differentiated them from other criminal elements was their cerebral approach to each new job. The detectives who investigated their crimes believe they got just as much of a thrill from subverting a target's security systems as they did from the take itself. The members of the School of Turin were not known for robbing at gunpoint, threatening a manager or owner into revealing a safe's combination, or bribing a security guard to look the other way. Instead, they outsmarted every security system they encountered, whether it was physical, electronic, or human. Ingenuity was a hallmark of their operations, and they always made the best of whatever resources presented themselves. In one famous example, they ditched the high-tech approach to learning the combination of a certain store's safe and instead sent one of their own to seduce an employee, who proved less than reliable when it came to keeping secrets from her lover.

Organizing a heist was a loose affair. A couple of guys would venture out to case a joint, often with at least one woman, someone's wife or girlfriend, serving as cover. Nicely dressed, they would go on what looked like a shopping expedition, but which was really a surveillance operation. Paying attention to the jewels gleaming at them from under the glass cases was only part of their focus. They would spread around the room pretending to admire just the wares, when actually they were sizing up the store's security: How many video cameras are evident? What is the make and model of the motion detector near the door? Which drawer does the clerk open to take out the keys to the display case? They also took careful note of the jewelry; perhaps the most important question in evaluating a heist was whether or not it was worth the risk.

From there, the plot would evolve organically along lines of communication that were well established in the underworld, through code words and innuendo placed with the right bartender in the right part of town. The men would gather in the back room to play cards and drink a few glasses of beer, making sure to keep their conversation as vague as possible in case the place was bugged. When they needed to go over specifics, a few of them would go for a walk around the block that might last as long as an hour.

It was then that they would go through the mental roster of who to involve. It was important that they worked with people they knew well or at least those who could be vouched for by already-trusted associates. It was a system of trust Notarbartolo would later discover in the legitimate diamond trade as well. The difference was that if the thieves picked the wrong people, they risked more than a deal going bad; they faced a long stretch in prison.

If the plan required a safecracker, they would compare notes on people they knew. They would debate the person's skill and reputation and try to remember whether he was in the city or in jail at the moment. It wasn't unusual that the first pick for the job was unavailable. Maybe he wasn't interested because he didn't like the risk, or maybe he was on vacation. Maybe he was involved in some other job at the moment. Sometimes a plan wouldn't come together because the right people couldn't be found to pull it off. Other times, a plot could be hatched in just weeks. And on occasion, they might formulate the perfect crime, but not commit it, preferring instead to sell the idea to someone else for a cut of the action.

After a job, that particular group might never work together again. Other times, the men might become fast friends who plotted their heists with each other in mind. Regardless, every job they pulled off added to each participant's reputation, and over time, Turin's thieving industry became well known even outside the realm of law enforcement. Gangsters from all parts of Italy paid a visit to its smoky cafés when they were in need of a skilled computer expert, alarm specialist, or jewelry fence.

Notarbartolo wasn't the only School of Turin member the police were watching. Out of dozens of criminals possibly involved in this nebulous ring, Martino's squad had identified several others that the mild-mannered jeweler associated with regularly. The best the police could do, however, was try keeping tabs on them; like Notarbartolo, they'd situated themselves just on the surface of respectable society as legitimate businessmen, retired pensioners, or honest laborers. They were careful to pay their taxes and keep proper business records. None of them wanted to risk arrest on something small; time in jail for any reason could scuttle a plan that had been in the works for months.

Because of the care the thieves took, police were powerless to do anything more than watch a suspicious business from a distance, rigging it with electronic eavesdropping equipment and watching it from the outside with video cameras. They did this with Personal Chiavi, a little locksmith store barely larger than a storage locker, which was owned by Aniello "Nello" Fontanella. Known in certain circles as the Wizard with the Keys, Fontanella had skills that extended far beyond making spare house keys for the occasional customer who wandered in. Fontanella was an expert lock picker. His business provided the perfect excuse to continually improve his craft. In his backroom workshop that was off limits to customers, he spent his days disassembling locks, manufacturing dummy keys, and perfecting the art of breaking and entering.

A regular at Fontanella's store was his friend Giovanni Spurgo. What Fontanella was to keys, Spurgo was to alarms. Spurgo studied motion detectors, heat monitors, and light sensors so he could understand their tolerance thresholds.

There were others the police kept an eye on, including a man who, at almost seventy years old, was the grandfather of Turinese thieves, the elderly Giovanni Poliseri. He went by the nickname John the Tunisian or the King of Thieves. The police also kept an eye on Pietro Tavano, a close friend of Notarbartolo's.

The one exception to the "keep a low profile" rule was Ferdinando Finotto, a master crook who was a jack-of-all-trades. According to the police, he knew a little about all the specialties, including alarms, locks, computers, and front companies. Where most of the other men moving in and out of this criminal orbit had, like Notarbartolo, perfected their ability to blend into their surroundings, Finotto couldn't help but leave a memorable impression, as no manner of dress could disguise his imposing figure. Finotto stood well over six feet tall and weighed somewhere in the range of two hundred and forty pounds. His head was shaped like an anvil, and he did nothing to mitigate it with the flattop buzz cut he preferred. Had he been inclined to make an honest living, he could have been a longshoreman or a lumberjack. Instead, Finotto was convicted of attempting to rob the KBC bank in Antwerp in 1997. At the time, the bank was located on Pelikaanstraat, right outside the Diamond District.

Finotto took his skills to Antwerp in 1995, in the wake of the Italian government's crackdown on 'Ndrangheta and other Mafia organizations through countrywide indictments that swept from Turin to Naples. With three hundred warrants issued and one hundred and fifty people arrested, it was the largest criminal roundup in Italian history. Authorities code-named it Operation Olympus—apropos, since some of the Mob's most important gods in its pantheon were nabbed, indicted, and jailed for life. Though the arrests didn't change much in the Mob's historical turf cities like Naples, the cessation of overt Mob crime in satellite cities like Turin meant Martino and his force finally had the time and resources to tackle the rest of Turin's problems. Suddenly, it wasn't such a good time to be a jewel thief in Turin.

Many Turinese criminals found refuge beyond Italy's borders, taking advantage of the city's location at the doorstep of the Alps. Anyone who needed to get lost for a while could hop in an Alfa and, with one high-speed run, be in France or Switzerland within the hour. It wasn't so dramatic for the School of Turin; those with businesses and homes had no need to flee or go underground. They just needed to find somewhere else to employ their extracurricular skills for a while.

Finotto chose to scope out the Diamond District; he set up a front company in Antwerp called Max Diamonds in order to open an account at KBC bank. For weeks, he and a few accomplices cased the bank thoroughly, using a small hidden video camera to film its every nook and cranny. On the night of the heist, however, the thieves got no farther than outside the building before they blew it. Around 8:30 p.m. on Sunday, February 2, 1997, while trying to disarm an alarm, they accidentally set it off. Finotto and his accomplices sprinted into the night, leaving their tools behind. By the time a security unit arrived to investigate, no one was there. The only clues were the burglary tools that had been left behind and some minor damage to a door. The bank opened as usual on Monday morning.

Finotto returned to Turin to lay low, but somewhere along the criminal pipeline, an informant told the police that the burly Italian was behind the failed heist attempt. A Belgian court convicted Finotto in absentia, since the law there allowed criminal defendants to be charged, tried, and convicted without being in custody. To avoid extradition, Finotto hired lawyer Monica Muci to plead his case to the Italian appeals court. Muci convinced the judge that Finotto's attempted bank robbery wasn't an attempt at all, but a scouting mission that went awry. They had triggered the alarm while just looking around, she argued. What they intended to do with the knowledge they gained was immaterial, she said, and, legally speaking, a scouting mission by its very nature wasn't an "attempt." The Italian appeals court agreed to throw out the conviction of "attempted bank robbery," though the Belgian court did not. As a result, Finotto was free in Italy, but risked jail in Belgium if he was ever caught there.

Though Finotto didn't score anything on the bank job, he didn't come away completely empty-handed. While posing as a diamond dealer, Finotto had rented an office in one building that didn't screen its tenants as vigorously as others in the Diamond District, the Diamond Center. Although he was working on his bank job, Finotto, like any observant thief, took careful note of the Diamond Center's security system and the general characteristics of its vault. He also sized up its take, guessing that there must be hundreds of millions of dollars' worth of diamonds stored in the underground vault at any given moment. Liquidating diamonds was harder than simply laundering the cash from a bank job, but diamonds were far more valuable by weight than cash, and they were considerably harder to trace. Luckily, he knew a jeweler in Turin who knew the particulars of the industry: Notarbartolo.

The few people Finotto entrusted with the vague outline of a plot were quickly addicted to the idea, enticed by its seeming impossibility. Their tempered experience, however, kept them from getting too swept away; they agreed to send a scout to check it out. Since it was out of the question for Finotto to wander the Diamond District as a wanted man, the obvious choice was to send the jeweler. They agreed to wait until Notarbartolo completed his initial reconnaissance before giving the plot the green light.

It was by far the biggest job the School of Turin had ever attempted. If they pulled it off, it would be the biggest heist of all time.

Chapter Three

PROBING MISSIONS

"Maybe I am a romantic lunatic who lives in his own world of dreams/fantasies, but money was the last thing on my mind. I was always waiting to reach something that was the top of its field."

— Italian crook Valerio Viccei, after being arrested for robbing the Knightsbridge Safe Deposit Centre in London of $65 million in cash in 1987

If he felt like a fool carrying a man-purse, Notarbartolo could at least comfort himself knowing that it would help make him incredibly rich. The little dark-leather satchel was triangular with a flat bottom and a handle on top so that he could carry it like a doctor's kit bag. What made it special, however, was the hole he'd cut out of the side. It was just the right size to accommodate the lens of a small video camera.

In the early months of 2001, as the School of Turin was deciding whether robbing the Diamond Center was doable, Notarbartolo traveled from Turin to Antwerp often. Cheap flights left daily from nearby Milan to Brussels. From there, Antwerp was just a short distance away. He kept the satchel in his Antwerp apartment so its obvious modification wouldn't lead to questions from airport security.

As he approached the Diamond District, he carried the little leather purse under one arm with the camera inside rolling. He walked slowly so the recorded image wouldn't jiggle too much.

Once at the Diamond Center, Notarbartolo badged through the turnstiles and made his way to his office on the fifth floor. Later, he took the bag into the elevator and down to the vault, filming the whole time. The resulting footage captured the elevator doors sliding open to reveal the stark white foyer before panning left to reveal the big vault door and the opening to the safe room covered by the day gate. He was keenly aware that at the same time, the Diamond Center video cameras were also filming him.

Once he was buzzed through the day gate, though, he needed only to wait until he was alone to film more openly and thoroughly. The vault was filled with riches, but also with blind spots that couldn't be seen on any of the building's CCTV cameras. This was to provide the tenants with privacy as they stored and removed their valuables in the safe deposit boxes, and it served Notarbartolo well. There were never any guards in the vault, so, once he was alone, he would need only to listen for the sound of the elevator door opening to know if someone was coming to open a safe deposit box. That they needed to be buzzed through the day gate gave him ample time to hide what he was doing.

Notarbartolo took his time filming the motion detector on the wall on the left side of the room, and he zoomed in to tape the details of the light detector attached to the ceiling. He panned slowly across the walls filled with the safe deposit boxes' rectangular doors, knowing that the footage would make his colleagues in Turin salivate at the thought of what they contained.

He couldn't do more than film the big vault door in passing, as it was in full view of the building's security cameras, but he didn't necessarily need to. The LIPS logo was stamped on the doorframe; knowing that and the building's date of construction was all the information the School of Turin's locksmiths needed to begin hunting down detailed schematics about its locks and security features.

Alone in the vault, Notarbartolo had the freedom to take a tape measure from his pocket and record the precise dimensions of the door, the tongue of the deadbolt, and the box. It was also an excellent opportunity to assess the structure of the room. Notarbartolo could tell simply by touching the walls that they were made of solid concrete. It's not hard to cut holes in concrete given enough time and the right tools, but not without shaking the foundation of the building. Notarbartolo assumed—correctly—that the floor and the walls were laced with seismic sensors to detect attempts to tunnel into the vault.

They'd have to find another way in.

◆ ◆ ◆

Ensuring that he filmed everything inside the Diamond Center in a way that would be instructional for the rest of the crew resulted in some awkward moments for Notarbartolo. With his little purse cocked under his arm, he was often seen on the security cameras tilting his upper body at odd angles, slowly turning in circles in the middle of hallways and walking stiffly like he had pulled a muscle. Much later, the police would watch the security tapes and laugh humorlessly at how in hindsight it was obvious that something was amiss with his behavior, but at the time, his clunky gait and what looked like spells of absentmindedness didn't attract attention.

For Notarbartolo, the possibility of looking like an idiot was one of the risks of his job. He had a long list of images he needed to film, and he knew he couldn't get them all at once. It would take him several trips over the course of months to film everything he needed. Each time he went back to Turin, his cohorts would have additional demands as they analyzed each new film. If they noticed a side door in one shot, they'd ask him to get a close-up of it on his next trip.

The men needed as much detail as possible about things that only a crook could be interested in. These included the type of lock on the door of the security control room; the specific makes and models of the video surveillance equipment, badge readers, and motion detectors; the manufacturer of the equipment that controlled the garage doors; and the type of lock on every door and safe between them and the diamonds. Standing around filming these things with a hidden camera was risky.

But Notarbartolo was nothing if not confident in his abilities, leading him to his most suspicious overt move to that point. During his reconnaissance, he stopped to talk to Julie Boost, wearing a slightly embarrassed expression and explaining that he had an unusual request for the building manager: he wanted a copy of the building's blueprints.

Notarbartolo explained that he was considering upgrading to a different office in the future, maybe a bigger space that could accommodate his supposedly growing business. The blueprints, he said, would help him decide which suite of offices would be best for his plans. As risky as it was, the request was an effective probing of the building's human defenses. Cameras and alarms are only as effective as the people monitoring them, and the Diamond Center staff had already shown themselves to be lacking by renting an office to him without bothering to check his background.

Diamond Center staff provided Notarbartolo with the requested blueprints, including those for level -2, where the vault was located. He could hardly believe his luck.

On the map, the safe room didn't look very impressive. It wasn't even the biggest room on the floor. There was also a workshop where staff members could make repairs to equipment, and a large storage room where unused furniture was piled among the furnaces, water heaters, and air-conditioner ducts. Each room was measured to the inch. The safe room, according to the blueprint, was twenty-seven feet wide by twenty-eight feet deep.

Getting the blueprints was the biggest testament so far to Notarbartolo's ability to pull the wool over anyone's eyes, even those like Boost who believed themselves to be hyperalert for scams and con artists. It didn't take newcomers long to figure out that Julie Boost was not well liked among the diamond dealers who rented offices in the Diamond Center. Part of the reason was that she was unusually nosy.

Though Notarbartolo didn't speak Dutch (or its local dialect of Flemish), he spoke fluent French in addition to his native Italian, and so was able to communicate easily with Boost and the other French-speaking staff members at the Diamond Center. Careful to stay under the radar by keeping his interaction with other tenants to careful nods and "bonjours," he maintained a relative silence that belied his acutely attuned ear. Notarbartolo was on the alert for every snippet of overheard gossip and idle chatter, and from what he could glean, it seemed many found Boost often unnecessarily stern, rude, and domineering. Her boss, Marcel Grünberger, had little interest in the daily affairs of the Diamond Center, preferring instead to focus on his diamond-trading business. She was given free reign to manage the building as she saw fit, and she ruled over it like the nosy superintendent of a New York

City apartment building. Given her habits, Notarbartolo must have been amazed when he thought about how well he'd snowed her.

Boost wasn't the only one on the staff Notarbartolo came to understand. There weren't many employees, and through a combination of overheard conversation and surreptitious observation, Notarbartolo began populating his mental map with personalities.

There were the two caretakers, referred to as concierges: Jorge Dias De Sousa and Jacques Plompteux. Although he was Portuguese, Jorge's name was pronounced "George" by nearly everyone, and Jacques was simply "Jack." They lived in separate apartments in the Diamond Center: Jorge, the more senior of the two, lived on the second floor of B Block. His apartment faced the vacant lots that were visible from Notarbartolo's office; on days when Portugal played an important soccer match, Notarbartolo could have looked down and seen the Portuguese flag flying from Jorge's second-story balcony. Jacques' quarters were on the fourth floor of C Block. One widely circulated rumor at the Diamond Center was that Jorge and Julie Boost were romantically involved.

Jorge and Jacques alternated weeks in which they were required to live in the building, so Notarbartolo knew that there was always at least one person there around the clock. They both had master keys to the building's entrances and internal doors and, most important, they were among only four people who knew the combination to the big vault door. The others were Boost and Grünberger.

Each weekday at 7:00 a.m., the concierge on duty took the elevator to the bottom floor, turned on the lights, and inserted a huge fairy-tale-style key into the LIPS door. The key was specially designed, something the School of Turin's lock specialists knew the moment they learned the door's make and model. The door was at least twelve inches thick, so the key's pipe needed to be nearly a foot long in order to reach the lock inside. Because such a thing can't be easily toted around in one's pocket, the key's stamp—the piece on the end that operated the internal tumblers—was removable. It was designed this way so that the vault keeper could leave the long pipe in a convenient location near the door while keeping the important part safely in his pocket. To open the vault door, there were two mechanisms that needed to be unlocked. The key had to be inserted and turned, and a four-number combination entered with a knob just above the keyhole. There were 100 million possible numeric combinations. The concierge then turned a wheel-shaped handle to retract the anchor bolts and the vault could then be pulled open for business.

Each weeknight at 7:00 p.m., the concierge closed the vault door and locked it by setting in place six stainless steel rods, each three inches thick, that extended from the door into the frame on the left and the right; and two more into the floor and ceiling. Then he'd flip off the lights before getting into the elevator. Until one of them opened it again, the vault remained as dark as a tomb.

Otherwise, the concierges' responsibilities consisted of being available to open the garage door if a tenant called and needed access to the building after hours. That happened only occasionally and usually only if a tenant needed to be at the office to conduct business with someone in a different time zone. In such cases, all tenants had a laminated business card printed with Jorge's and Jacques' phone numbers and a schedule of who was working which week. The dates on the calendar were color-coded in black and red to make it easy to tell who was on duty.

Overall, it was a cushy assignment. Once the building was closed for the night, they had free reign of the Diamond Center and its three buildings, but they weren't required to patrol the hallways, check that office doors were locked, or even watch the video monitors in the ground-floor control room. Most of their time was spent in their apartments watching television.

Despite the undemanding nature of the job, the men were often annoyed when they were interrupted by tenants requiring access to the building, especially considering how tempting it may have been on slow nights to sneak around the corner to the plaza for a late night beer or two. Smart tenants knew to slip the concierges a few euros for the trouble of doing their job, just so they could stay on their good sides.

Notarbartolo also became familiar with men named Andre and Kamiel, the putative daytime security guards. Andre was technically head of security, but when Notarbartolo rented his office, Andre had for six years simply performed the duties of a doorman. He spent his days in a small glass-walled security control room inside the garage, his responsibilities essentially limited to raising the arm bars for tenants with parking spaces and watching the video monitors as they badged through the doors that led from the parking deck to blocks A and B. The entry door to C Block was accessed with a key, not a badge; tenants were not supposed to use that door, so there was no camera observing it.

Kamiel was arguably the busiest of the four guards. He sat in the security booth at the main entrance on Schupstraat watching the video monitors and the foot traffic swarming in and out of the Diamond Center during business hours. He checked visitors' IDs and issued temporary passes, phoning the receptionists in the diamond businesses upstairs to confirm that strangers had legitimate appointments. It was his job to buzz open the fenced day gate to the safe room when tenants wanted access to their safe deposit boxes. At the end of the day, he rewound the videotapes that recorded all the images from the video monitors, labeled them with the date, and put fresh tapes in the VCRs.

Neither Andre nor Kamiel patrolled the halls. According to an account of their later statements to police, they relied purely on technology for the building's security. Ironically, although he controlled access to the vault for more than one hundred tenants who stored invaluable wealth in their safe deposit boxes, Kamiel had never even gone to the bottom level of the Diamond Center. All he knew of the vault was what the video monitors showed him.

The picture that took shape in Notarbartolo's mind was one of a staff that had grown dangerously complacent. The Diamond Center had never been robbed, and, based on what he could discern about the staff's habits, no one expected it to be. They trusted the security of the Diamond District in which the building was located to deter most clear-thinking thieves, and they were certain that the impressive vault with its bombproof door would keep out anyone foolhardy enough to try anything.

Sitting alone in his office, Notarbartolo assembled something of a multimedia treasure map. The videotapes, the blueprints, and the reams of sketches he drew in the long hours spent sequestered in his office pretending to trade diamonds were equal parts informative and tantalizing. Through them, the School of Turin could easily imagine following this treasure map to riches.

◆ ◆ ◆

Notarbartolo's reconnaissance proved to the School of Turin that it had picked the right building to knock over. The staff's lax approach to security stood in stark contrast to the other main diamond office buildings in the district, the four bourses. It was highly unlikely that Notarbartolo would even have gotten into the trading hall of a bourse to see for himself just how soft a target the Diamond Center was in comparison.

On any given weekday, the tables in the main trading hall at the Beurs voor Diamanthandel, which was founded in 1904, could be found scattered with coffee cups, crumpled napkins, mobile phones, day planners, and gemstone loupes. What a visitor noticed, however, wasn't the cafeteria-style trappings, but the diamonds blinking like white Christmas lights in the sunlight cascading from the room's twenty-five-foot windows. The loose diamonds were laid out on small white velvet pads or in little tissue-paper packages known as diamond papers unfolded into the shape of a paper box. They were handed around casually like someone passing the salt; when they were poured into metal measuring cups at the electronic scale on each table, they sounded like marbles being poured into a skillet.

The diamonds traded here and at the three other members-only bourses in the Diamond District were often sold in packages of hundreds of carats at a time in values that would blow the mind of anyone not accustomed to making transactions involving true wealth.

Diamonds are the most valuable commodities by weight known to man. A pocketful of ten single-carat brilliant-cut diamonds with exceptionally good color, cut, and clarity—altogether weighing only two grams, about the same heft as a pencil—is worth as much as $200,000 at retail. A kilogram of the same type of diamonds, weighing the equivalent of a liter of water and taking up as much space as a jar of peanuts, would retail for $200 million. Because of their small size, their enormous value, and their liquidity, diamonds are among the most coveted forms of wealth in the world.

They may be a girl's best friend, but because of their return on investment—of time and planning—they're also a thief's. Because the diamond merchants in Antwerp were aware that, at any given moment, a plot was in the works to rob someone, there was a cautionary saying all along the diamond pipeline, from mine owners to diamond traders to the mom-and-pop jewelry store: "If they can touch it, they can steal it."

Considering that, it was remarkable that the men gathered at the tables in the bourse could be so relaxed when dealing them from hand to admiring hand. It was common practice to temporarily part with your goods—whether to have them analyzed for cutting or to entrust them to a broker to sell for a specific price—and, therefore, merchants were often in possession of stones they didn't own, perhaps from several different sources. These stones could easily be worth hundreds of thousands or even millions of dollars. There weren't even formal records of who had exactly what in their safe deposit boxes from one day to the next. Of course, this would only happen between people who trusted each other. Trust was the cornerstone of the diamond industry, and it acted as an antitheft device more powerful than the most advanced surveillance system or biometric lock.

This was one of the enduring paradoxes of the industry. Those who worked with diamonds were thoroughly paranoid about theft and yet, in order to do any business, they had to take one another at their word. It was an ancient and powerful tradition in the diamond industry that deals hinged on the weight of one's reputation. Generally, this practice worked well, in large part because the industry was tightly cloistered. The ownership of many diamond companies spanned generations, and memory in the Diamond District went back just as far. Anyone tempted to run a scam on a fellow diamantaire risked not only his own reputation, but also his extended family's.

This wasn't to say that scams didn't happen. Quite the contrary, they happened regularly enough that Antwerp had a dedicated unit of federal police detectives solely devoted to investigating crimes involving diamonds. They looked into everything from allegations of smuggling and money laundering to bait-and-switch schemes and other rip-offs. By and large, the latter con occurred when diamond merchants weren't as vigilant as usual about with whom they did business.

Sleight-of-hand cons were common, in which someone examined a stone of a particular size and shape and deftly swapped it with a diamond of lesser value or a cubic zirconia, making off with the original before anyone noticed. In one particularly crafty switch, a man posed as a buyer for several meetings with a merchant selling a small parcel of stones. They came to an agreement on price and, as was typical, the merchant sealed the diamonds in a small envelope, scrawled the buyer's name and the details of the stones on the outside, and placed it in his safe. When the buyer returned within twenty-four hours with the money, as had been agreed, he asked to take one more look at the goods. He was handed the envelope, but before he opened it, he patted his pockets as if he'd forgotten something. Looking embarrassed and apologetic, he handed the envelope back and said that he'd left his loupe in the car and that he would return momentarily. No one ever saw him or the diamonds again; in the brief moment he'd held the envelope, he'd switched it with one that was identical, except in one respect: it was filled with gravel, while the one he took had the diamonds.

Diamonds purloined like that were traded quickly, often before the end of the day just across the street from where they'd been stolen. By the time a ruse was reported to the police, the likelihood of ever getting them back was between slim and none. The new buyer most likely had no idea the diamonds were stolen from their previous owner; even if he did, it would not necessarily prevent a sale. It just meant an unscrupulous merchant was then in a position to negotiate a handsome discount for not asking too many probing questions. As always, there were people in the diamond business willing to make an easy profit by turning a blind eye.

Because of both tradition and the high volume of quick trades, diamond transactions involved no lawyers and no contracts and almost never any lawsuits if a deal went south. Two men simply agreed on a price for a certain parcel of stones, signed the envelope containing the stones, and shook hands. The Yiddish phrase *mazel und broche*—luck and blessing—sealed the deal no matter what one's ethnicity. Even an Indian and a Chinese trader doing a deal in Dubai would use this expression.

After that point, backing out or changing the terms was as good as packing one's office and getting into the cubic zirconia business, because one's reputation as a diamond dealer would be sorely blighted. In the event of legitimate disagreements or misunderstandings, the bourse served as arbiter. This system was established by Antwerp's first bourse, the Diamantclub van Antwerpen, which was founded in 1893, and it worked so well that as few as two disputes in its first thirty years had to be settled in civil court.

As long as you knew the person you were dealing with, there wasn't much concern about lending someone a parcel with eighty carats of polished diamonds while he looked for a buyer for it. Few legitimate diamond dealers would give in to the temptation to swindle someone out of a mere $300,000 worth of diamonds when there was so much more to be had over the course of a lifetime.

Of course, that wasn't true with everyone, which was why such robust security measures were deployed throughout the district. Trust would be exponentially harder to extend if it weren't conducted within a web of security that included electronic surveillance, a platoon of police officers, and a fleet of armored cars.

Before technology allowed such a comforting dome to be placed over the Diamond District, confidence, trust, and a certain degree of courage were all a diamantaire had to rely on, and it resulted in practices that would be seen as ridiculous—even suicidal—today. At the turn of the twentieth century, long before the Diamond District contracted within its current borders, Jewish diamantaires and visiting traders from outside Antwerp simply set up shop at the cafés, diamond clubs, and restaurants on Pelikaanstraat just across from the train station. They would drink tea and wait for customers to arrive from Brussels or Amsterdam. Diamonds were bought and sold across the lunch table without a police officer in sight.

"I remember times when there was absolutely no security," said Fay Vidal, an employee of IDH Diamonds, which had its offices in the Diamond Center. Vidal's father and grandfather had also been in the diamond business, dealing stones on Antwerp's streets long before there were surveillance cameras and specialized police forces. She was respectfully referred to as "Madame Vidal" by anyone who knew her, and she was something of an institution in the Diamond District, an old hand who knew the industry inside and out. She carried herself with an imperial flair and, although proudly Belgian by birth, could be mistaken by her accent and her demeanor for having royal French blood in her veins. "You'd put [the goods] in your drawer, or you had a little safe in the office, but we went on the street with millions of dollars' worth of diamonds."

After a sale, customers would jump back on a train with their pockets filled with diamonds, and the diamantaires would bicycle home at the end of the day with their goods in a briefcase jiggling in the front basket. The thought of such an open and trusting system would make today's thieves go cross-eyed at the possibilities. Indeed, the threat of pickpockets, muggers, and scams by unsavory traders eventually imparted some common sense to the trade. The bourses formed in the late 1800s and early 1900s as clubs where diamantaires could wheel and deal with people who had been vetted by a membership committee.

The men in the Beurs voor Diamanthandel—as well as the three other bourses in the district: the Antwerpsche Diamantkring, the Diamantclub van Antwerpen, and the Vrije Diamanthandel—could be as casual as their Pelikaanstraat forebears because membership in the bourse was as reassuring as a Brinks truck. Someone walking in the front doors of any of the bourses would not get through the turnstiles in the lobby unless he was either a member or the guest of a member. Once inside the building, an invited guest could visit a private office but could not enter the trading hall itself unless he was a member of another bourse. The World Federation of Diamond Bourses represented twenty-eight of these members-only establishments worldwide.

Bourse memberships were not granted easily; one couldn't even apply without two current members willing to vouch for them as sponsors. When a new application was received by a bourse, it was posted along with the applicant's photograph on a cork bulletin board on the main trading floor of every bourse in the world. The members browsed these boards not out of curiosity but for security. They looked to see if they recognized anyone who might have screwed them in the past. If they did, they detailed their unsavory experience in a memo to the bourse membership committee. The allegation was investigated, and if substantiated, the application was denied. A record of the denial was entered into a database accessible to all bourses, along with the reason.

If an applicant survived two months on the bulletin board without any complaints, he was granted a provisional membership, which was susceptible to revocation. Even after he passed the trial period, he had to continue to operate aboveboard; if he was ever caught so much as failing to pay his taxes he could get kicked out of the bourse. And if a diamantaire was canned at one bourse, he would never get into another. It was a system that encouraged honest dealings; the trust displayed on the trading floors was well earned.

And indeed it must have been, if only for the sheer volume of goods that flowed through its door. It wasn't only diamonds that were on hand, but also millions of dollars in cash. In keeping with the old traditions, diamonds were paid for with cold hard cash, usually American dollars.

To accommodate this concentrated crush of wealth, the bourses all had underground security vaults with giant safe doors. Like the Diamond Center, the Beurs voor Diamanthandel had a LIPS door, but the other major brands were also represented. The Diamantkring kept its wealth behind a Tann door, while the Diamantclub van Antwerpen and the Vrije Diamanthandel, which were in the same building, entrusted their goods to the security of a Fichet. Considering the number of businesses in the Diamond District, vaults were surprisingly rare. Aside from the bourses and the Diamond Center, at the time that Notarbartolo was operational, the only other building within the secure zone with a vault for its customers was the CBS-Brachfeld Building, which had both a LIPS and a Fichet.

All of the vaults were highly secure, with multiple redundant security measures to prevent theft, but the highlights were the doors themselves. The LIPS door that protected the Diamond Center's vault, for example, could only be opened with its long key and the four-number code with 100 million possible combinations. No bomb could blow it out of its moorings without bringing the whole building down.

Had he been able to visit a bourse, it would have been obvious to Notarbartolo that the vault door was perhaps the only thing a bourse had in common with the Diamond Center, aside from the wealth that flowed through its doors. Compared to the bourses, the Diamond Center was a virtual sieve, the security of its tenants' diamonds and cash entrusted wholly—and foolishly—to electronics and heavy slabs of steel.

Notarbartolo didn't know it, but someone else in the Diamond District had already reached that conclusion, someone who knew more about the various security features of its buildings than anyone else.

♦ ♦ ♦

Insurance investigator Denice Oliver turned heads on the streets of the Diamond District, but not because of her crisp British accent, long blond hair, or distinct freckled complexion. She was well known because diamond dealers were all too aware that her reports to insurance agencies determined the price they would pay in premiums and how much of their business stock would be covered in the event of a theft. Those coverage amounts had a direct impact on how much business they could do. If they were covered up to $10 million, any amount of diamonds they had on hand above that would be gone with the wind should they be robbed.

The coverage amounts, however, were usually the least complicated aspect of typical insurance policies, which were tailored to individual diamond companies. Oliver's job was to conduct a thorough review of a company's security policies in order to analyze the risk. In this regard, her job was not so different from Notarbartolo's.

The first thing she took into account was where the diamonds were physically located. If the diamond company applying for coverage was located inside the SADA, the likelihood that the underwriters would agree to cover the goods was much higher; if it was outside the SADA, it might have been tougher to get a good policy, or the company might have been required to pay a higher premium. Alternatively, the company could have been required to install its own hard-hitting security in its private offices, which was expensive.

Oliver inspected the building where the diamond company was located, checking to make sure that its security features complied with Belgian laws specific to the diamond industry. For example, laws required motion detectors to be anti-masking, meaning they couldn't be subverted by being covered with a transparent film or gel. Magnetic alarms had to be polarized. A company's security team had to be licensed and vetted with background checks.

Oliver examined all the entrances and exits, and noted the times the building opened and closed. She walked all the hallways and counted the video cameras. She interviewed everyone who could unlock the safes, and she quizzed the people with access to diamonds about their daily movements between home and work to assess how susceptible they were to kidnapping. She found out if they drove armored cars or "soft" cars. She visited the vault room and made a detailed list of its protection. She noted the brand of vault door and found out if there were seismic alarms to prevent tunneling from below. She examined the inventory and saw proof of how much business, in both volume and value, a company did each year. She learned every step the diamonds took from the moment they came into a company's possession to the time they were sold.

Oliver was paid to think like a thief, because in the event of a theft, she was the one who analyzed the claim. Policyholders who were robbed had to prove both to the police and to Oliver that they weren't complicit in the crime. If they hoped to see an insurance settlement, they also had to show that they had complied with the terms of their policy and that the theft wasn't due to negligence on their part.

This scrutiny resulted in policies that could be extremely complicated, and no two of them were the same. It wasn't unusual for insurance companies to decide that there were too many risks to offer coverage. Some business owners could get insurance for just a fraction of what they handled on a regular basis. Still others could get no insurance at all unless they implemented extensive upgrades to their personal security infrastructures.

Those who obtained insurance had a complex set of rules to follow for the insurance to be valid. These rules could range from employing security firms with up-to-date personnel records to upgrading an interoffice CCTV system so that images were digitally stored on a remote computer server rather than on flimsy videotape. Or even replacing a cheaply made safe with something like a Fichet or a LIPS. Policies could also dictate that the diamonds never leave the SADA. The diamantaire who went to lunch on the plaza near the train station forgetting that he had a pocketful of gems was out of luck if he got mugged.

An example of a typically complex policy was the one that Oliver negotiated for the Antwerp Diamond Museum, a four-story building a few blocks from the Diamond District housing a permanent exhibition of priceless jewels. The policy was so detailed that it dictated where security guards were required to stand during the day. When a visiting exhibit was stolen in a smash-and-grab in 2003, Oliver denied the museum's claim because the guards had not been where they were supposed to be. If they had been, she argued, they would have prevented the theft or at least caught the perpetrators before they could run into the streets with a million dollars in stolen jewels.

Oliver had analyzed the security measures of most of the major buildings inside the SADA. She considered only five of them, including all the bourses, to be "acceptable" according to the standards set by the insurance underwriters she represented.

The Diamond Center at 9–11 Schupstraat was not among this group, despite being one of a handful in the Diamond District with a vault. This was primarily because Marcel Grünberger and Julie Boost never allowed Oliver to inspect the vault and analyze its security protocols. Even if they had, it's not likely the building's rating would have improved; just the fact that practically anyone could rent an office there and, therefore, have access to the vault, would probably have rendered it as "unacceptable" in Oliver's book. Unlike at the bourses, no background check was required to do business from the Diamond Center, and no one asked for references. As Notarbartolo discovered, there were no requirements for prospective tenants other than the ability to pay the rent.

The only way many insurance companies would do business with diamond dealers that had offices in the Diamond Center was if they fortified their own property, or if they agreed to store only small portions of their stock in the vault.

A good example was longtime diamond insider Fay Vidal's employer, IDH Diamonds, which occupied the entire third floor of B Block. When you stepped off the elevators, it was easy to forget you were in the Diamond Center. Unlike the grim, prison-like corridor of the fifth floor, where Notarbartolo's office was located, the third floor was redone entirely in blond wood and bright tile. Visitors entered a small foyer where they pressed an intercom button next to IDH's main entrance to get further.

Cameras watched the door, and a receptionist buzzed visitors into a small area that was called a "rat trap" in security parlance. There was another camera in this entryway and yet another door that had to be buzzed open to get to the inner sanctum. Inside, the open area was expensively adorned in wood with marble countertops, fresh flowers, modern artwork, and abundant recessed lighting. Glass-walled offices looked out onto the central area. Video cameras were subdued but still obvious, even in the corner conference room. It was a safe assumption that the offices were wired from top to bottom with alarms.

IDH dealt exclusively in rough uncut diamonds, and moved them in and out of Antwerp in great volume. The company bought rough from major producers throughout the world and distributed them to smaller manufacturing companies, actively doing business with some three hundred firms. On hand at any given time were millions of dollars of uncut stones, which were sorted by size and color and kept in large resealable plastic bags, which in turn were kept in several safes, one of which was the size of a kitchen refrigerator.

Though it may have looked like a graphic design firm, the company was a fortress; its security top-notch. None of its vast wealth was kept in the Diamond Center's vault; the underground safe deposit boxes IDH rented were used to store documents and business records, not diamonds, cash, or jewelry.

The Diamond Center was considered "unacceptable" by Oliver's standards, owing to the fact that she hadn't been allowed to inspect it, but that didn't mean it was impossible for businesses located there to get insurance. Some insurance companies were strict about not insuring diamonds kept in the vault, but others were happy to do so for a higher premium or by offering only limited coverage. Of course such insurance was optional, and there were many companies with offices in the Diamond Center that felt it was unnecessary. The vault, in their view, was insurance enough against theft.

♦ ♦ ♦

After every trip to Antwerp, Notarbartolo returned to Italy smarter and more confident than when he left. As eager as he was to debrief his colleagues, he was just as eager to simply surround himself again with the comforts of his home. Living undercover in Antwerp left a lot to be desired. As his friend Antonino Falleti said later, "Belgium is great for beer, but not for anything else."

For Notarbartolo, as for many Italians, food was among life's top priorities, especially after the relatively bland fare on offer in Antwerp. There was an Italian restaurant on the plaza near the train station, but it was a garish mockery of Italian restaurants, all red-and-white-checkered awnings and tablecloths, with a plaster statue of an Italian chef greeting patrons at the door.

For a man whose pleasures were among the simplest—good food and the company of family and friends—Notarbartolo's home in the Alpine foothills town of Trana was a sanctuary that was nothing like the depressing apartment he rented in Antwerp. Located between Turin and the French border, Trana shamed any Belgian village purporting to be "quaint." Huddles of red-tile-roofed homes settled in the dells of towering hills like water in the recesses of rocky ground. The highest structure in Trana, as in the villages around it, was the church, and the town reached toward the Piedmont forests with fields of corn, grapes, cattle, and horses.

Notarbartolo's house was nearly hidden in a small maze of rural dwellings situated on a modest hump of rolling hills. It was off the main road leading away from Trana toward the larger town of Giaveno, past haystacks carefully covered with tarps to protect against snow and rain, brick barns crumbling just so, and neighbors in rubber boots and wool sweaters burning leaves in their fields. Although his direct neighbors had horses and goats, Notarbartolo's property was more country estate than country ranch. It wasn't lavish, but it was more than modest. It befitted his image as a city jeweler who preferred the peace and quiet of the countryside.

The square one-acre property was fronted by a knee-high stone wall facing the narrow road, topped with a four-foot wrought iron fence interlaced with shrubbery and rosebushes. Eight-foot hedges separated his property from that of his neighbors, providing an impenetrable privacy screen. A more workaday fence defined the back border; beyond it, lush forest fell down a long slope, opening the view to a stunning valley scene that looked several miles across farmland dotted with brick homes and, in the winter, their curling gunmetal columns of chimney smoke. The wide back patio, perfect for sipping wine, completed the estate's mini-villa appeal.

In the backyard was another small structure, Notarbartolo's workshop. As much as his life as a jewelry store owner served as cover for his criminal activities, the irony was that he very much enjoyed the craftsmanship of making jewelry. Stealing necklaces, rings, and watches made him rich, but he hoped that designing them would one day make him famous. Amid the maps, diagrams, and to-do lists that occupied his lonely days sequestered in the office at the Diamond Center were sketches of wedding bands, pendants, and earrings, many undoubtedly inspired by pieces he saw during his forays past the retail stores on Pelikaanstraat. It's not hard to imagine him retiring to the workshop with a glass of wine—he preferred the local vintages, Barolos and Barberas—to tinker with the tools of a trade that, for him, was more than just a façade.

But before long, it was time to get down to business. He became less Harry Winston and more James Bond. When he called Tavano, Finotto, and the others, he switched his personal SIM card in his mobile phone—the one with the phone number he assumed was known by the police—for a different one with an anonymous prepaid Belgian phone number that couldn't be traced back to him. No one who was in on the crime ever called the others except on these secret numbers that couldn't be traced. The gang was then summoned to a meeting.

Even today, the police don't know exactly where the School of Turin plotted its operation. Because Personal Chiavi, Nello Fontanella's locksmith shop, was wiretapped and videotaped, they know it wasn't there. Police believe the most likely spot for such a meeting was at Notarbartolo's house. It was comfortable—the billiard table downstairs would be the perfect place to spread out documents—and it was remote. There was plenty of room inside the driveway gate to accommodate three or four vehicles. Nosy neighbors wondering about the visitors could easily assume they were there to watch a soccer game on television. The house was not under police surveillance. The School of Turin had free reign at Notarbartolo's villa as the plot took shape.

Generally speaking, there were two ways to rob a place like the Diamond Center: the gangsters could come roaring in with guns blazing, hoping to overwhelm the guards in a blitzkrieg of terror, or they could try tiptoeing through the security network like phantoms to make off with the loot behind everyone's back. On first glance, both approaches had their challenges, but the strong-arm strategy was ruled out immediately. The School of Turin operated according to a strict code: no violence. Any thug could stick a gun in someone's face and make off with his money and diamonds, but crooks like that were at the bottom of the food chain. Stickups were the crudest form of thievery, requiring nothing but guts or the right level of desperation.

That's not to say strong-arm tactics didn't work. The biggest benefit to barging in and demanding money was that it required minimal preparation and it was usually over very quickly. The thieves could be in and out, hopefully vastly enriched, before the adrenaline had tapered off. One such robbery resulted in what was, at the time the Turin gang was gathering its intelligence on the Diamond Center, the largest diamond heist thus far. Bandits firing machine guns stormed the Carlton Hotel jewelry store in Cannes, France, on August 11, 1994, just before closing time. They pocketed the loot and were gone before anyone realized they were shooting blanks. Brutish, yes, but it was also highly effective. In just minutes, they were gone with an estimated $45 million in jewelry.

An even more dramatic robbery had taken place seven years before the Carlton Hotel heist. In that case, flamboyant Italian criminal Valerio Viccei—who like Notarbartolo had a weakness for fast cars and flashy clothes—had led a group of accomplices into the Knightsbridge Safe Deposit Centre in London and held up the staff at gunpoint. They flipped the sign on the front door to read "closed," emptied the safe deposit boxes of an estimated $65 million in cash and gems, and then just walked away. The police found one of Viccei's fingerprints in the Safe Deposit Centre and arrested him and everyone involved a month later. Viccei was convicted and sentenced to twenty-two years.

The Turin gang undoubtedly knew of Viccei—he was Italian, after all—but they probably considered themselves more closely aligned with Albert Spaggiari, known for spending Bastille Day weekend in 1976 pillaging four hundred safe deposit boxes inside the Société Générale bank in Nice. Spaggiari, a Frenchman, was a legend to sophisticated criminals everywhere.

After renting a safe deposit box at the bank, Spaggiari and a team of trusted accomplices had spent two months burrowing a tunnel from the city sewer system into the vault. The sewer was big enough to drive a Land Rover inside; the thieves filled the truck with excavated dirt that was then dumped miles away.

Before committing to this arduous task, Spaggiari had put a loud alarm clock in his safe and timed it to go off in the middle of the night. He wanted to see if the vault was protected with acoustic or seismic alarms that would detect the noise and vibration of their work. It turned out that the vault had no alarms at all because the bank owners considered it to be utterly impregnable.

Once Spaggiari's men tunneled up into the vault, they welded the vault door shut from the inside and held a looting party, complete with wine and pâté, as they raided the safe deposit boxes. In some of the boxes of prominent citizens, they discovered compromising photos. As an extra touch, the thieves taped the photos to the wall for all to see, and then escaped with $18 million worth of cash, jewels, and precious metal. They left behind a note with a sentiment that the School of Turin would have admired. *Sans armes, sans haine, et sans violence,* it read. "Without guns, without hatred, and without violence."

The police eventually caught Spaggiari, but even that part of the tale was stamped with his special flair: he escaped from custody during a hearing by jumping out a third-story courthouse window and taking off on a motorcycle. Legend has it that he mailed a check for the equivalent of six hundred dollars to the owner of the car he damaged when he landed on it. He was never recaptured and was rumored to have died in Italy's Piedmont, where the School of Turin planned the ultimate heist two and a half decades later. Certainly, it was one Spaggiari would have admired.

Even if they didn't consider a holdup as being beneath them, there were practical reasons the School of Turin rejected the direct approach of an armed robbery. Storming the building was simply out of the question. Notarbartolo didn't need to be operational in Antwerp long before taking stock of the overwhelming arsenal at the hands of the Belgian police and the private security guards who roamed the district's streets. Some carried Belgian-made FN P90 submachine guns and wore body armor.

Between his apartment and the Diamond District, Notarbartolo walked past a full-service police station every day, counting as many as a dozen cop cars out front at times. At most, it would take four or five minutes before as many as fifty heavily armed cops dropped into the Diamond District like paratroopers. The vehicle barricades meant raiders would have to arrive and depart on foot. Without question, there would be a bloody shootout with very little hope of leaving with anything of value; it would simply take too long to get down to the vault and open enough safe deposit boxes to make it worthwhile. A plan like that also assumed they could figure out how to get into the safe deposit boxes quickly, a problem they hadn't even begun to address.

Notarbartolo and his accomplices could kidnap someone and force him to open his or her box—or, just as effective, kidnap someone's wife or children—but whom would they target? There was simply no way to tell which boxes held enough treasure to justify such means. Boxes that Notarbartolo spied filled with jewelry one day might be empty the next. If they kidnapped a relative of one of the staff to get keys, codes, and combinations, they risked the police finding out, a hostage escaping, or getting hurt. Plus, when one resorts to violence, the penalty for failure steepens acutely. The School of Turin knew if they were not killed in the commission of the crime, they could go to prison for a very long time.

No, the Turin gangsters agreed, stealth was the only acceptable route. As much as they wanted to successfully steal as much as they could carry, as Spaggiari had done, they wanted to do it with some élan. The School of Turin had never tried a job this big before. Most of their previous heists targeted retailers, minor league compared to what they were plotting now. But as far as the thieves were concerned, there was no such thing as an impregnable vault.

However, creeping through the shadows and robbing the place in secret had obvious risks, including silent hidden alarms, a night watchman with insomnia, or trigger-happy cops who might mistake a crowbar for a shotgun in the dark of night. Missing one small detail would spell their doom.

Minimizing those risks was the entire point of their extensive preparation. The satisfaction of penetrating what was supposedly impenetrable would make spending the millions they hoped to steal all the more enjoyable.

Chapter Four

WHERE THE DIAMONDS ARE

"What do I know about diamonds? Don't they come from Antwerp?"

— *Snatch* (2000)

Word of the heist spread like a brush fire. From one end of the Diamond District to the other, the news on every pair of lips was that thieves had robbed one of its fortresses. The warbling of police radios and the high-frequency shrill of sirens added to the sense of disaster in the district. Panic struck in the streets of Antwerp with traders wondering if their safe deposit box had been emptied or if any of the stones they had lent a fellow trader had been stolen.

It was a Thursday morning in December 1994, and the target had been the Antwerpsche Diamantkring, one of the four bourses. One of its members had gone to the vault and discovered his safe deposit box had been emptied. It took uniformed police officers about thirty minutes to cordon off the entrance and get control of an increasingly desperate crowd of diamantaires and bourse members who were churning the few details they knew into a thick butter of gossip and innuendo.

The police were clueless. It was a clean heist and they considered it fortunate that the thieves had raided only five of the bourse's 1,500 safe deposit boxes. Because it was such a well-done job, the initial suspicion was that an insider was involved. The first step of the investigation was to look carefully at the employees, and then turn to the tenants who had access to the vault. With so many people to interview, it was going to be a long process.

Meanwhile, as insurance investigator Denice Oliver tells the story, two Orthodox diamond dealers were having their own crisis in the midst of it all. They hadn't lost anything in the robbery. It was just the opposite: they had much of the loot. They were in on the plot with an Israeli named Amos Aviv who had rented an office in the bourse. Aviv had spent eighteen months casing the building and its vault while acting as a diamond dealer and recruiting the help of one of the security guards. With the guard's assistance, Aviv was able to make impressions of the safe keys, which is usually done by pressing the key into a block of modeling clay. It's not hard for a locksmith to create a key from the cast. Aviv and two others opened the safes and immediately handed over the cache of diamonds to the two religious men, who were simply supposed to hold onto it until the heat died down.

Aviv and his associates may well have gotten away with the heist if these diamonds hadn't seared a hole in the men's consciences. They were distraught, simultaneously riddled with guilt for their complicity in ripping off fellow diamond dealers and terrified of being arrested if they confessed. They eventually decided to tell a rabbi everything and ask for his help and guidance.

The rabbi was stunned by what his followers had done but heartened that the men had done the right thing by confessing. He absolved them of wrongdoing, forgave them their sins, and volunteered to take the diamonds to the police. The rabbi took the cardboard box filled with 10.3 pounds of diamonds worth $4.7 million, strapped it onto his bicycle with bungee cords, and pedaled to the downtown police department where the investigation into the heist was being run.

The officers took one look at the rabbi, shabby and red-faced after biking through the winter weather, clutching a ragged box, and decided that whatever his complaint, it was less important than the diamond crime they were investigating at the moment. He was told to take a seat.

It was only hours later, when it became clear that he was resolved to stay until he could speak to an investigator, that the rabbi was interviewed. He opened the box and poured out the contents on a desk to the amazement of the officers. In addition to the rough and polished diamonds, there was the equivalent of half a million dollars in fifteen different kinds of currency. The loot they'd been looking for had been sitting in the waiting room all along.

The story didn't end as the rabbi had hoped. The detectives were not so accepting of the accomplices' change of heart, and they were entirely unmoved by the rabbi's insistence that the matter was closed because the men had repented and he had forgiven them. He was browbeaten and interrogated for hours more, as police tried to extract the names of the accomplices from him. "The rabbi was about to get his nails pulled out," as Oliver put it. Finally, he identified the men. They were arrested and eventually confessed to everything. Aviv and his accomplices were also arrested.

That situation was played as a huge win for the police despite that the crime was solved only because two of the perpetrators had a crisis of conscience. In the halls of justice, that didn't matter because heists don't usually end so cleanly, with the loot recovered and the perpetrators jailed. The police were happy to take their victories where they could.

♦ ♦ ♦

Tales of such criminal derring-do flowed like water through the offices on the fourteenth floor of the federal police building located on the outskirts of Antwerp. Home to a special unit of federal detectives who investigated only crimes involving diamonds, its shelves were filled with books about diamonds and its walls with mug shots of men who were wanted for stealing them.

In the office shared by unit commander Agim De Bruycker and detective Patrick Peys, one wall was filled with Polaroid snapshots of the unit's men conducting investigations in various cities around the globe, from the seedy to the ritzy. These six "diamond detectives," as they were known, traveled to the corners of the earth following the trails of Lebanese financiers, Israeli rip-off artists, and Belgian middlemen working for Al Qaeda cells. They ran down diamantaires who smuggled goods in and out of the country to avoid taxes. They investigated allegations of money laundering and trafficking in conflict goods used to finance African wars. Because diamonds are used to pay spies, gunrunners, and soldiers of fortune, the detectives also functioned as a de facto organized crime and counterterrorism squad, and they worked closely with the U.S. Federal Bureau of Investigation, Europol, Interpol, and the International Criminal Court. Both De Bruycker and Peys looked the part, although from different genres—De Bruycker had a passing resemblance to

Patrick Swayze and looked like an action hero; Peys, with his thick salt-and-pepper hair and walrus mustache, looked like Peter Sellers's famous *Pink Panther* detective Jacques Clouseau.

Despite the prestige of their jobs, the men felt underappreciated—and often openly resented—particularly in the narrow confines of the Diamond Square Mile. While the detectives were the first ones diamantaires turned to in the event of a theft, they were also often the last ones the diamantaires wanted to see at any other time. The diamond industry was tightly insulated and highly protective of its reputation. From the industry's point of view, the diamond detectives were tolerated because they were necessary to investigate crimes *against* it, but whenever they made headlines by looking into crimes *within* it, they were a threat to the reputation of the whole industry.

The diamond industry had already withstood some sizable blows to its reputation. In 2000, news of conflict or blood diamonds made buyers aware of the very real connections between diamonds and war. Industry titan De Beers quit buying diamonds on the open market in order to quell criticism that it was funding wars in Africa, particularly in Sierra Leone, Angola, and the Democratic Republic of Congo. As of 2000, the diamonds De Beers sold were certified by the company to be conflict free. It vowed that, in the future, its cache of rough goods would come only from mines it controlled or from companies or governments it partnered with.

As if that weren't bad enough, a *Washington Post* investigation in late 2001 tied Sierra Leonean rebels to Al Qaeda, which was buying diamonds from the African guerillas in preparation for its September 11, 2001, attacks on the United States. Osama bin Laden's group needed a major cache of highly liquid assets, since it anticipated one of the first responses from the United States and its allies would be a freeze on its international bank accounts. According to the *Post*, the scheme worked, and Al Qaeda had in its possession tens or even hundreds of millions of dollars' worth of diamonds that could be easily converted to cash as it launched its attacks.

For the diamond industry, this was a nightmare. There could be no worse possible association for the products it sold than Al Qaeda. The diamond industry wanted to distance itself as much as possible from any ties its products might have with terrorism, but, unfortunately for Antwerp, two of the men alleged to have acted as middlemen for the Al Qaeda diamond transactions were found right in the middle of the Diamond District.

When the *Post* story broke, the diamond detectives asked Belgium's major banks to scour their records for unusual transactions. Artesia Bank noticed that one company had done very little business in the late 1990s, and then suddenly turned over $14 million in 2000 and more than $1 billion in the portion of 2001 preceding the September 11 attacks. The company had then stopped recording diamond sales in Antwerp—the opposite of what would be expected with such a sudden surge of money through its account. The ensuing investigation linked the company to Lebanese diamond dealer Aziz Nassour and his cousin Samih Osailly. Osailly and Nassour were convicted of dealing with conflict diamonds and belonging to a criminal organization and were sentenced to three and six years, respectively.

Since Antwerp had a policy of zero tolerance for trafficking in blood diamonds, there was nothing to do but grit its teeth that one of its own businesses was involved in it and assure anyone who asked that it was an isolated incident.

To be sure, there's no evidence that most of Antwerp's 1,500 diamond businesses were anything but perfectly aboveboard. But just as in any industry, there were those for whom that definition was flexible. It's not unlikely that a diamantaire who considered himself to be perfectly scrupulous still had a stash of "black diamonds"—diamonds bought and sold off the books, on the black market—hidden in a safe somewhere. This was sometimes done to avoid value-added taxes or sometimes because a diamond's pedigree wouldn't survive close scrutiny. Maybe they had been stolen or maybe they'd been smuggled. Regardless, trading in black diamonds was hardly uncommon; it was a means of padding the bottom line. It's not unlike claiming the maximum amount of charitable donations on one's tax return up to the point at which the IRS requires proof: if the value of the donations is inflated, while it's still illegal, the penalties are minute, and it's almost impossible to get caught.

If a diamantaire were to be caught trading in black diamonds, however, it would be the diamond detectives who would catch him. That's why, unless they're the victims of a theft, few diamond merchants would welcome a call from the fourteenth floor of the federal police building. Even if they were the victims of a crime, some would rather say nothing than open their books to these detectives. Peys summed it up even more succinctly when he said, "Some of them wish we'd all drop dead."

Be that as it may, there's little question that the diamond industry requires policing both internally and externally. As a form of currency, diamonds have no equal. They are untraceable, are easily concealed, and retain their value anywhere on the globe. It's well known by law enforcement and thieves alike that you cannot trace a diamond backward. Serial numbers inscribed by lasers can also be removed with lasers. Certificates detailing cut and weight are rendered meaningless if a stone is recut to shave off a tenth of a carat. A thief can simply submit the altered stone for grading and get a new certificate. These are among the reasons thieves have plotted to steal diamonds since practically the moment that humans decided they were valuable.

Diamonds are precious for both the characteristics nature has bestowed upon them and the mystique humans have attributed to them. They are the hardest substance found in nature, formed over the course of almost a billion years to 4.25 billion years deep beneath the earth's surface in what geologists call the "diamond stability field." At that dark and violent subterranean level, about 90 to 120 miles deep, the extreme pressure and heat of the upper mantle combine in the correct proportions to fuse carbon molecules together in the strongest elemental combination possible.

Other carbon materials aren't nearly as strong. For example, graphite has strong carbon bonds in layers, but these layers have very weak connections between each other. That's why graphite transfers so easily to a sheet of paper from the tip of a pencil. But the carbon in diamonds is linked in a three-dimensional structure, with each atom bonded in the strongest way possible. As a result, they have a unique octahedral crystalline structure. The bonds between the atoms of a diamond can only be broken by another diamond. That's why diamond polishers use saws and grinders dusted with diamond powder to cut and shape rough diamonds.

Even before the 1400s, when Belgian craftsmen invented the techniques for cutting diamonds into the shapes that are well known and treasured today, the stones were considered priceless and powerful. Because of their hardness and their ability to refract light, they were often considered to have mystical powers, such as invisibility and immortality.

No one is certain when diamonds were first discovered. The first mention of them is found in the *Arthashastra*, an economics manual from India believed to have been written around the fourth century BCE. For thousands of years, India was believed to be the sole source of diamonds. Then they were discovered in Brazil in 1725. Even as early as the late nineteenth century, these two countries were considered the only places to look for diamonds.

Diamonds, in fact, can be found the world over. Back when life on Earth consisted of single-celled organisms, diamonds were propelled from their subterranean birthplace during the volcanic throes of a young planet's growing pains. As the earth ventilated itself, volcanic eruptions spewed through the earth's crust, showering ash, magma, and rocks for dozens, and even hundreds, of miles. The deepest of these explosive events originated far below the diamond stability field and punched through successive layers as they rose to the top. Anything intercepted along the way, including diamonds, was mixed together and went along for the ride.

Not all diamonds survived the trip up a river of magma. It was a precarious journey that required everything to go right for them to make it to the earth's surface intact. Eventually, these former magma flows developed into kimberlite or lamproite pipes. Shaped like carrots, these diamond pipes tended to be much younger than the diamonds they carried, anywhere from 50 million to 1.6 billion years old. If the magma did not travel upward fast enough, the diamonds turned into graphite by the time they finished their journey.

These ancient volcanoes are gone, but the pipes they created are still there, lined with the long-ago cooled and hardened miasmic stew of geological debris of kimberlite. Not all volcanoes contained kimberlite, and not all kimberlite contains diamonds—but plenty does.

Centuries of erosion have loosened these eight-sided super-hard crystals, allowing them to migrate across spans of hundreds of miles. The resulting alluvial deposits produce diamonds from just under the ground, sometimes from beneath just a foot or two of dirt over broad areas. The diamond-bearing kimberlite pipes themselves can contain the stones as far down as men can dig.

Diamond pipes are found in countries all over the world, including Australia, Canada, the United States, Brazil, India, Russia, and throughout Africa, but geologists didn't learn how to start actively looking for them until diamonds were discovered in abundance in South Africa in the 1860s. By that time, the diamond industry was well established, particularly in Antwerp.

There was lingering disagreement over where, exactly, the practice of cutting and polishing diamonds into gemstones had first taken root, in Brugge or Antwerp. There were partisans on both sides of the issue, but Antwerp seems to have won the right to claim that it was the birthplace of modern diamond manufacturing. Its merchants in the late nineteenth century sold expensive diamond rings to captains of American commerce to give to their spouses, but they also sold low-quality diamonds suited for industrial uses, particularly to manufacturing companies.

Now as then, diamonds' hardness makes them valuable as tools. The Chunnel between London and Paris, for example, was created with a bore drill the size of a house that was studded with thousands of diamonds, making it strong enough to chew through solid rock like a spade through soil. These were not, however, the sort of diamonds that would ever have been found around Elizabeth Taylor's neck—they were low-quality stones whose characteristics weren't conducive to being fashioned into gemstones. In fact, 80 percent of all diamonds pulled out of the ground are not bound for jewelry companies, but for equipment manufacturers.

The price for industrial diamonds is not high compared to that of gemstones. Because of their rarity, for a long time gem-quality diamonds commanded prices that few outside royalty could afford. It wasn't until 1866, when a young Boer shepherd found a large diamond in South Africa, a fortuitous discovery that led to a diamond-mining boom there, that they became far more common than anyone expected. As any student of economics knows, the first thing that happens when a market is flooded with goods is that the price plummets.

But one Englishman, and one company, prevented that from happening.

Cecil Rhodes established the famous Rhodes Scholarship at his alma mater, Oxford University, and expanded the British Empire in Africa with the formation of a country that also bore his name, Rhodesia. But for diamond merchants the world over, his most important accomplishment was the foundation of De Beers Mining Company in 1880. De Beers maintained price stability in the global diamond market for more than a hundred years and laid the foundation for the modern diamond industry.

When Rhodes arrived in South Africa in 1871, he was an asthmatic eighteen-year-old who hoped the country's climate would be kinder to his delicate health than the damp chill of Europe. At the diamond fields, he discovered a frontier town of vagabond diggers who bored like termites into once-bucolic rolling hills and farmland, transforming the Orange and Vaal river valleys into a barely navigable series of pits and trenches that extended to the horizon.

Miners lived in tent cities and walked to their claims over wooden boards spanning deep holes, as it was an offense often punishable by violence to even walk on someone else's claim, lest a diamond become embedded in the soles of hobnailed boots. Every inch of dirt contained a potential lifetime's worth of wealth, and removing the soil from the pits took impressive ingenuity. Some prospectors strung parallel cables from the surface on which to balance the special wheels of jerry-rigged carts that were filled with dirt and then winched to the top. It often proved worth the effort. One of these holes, after it was expanded to include surrounding claims, eventually produced almost three metric tons of diamonds.

Rhodes saw early that there were so many diamonds to be had under the South African soil that if the disorganized mob of miners sold them all, the market would flood and prices would crash. In fact, prices per carat dropped from $14 to $3.75 by 1885. The secret of Rhodes's success lay in his ability to buy out and consolidate the claims of the numerous miners who had preceded him to these rich diamond mines. He also established his first monopoly, one over the water pumps for three Kimberley area mines. When flooding occurred, miners had to deal with him to save their claims. As miners spent all their cash paying his rates, they eventually had no choice but to exchange shares in their claims for the use of Rhodes's water pumps.

Between 1874 and 1875, depression hit Kimberley, with most miners thinking that their claims were depleted. Rhodes, and his main competitor Barney Barnato, though, believed the opposite—that these claims would grow richer with the removal of the soft "yellow dirt" on the surface as miners reached the hard "blue dirt" that lay underneath.

After the small players had been bought out, Rhodes then moved on to the large players and convinced his most powerful competitors to unite under the umbrella of his company, De Beers Consolidated Mines Limited, in order to control diamond production. Once he controlled the known South African mines, Rhodes drastically cut back on mining. As a result, he was able to increase the price of diamonds by 50 percent.

By 1890, while still in his mid-thirties, Rhodes was the most powerful mining tycoon in the world. He controlled more than 95 percent of the world's production of rough diamonds.

Rhodes died at the age of forty-nine, but De Beers endured as one of the most successful monopolies in the history of human commerce. Almost a century after Rhodes's death, in March 1999, Nicky Oppenheimer said in a remarkably frank speech, "I am [the] chairman of De Beers, a company that likes to think of itself as the world's best known and longest running monopoly. We set out, as a matter of policy to break the commandments of Mr. Sherman [the U.S. senator for whom the Sherman Antitrust Act is named]. We make no pretense that we are not seeking to manage the diamond market, to control supply, to manage prices, and to act collusively with our partners in the business."

Thanks to its aggressive marketing, De Beers defined cultural traditions for generations of husbands and wives, who formalized their love by exchanging diamond rings. And because it aggressively pursued new acquisitions throughout the past century, it artificially kept the price of diamonds higher than they would have been under a purely market-driven supply-and-demand model.

The mechanism for controlling the price was simple. As new diamond fields were discovered throughout the world, De Beers bought the claims or developed agreements with the mining company to sell their diamonds only to De Beers. The pitch made sense economically: selling to De Beers took the diamonds off the market, meaning they were worth more in the long run. Should the mining company decide to ignore De Beers's offer and sell directly to wholesalers, it could depress prices across the industry if too many diamonds were in the market. That would benefit no one.

In 1889, Rhodes made a deal with a buying syndicate in London to handle all of the rough diamonds that De Beers mined. Ernest Oppenheimer, with his Anglo American Corporation of South Africa, used "the syndicate," as it was known, to eventually take over De Beers itself. Once he did, Oppenheimer abolished the syndicate and replaced it with a single-channel distribution system within De Beers itself—the Central Selling Organization (CSO). This distribution system remains intact today as the Diamond Trading Company (DTC) and Oppenheimer's descendants still run De Beers.

Historically, De Beers hoarded its rough diamonds in a vault in London. They came from mines in South Africa, Botswana, and Namibia, among others. De Beers's agents also patrolled independent selling markets in West Africa, including Liberia, Ghana, Angola, and Sierra Leone, among others, to snatch up diamonds that came from mines it did not control. Those too went into the stockpile.

In London, the rough diamonds were sorted, valuated, and then sold by the DTC and its predecessors in amounts that were carefully calibrated to market conditions to a small group of preferred customers. The number of these customers fluctuated over the years. but were generally between one hundred and two hundred. The sales took place every five weeks.

The sales were called Sights—and the customers, Sightholders—but the name was misleading because the diamond purchases were arranged in advance, sight unseen. For the Sightholder, this was far from ideal. There were occasions when a Sight parcel was a disappointment considering the price paid. On others, however, Sightholders would be rewarded with a box filled with what were called "specials," large diamonds that could be cut into several smaller ones. This system allowed De Beers to exercise a degree of control over those it did business with by rewarding them with specials or penalizing them with less than stellar boxes.

Although it was geared to favor De Beers, the system nevertheless made many people extremely wealthy. Diamantaires may have legitimately complained that De Beers treated them unfairly, but they couldn't complain much about the industry De Beers had fashioned. The product they sold was artificially overvalued, but De Beers itself ensured throughout most of its existence that demand for it remained high with its unrivaled marketing clout. In short, De Beers transformed diamonds into the most treasured and valued gemstone throughout the world, and ensured that those who sold it became, by and large, immensely wealthy.

But it's precisely because of the artificial value De Beers has bestowed on diamonds that they are targeted, as they have been throughout history, by bandits and thieves. Their small size and their portability can be both a blessing and a curse for diamantaires: a blessing because getting into the business requires very little investment in infrastructure compared with other valuable commodities like oil or timber, and a curse because the same small size allows them to be pocketed, or even swallowed. Because it's possible to ingest millions of dollars' worth of diamonds, theft becomes difficult to detect.

To combat the ease of theft, De Beers has developed increasingly stringent antitheft measures at its mines. In the days of Rhodes, the process diggers used to steal diamonds was as simple as waiting until the foreman looked the other way before pocketing or swallowing the stones rather than handing them over. Modern mining companies have all but eliminated the chance of theft in this manner. At kimberlite pit mines, gangs of men with pickaxes and shovels have been replaced by heavy machinery that excavates dirt by the ton. The dirt is no longer sorted by hand, with miners' trained eyes picking out the diamonds from the quartz; these days, mechanically crushed rock is sifted along a conveyor belt that winds through a recovery plant. X-rays illuminate the diamonds amid the rubble, triggering little tubes along the belt that puff out quick bursts of air as the diamond goes by, blowing it into a bin. The rest of the soil is loaded into dump trucks and scattered back on the ground.

The problem of theft remains high, though, with deposits where the diamonds are scattered throughout the soil on the ground. In these enormous areas, diamonds have been scattered by eons of wind, rain, glaciers, and shifting soil. There is no cost-effective way to excavate an entire region of a country, so mining here requires that humans look for the diamonds. As a result, the potential for theft skyrockets.

Take, for example, De Beers's operation in Namibia, where the huge stretch of alluvial deposits was located on the coast, an environment that caused them the most grief over the years in terms of theft. Once known as the "forbidden territory," the sands and sea of Namibia's Diamond Area 1 were the source of some of the highest-quality diamonds to be found, but because of the landscape and its access by sea, it was also one of the hardest to secure. The company ringed the area with high barbed wire fences and private security guards armed with rifles. Workers were subjected to full body searches that included random and frequent scans with low-dose X-ray machines. All employees had computerized security badges that tracked their movements through the compound; some were even required to live there in on-site dorms for up to six months at a time. That way, they only had to be searched via X-ray once in that period of time, on their way out. De Beers even instituted a policy of keeping machinery in the area permanently, a response to the discovery that one ingenious worker had smuggled diamonds out in the hollow bolts of his car. From that point forward anything that entered the diamond complex's perimeter stayed there until it rusted away.

As resolved as De Beers was to hold onto each and every diamond discovered in Diamond Area 1, criminals were equally determined to steal them. One man swallowed 51 stones worth $2.5 million before X-rays revealed a small mountain of gumball-sized diamonds in his stomach. Some miners tied small leather bags filled with diamonds to the feet of homing pigeons to fly them out of the mining compound. It was a good plan, but one of the men spoiled it for the rest by being overzealous; he loading his bird with so many diamonds that it couldn't fly over the fence. Guards found the poor creature flapping futilely on the ground, relieved it of the diamonds, and released it. Since the pigeon was trained to return to its coop, they followed it to its owner's house, where he was arrested. Guards were subsequently ordered to shoot pigeons on sight.

Still other thieves filled the hollow shafts of crossbow bolts with diamonds. That anyone could smuggle a crossbow inside is itself a testament to the thieves' ingenuity and determination. This method came to an abrupt end, however, when an errant bolt heavy with stolen diamonds punctured the tire of a jeep doing a security sweep of the perimeter.

♦ ♦ ♦

While diamond mines provided temptation to thieves, Antwerp had much more than the occasional diamond to offer them.

It was obvious from the start that diamonds were only one form of wealth in abundance in the district. The Diamond Square Mile was also home to numerous jewelry designers and was, therefore, awash in gold, platinum, titanium, and silver. Some of the best names in fashion, including Cartier, TAG Heuer, Rolex, Tiffany, and Harry Winston, had a presence and employed private designers to fashion jewelry, watches, and accessories in which to embed diamonds. Businesses that specialized in precious stones other than diamonds—including rubies, emeralds, sapphires, tanzanite, tourmaline, opals, and onyx, among many others—were found throughout the streets surrounding the district. Given that many businesses had been handed down through the generations, Notarbartolo suspected that some safe boxes might contain ancient treasures that he could only guess at—priceless Roman coins, maybe, or royal jewels. And of course there was no shortage of cold hard cash circulating through the district's offices and banks.

But it was diamonds, both rough and polished, that all but paved the streets in Antwerp. That was especially the case once every five weeks, after the most important diamond sales in the world, the De Beers Sights, which ranged in value anywhere from $500 million to $700 million. The vast majority of the stones came to Antwerp to be quickly resold by the Sightholders to the companies that cut and polished them into the precious gems displayed in retail stores around the world. And so, every five weeks, Antwerp swelled with diamonds like a mountain stream filled with spring runoff.

Rough diamonds may be interesting, but polished diamonds are spectacular. Because of their unique molecular composition and clear white color, diamonds can be cut and polished in a way that they refract light like no other gemstone, causing them to sparkle with all the colors of the spectrum. The more it sparkles, the more a diamond is said to have "brilliance." And the greater a stone's brilliance, the higher its value.

A dealer in rough stones needs to be able to imagine what polished diamond or diamonds lay within a given stone. Often a lesser cut is required in order to maximize the size of the polished diamond or to accommodate an irregularly shaped piece of rough. Cutters spend most of their time carefully analyzing diamonds with computers and with strong magnifying loupes to figure out where to cut. Internal flaws usually dictate this; if the diamond is fractured inside, it can explode if it's cut in the wrong place, turning a once-precious piece of rough into worthless fragments. The location of a diamond's first cut, called the "cleave cut," is marked on its surface with a black marker.

Throughout the Diamond District and on the streets surrounding it, cutting factories specialize in this important but not so glamorous work. Long tables are filled with diamond saws reminiscent of machines from a Dr. Seuss book. Rough diamonds are clamped in a vise, and a circular saw blade dusted with diamond powder is lined up with the black mark on a diamond for the precious stone's first cut.

Because diamonds are so hard, the process of making the first cut can take weeks. The saws run around the clock and they're carefully watched. The cutters recognize when a diamond is almost cleaved by the sound a saw makes. When the saws start emitting a barely audible, high-pitched whine, the cutter knows to watch them carefully—because of the pressure of the vise, the diamonds can pop out and ricochet around the room once they're cut.

From there, the diamonds are buffed in a special machine before being handed to the polishers. Each of these men spends his days hunched over a diamond-dusted grinding wheel, perfecting a diamond's facets down to fractions of a millimeter, following instructions scrawled by the owner on the small paper the diamonds were delivered in. The machinery looks like what you'd expect to see in an auto garage, greasy and smudged from years of heavy use, but from it the polishers coax some of the most beautiful diamonds in the world. Because of all the grinding and polishing, the finished product can be up to half the carat weight than when it was a rough stone.

The diamantaires are consulted frequently along each of these manufacturing steps to ensure that their specifications are being met. It can take dozens of visits to the polishing houses to get a stone just right. Once they are perfect, diamonds are usually taken to a certification company in the Diamond Square Mile, laboratories that analyze a diamond and verify its four Cs: carat, color, clarity, and cut.

This process is the equivalent of having a car inspected before it's driven off the lot. Once it's verified as being a real diamond—an important first step since it's not always easy to tell the difference between a diamond and a cubic zirconia, even for professionals—the stone is graded in each of the four categories. "Carat" refers to a diamond's weight; "color" is a measurement of the yellow or brown hue all white diamonds have, the less the better in terms of value; "clarity" is a grade based on the number and size of a diamond's internal flaws; and "cut" is an evaluation of its shape, symmetry, and finishing qualities.

Throughout most of the history of diamond trading in Antwerp, buyers and sellers agreed on the four Cs after much haggling in the bourses' trading rooms or in the cafés on Pelikaanstraat. If you could convince a seller that his diamond was more of an F in color than a D—the scale goes from D, which is perfect white, to Z, which has a light yellow or brown tint—then you could probably knock a few thousand off the asking price.

The HRD (Diamond High Council) began offering uniform certificates in 1976 that were quickly adopted as the industry standard. When the certification is complete, the diamonds are individually sealed in numbered, plastic blister packs about the size of a typical business card. A certificate is issued that corresponds to the assigned number; it features a wealth of information about the diamond, including the four Cs. Diamonds with certificates are easier to sell as the buyer no longer requires a lifetime of expertise to judge a loose, polished diamond. With the certificate, he knows what he is getting, and this enables deals to be done over the Internet without the buyer even seeing the stone.

Although the certificates are numbered, the number can only be traced to the person who requested the certificate in the first place. Since diamonds change hands so frequently throughout the day, the numbers are almost always meaningless to someone hoping to prove a diamond's ownership. In practically all situations, a buyer would never think to ask a seller to prove a diamond's chain of custody; what's important from the buyer's point of view is the certificate, which allows him to accept a diamond's merits at face value so they can quickly move on to the one thing that matters most, the price.

Still, if a thief prefers not to take the slim chance that the certificate might be traced, he can use the information on the package to order minor adjustments that will remove any trace of its former identity. If a certificate says a diamond weighs 1.02 carats, the thief could take the stone to a polisher and ask him to grind off one one-hundredth of a carat. Then, for only €75, the diamond can be certified again, this time as a 1.01-carat diamond.

It would be slightly less valuable than it was previously—perhaps by a few hundred dollars—but what was even more valuable to the thief was that, to the rest of the world, it would be a completely different stone, legitimized with its own unique certificate. A stolen diamond going through that process is gone for good, because there is then no way at all for a former owner to prove it was once his.

Detective Patrick Peys knew this as well as Leonardo Notarbartolo. This was why diamonds were rarely recovered after a heist. If the detectives were provided with a detailed list of what had been stolen, complete with certificate numbers, they would have to solve the crime and catch the thief before he had a chance to have the diamonds reworked or even removed from the blister packages. You couldn't always count on the accomplices confessing to a rabbi.

Chapter Five

THE PLAN

"Obviously crime pays, or there'd be no crime."

— G. Gordon Liddy

When Notarbartolo's watch showed that it was just a few minutes before 7:00 p.m., he picked up his attaché case, locked his office door, and headed to the elevator. It was nearly the end of the business day at the Diamond Center, but Notarbartolo wasn't quite done with his work. He pushed the elevator button for -2, and disembarked moments later in the echo-chamber foyer on the vault level. He paused for a moment at the locked day gate, waiting for the guard upstairs to buzz him into the safe room. Once inside, he walked directly to his safe deposit box and opened it. He took nothing out and put nothing in. His mission was simply to stand there pretending to be occupied with its contents until the concierge came to lock the vault door for the night. Notarbartolo wanted to see exactly how it was done.

An end-of-day trip to the vault such as this was one of a few theories detectives later would have on how Notarbartolo was able to learn about the nightly locking procedure. It was one of the least suspicious ways to gather information because it wouldn't have been odd for the concierge to find someone still in the vault at closing time. Sometimes there was a last-minute scramble as diamantaires gathered the goods they'd been working with during the day to place them in their safe boxes before the big door was shut. But most of the men doing legitimate business quickly wrapped up what they were doing when Jorge or Jacques exited the elevator and announced it was time to leave. Not so for Notarbartolo; this was showtime for him. As with Boost, his goal was to get information without his mark knowing he was giving it. And so Notarbartolo did whatever he could to linger in the foyer as the lights in the vault were turned off and the day gate was pulled tight.

The giant vault door closed with a definitive boom, and the wheel operating its massive bolts was turned to anchor them in place. Using the keypad next to the door, the concierge armed the sensors protecting the room and then unlocked a plain door to the left of the vault. Inside were some paint cans as well as the stock of water bottles used to refill water coolers on the upper levels. This was clearly a storage room. Notarbartolo would have assumed the concierge stored the long key-pipe there while slipping the detachable stamp safely into his pocket, as basic security precautions dictated that the stamp and the stem be safeguarded separately. The concierge locked the storage room and turned off the foyer lights as he and Notarbartolo got in the elevator and took it up to the ground floor.

At 7:00 p.m., the staff on the main level prepared to seal the building for the night. Notarbartolo headed for the entrance in no particular hurry; information was rushing at him and he wanted time to capture as much of it as he could. In the control room, the guards were turning off video monitors. Notarbartolo was thrilled to see that, as they prepared the security system for the night, they swapped fresh cassette tapes for the full ones in the recording system; a VCR would be much easier to access than a computer's hard drive.

Notarbartolo swiped through the turnstile. Though he was among the last who pushed through the plate glass doors, he lingered outside. He watched with studied nonchalance as, inside the entry foyer, a guard opened one of the glass doors and reached up to pull down a rolling garage-style door. It slammed to the ground with a rushing bang, followed by the distinct clacking of a lock being engaged. Notarbartolo assumed that the glass doors were also locked behind it.

He had watched this mundane ritual more than once so that he could be sure that what he saw was the standard operating procedure. While doing so, he was careful to spread out his observations so that no one would remember that he was often the last person in the vault.

When on occasion he stayed later than 7:00 p.m., which was allowed for tenants working in their offices without need to access the vault, Notarbartolo found that the main corridor on the ground floor was already dark by the time he left for the night. The control booth was unmanned and locked; the building's video cameras were dutifully recording all the areas they covered, but no one was watching the images. To exit after hours, he used his badge to open a door near the elevators that led to a short corridor cluttered with garbage cans and bits of loose lumber. The corridor led to the parking garage. He noted that tenants were required to use doors that were badge controlled to come and go from the garage, but that there was also another door connecting the garage to C Block that was locked with a key. Entering or leaving through that door, if a key could be fabricated, wouldn't leave an electronic trail, as would the doors that opened only with a badge.

Because the garage doors facing Lange Herentalsestraat were closed after hours, late-working tenants were supposed to call the concierge to open the door for them. Notarbartolo, however, found he could open the garage door without the help of the concierge: a key was left permanently inserted in the manual door opener on the wall. One twist to the right opened the door; one twist back to the left and the door closed. Notarbartolo found that to exit the garage unaided he needed only give himself enough clearance, then turn the key to the left and hustle through the opening as the door began to roll back down.

The intelligence gleaned from these late nights at the office might not have seemed like much to those who weren't professional thieves. But in the hands of a master like Notarbartolo, these small tidbits were invaluable.

◆ ◆ ◆

It's been said that there are as many cafés in Turin as there are Catholics, and it isn't hard to believe. Turin's storied cafés have always been important meeting places for people with big ideas. Whether they were planning a revolution or debating the merits of Torino FC over Juventus, men have made their arguments in cafés, as the constant influx of traffic makes the perfect front for anonymity. Historically, these places have served as petri dishes for all sorts of sordid plots and plans, and they have also been good for recruitment. In fact, Count Camillo Benso di Cavour, who masterminded Italian unification after Napoleon Bonaparte exiled the Savoys, did so from the cafés around the palazzo that bears his family's name.

The cafés throughout the Quadrilatero Romano in the old city are like miniature wedding cakes: no matter how small they are, every inch is well tended and tastefully decorated, chock full of coffees, teas, wines, liquors, chocolates, and pastries. One can usually find the owner himself polishing the brass filigree or waxing the marble countertop until it is as reflective as the surface of a lake. For customers, standing at the counter to sip their espresso is *de rigueur*, but also practical; if there are tables at all in the smaller cafés, there are usually no more than two or three, and those are almost always occupied.

Farther from the city's center, café culture becomes no less important, but the cafés themselves take on more of a workaday nature. The farther you get from the historic churches and cobbled streets, the more likely you are to take your coffee in a rundown little storefront. That was the case with the café near Fontanella's locksmith business and several of the cafés within paces of Notarbartolo's jewelry stores. While investigators believe the big meetings took place at Notarbartolo's house, the passing of smaller bits of information and intelligence undoubtedly happened over a thimbleful of espresso and a plate of cannoli amid the din of the lunch crowds. Had any of them been under surveillance, the police would have seen nothing criminal, or even odd, about two or three of them meeting for thirty minutes of drinking and conversation once every three or four weeks.

It may have been in one of these little cafés where Notarbartolo shared the good news with the others: Yes, there were active video cameras recording what happened everywhere they needed to go, but what had become obvious during Notarbartolo's observations at closing time was that no one watched the monitors overnight. With no one watching them, the video cameras were as good as blind. The recordings were for watching later, only after a catastrophe struck. Videotapes were stored for a few weeks and not viewed unless something happened, which it hadn't the entire time Notarbartolo was there. Removing evidence of their crime would be as easy as breaking into the control booth and stealing the tapes that recorded the break-in. Best yet, the guards clearly marked the videotapes with the month and day—rather than a code—so it would be simple to steal the correct ones.

Notarbartolo also told his colleagues the stunning ease with which someone inside the Diamond Center could open the door to the garage. Opening it from the outside would be trickier, but they had an idea of how it could be done. Based on Notarbartolo's description of the garage door opener and the secret films he had made of what could be seen of the mechanism inside the garage, it was likely that the opener was as old as the building itself. If it was true, then that meant the garage doors operated on one of 1,024 radio frequencies that were preprogrammed into the circuitry on a series of twelve toggle switches. They could simply use an electronic scanner to run through all the possible frequencies to find the right one. It would take, at most, thirty minutes. Once they knew the frequency, they could make their own remote control using an RF transmitter and circuit boards they could buy at any hobby store or electronics retailer.

Although they were closer by half to the police kiosk than the main doors on Schupstraat, the garage doors were not in the officers' line of sight. The Diamond Center had cameras monitoring the garage doors, but they broadcast their images inside the building, not to the police. He'd studied the street intensively for signs of other businesses' cameras that might cover the garage doors, but he'd seen none. The offices facing C Block across Lange Herentalsestraat didn't have external cameras that covered the Diamond Center's garage entrance, with the exception of a nearby gold company.

If the sound of the garage doors opening and closing was overheard by the police inside the kiosk on Schupstraat, it wouldn't arouse undue suspicion. It was not uncommon for the concierges to open the garage at night to let in those who needed to work after regular business hours.

Entering through the garage clearly beat the front door. The rolling gate covering the front door was locked from the inside. Even if they could have found a way through it, it was in full view of the police's video cameras which, unlike the Diamond Center's, were actually being watched live. Additionally, the front door was within sight of the police kiosk on Schupstraat, which was manned around the clock. And if that weren't daunting enough, it would have been impossible to bring a getaway vehicle around to the front.

The first step of their infiltration began to take mental shape: Three or four darkly dressed men could blend into the shadows as they walked single-file toward the garage doors from Lange Herentalsestraat. Once they were a few paces away, they would trigger the door with their homemade remote and slip inside. It would take mere seconds for all of them to be safely inside and they would immediately click the remote again to roll the door shut. Once inside, they would have virtual run of the place.

The thieves' daydreams of getting this far relied on a whole chain of what-ifs clicking as perfectly into place as the combination on the vault door. Their plan assumed they could learn the frequency of the garage door opener with an electronic scanner, which would require someone to loiter nearby for up to thirty minutes while fiddling with a suspicious-looking mechanism, and then trigger it a few times to be sure it worked properly. That was also assuming the building hadn't upgraded to a more difficult-to-crack rolling-frequency transmitter, which automatically changed the code after every use. It assumed that the police wouldn't be suspicious of the sight and sound of a garage door opening in the middle of the night. It assumed that a passerby wouldn't happen upon them and question their activities. It counted on the concierge staying in his apartment, preferably sound asleep.

There were a score of unknown elements as well. As far as they could tell from Notarbartolo's reconnaissance, there were no alarms on the door to C Block from the garage—the one that required a key that the School of Turin's locksmiths would fabricate—or any motion detectors in the hallways. But there was always the chance that there was some alarm or sensor he'd overlooked.

And, although they felt it was a safe assumption that the concierge on duty would stay in his apartment, there was also the chance that he had some sort of after-hours ritual Notarbartolo didn't know about. For all they knew, the men liked to roller skate through the empty hallways before turning in for the night. Even if the concierges didn't roam the halls as part of their nightly routines, there was the possibility that they would be called to open the garage for a late-working tenant, introducing yet more people into the building's corridors and stairwells. It was all a game of chance.

Ironically, the safest place for the thieves would be on the vault level. With the magnetic alarm engaged on the vault door, there would be no reason at all for a tenant or the concierge to descend to the basement, no matter what the emergency. The concierges knew that opening the door at any time other than 7:00 a.m. on a weekday would send an alert to Securilink, the company that monitored the alarm, who would then call the police on the assumption that the concierge was being forced to open the vault. The tenant who left his passport in his safe deposit box prior to a weekend trip was simply out of luck; he'd have to wait until the start of the workweek before the vault would open again. For the School of Turin, it meant that there would be no traffic on the vault level from 7:00 p.m. every Friday to 7:00 a.m. the following Monday. They had a window of sixty hours.

♦ ♦ ♦

The slow pace and tedium of planning a heist is something most Hollywood movies rarely depict. Heist films never show the frustration of needing to wait a month or more to get a critical piece of information from the inside man, such as confirmation on the number of security guards who work during the day. They don't show the gnawing fear that something is being overlooked, or that their ideas might not work. And they don't show the interminable hours staring at blueprints and watching videotapes over and over and drawing a blank.

If the men in the School of Turin watched such films, they likely would have gotten a laugh out of what they all seem to have in common: heists that are complicated to the point of absurdity and which leave far too much to chance.

To gain access to the underground vault of the Bellagio hotel in Las Vegas, the *Ocean's Eleven* crew had to first steal a high-tech magnetic superconductor from a scientific installation to kill the power to the entire city. In the original version of *The Italian Job* (which, incidentally, took place in Turin), Michael Caine's gang snuck into the city's traffic control facility to take over the computer system that controlled the stoplights, then stole a load of gold once its delivery truck got mired in immobile traffic. The gang then escaped through an entirely implausible route in Mini Coopers. In *The Score*, Robert De Niro's plan to steal a priceless French scepter from a safe in the basement of the Montreal Customs House relied on his accomplice—a man he didn't know well or trust—hacking into the security network using a laptop. A lynchpin of the plan was De Niro's ability to crack the safe in less than fifteen minutes.

Another hallmark of these fictional jobs is that they take only a few weeks to plan and pull off. By the time the School of Turin was ready to rob the Diamond Center, Notarbartolo would have spent twenty-seven months on his surveillance mission. And in the movies there is usually some sort of devious double-cross, pulled at the height of the crime, but which the hero invariably has the foresight to predict and thwart.

The School of Turin knew that real-life jobs were hard enough without the added drama of split-second timing, complicated disguises, and interpersonal subterfuge. And they knew that at the heart of every successful heist was a near-religious devotion to research.

Figuring out how to get into the Diamond Center was relatively easy compared to what they faced once they did. Once inside, they had to contend with a series of locked doors between them and the loot, most dauntingly the silent, immobile sentinel whose sole purpose was to keep men like them out of the safe room: the LIPS door. If they were able to open it without setting off any of the several alarms monitoring the vault, they'd have to figure out how to gain entry to the nearly two hundred locked safe deposit boxes that contained what they hoped to steal.

So far, no one had any idea how to do it without getting caught.

◆ ◆ ◆

The vault door in the Diamond Center was an elegantly designed masterpiece of engineering. Its locks incorporated the most basic principles of physical safeguards as well as a number of ingenious countermeasures that were in place to prevent those safeguards from being subverted.

The schematics for the vault door and its inner workings are available from a number of sources, most notably from old locksmith manuals that legitimate safecrackers keep on hand in the same way auto mechanics keep repair books for old or rare engines. The School of Turin could also have ordered them from the manufacturer, which likely wouldn't have hesitated to provide them to a legitimate locksmith outfit like Fontanella's Personal Chiavi. But if obtaining the plans would be simple, figuring out a way to actually open the door would not.

From the plans, the thieves would have seen that the combination dial was connected to a long rod that operated a drive cam inside the door. The drive cam was connected to a stack of four round wheel plates, each with a notch in it. Each of the wheels corresponded with a number on the dial. As the correct numbers were dialed, the cam "picked up" a different wheel with the notches aligned and spun them in tandem. Once all four were lined up, it allowed a "fence," or metal bar, to fall into the notches and out of the way of the key mechanism. Now the key could be inserted and turned to retract the bolts that anchored the door to the jamb. Without the right combination, the key could not be turned.

The key itself, which was assembled from the pipe and the removable stamp, operated a sturdy lock. The double-bitted stamp aligned with grooves and wards cut into a stack of sixteen steel plates. The lock was designed to be unpickable.

Without knowing the combination, a safecracker would have quite a time opening the door, even if he had the key. It could, nevertheless, be done. The first step would be to discover the combination. One way of doing that would be to drill a peephole into the door so that the safecracker could use a special eyepiece called a borescope to see the notches on the wheels. Doing so would require the safecracker to be intimately familiar with the door; he would need to drill the precise distance needed to view the wheels and no farther. If he were to accidentally drill into the wheels themselves, it could warp them and prevent them from turning properly. If he drilled the hole to the precise depth, then it would be just a matter of watching through the borescope while turning the dial back and forth until the notches lined up.

Drilling the hole, however, would not be nearly as easy as it sounds. The vault door was made of steel, and, depending on the model, backed by ultra-hard metal plates made of tungsten carbide or aluminum oxide around the combination mechanism. The LIPS company called them "torch and drill resistant layers," or TDRs. Titanium- or diamond-tipped drill bits could eventually bore through these plates, but doing so would burn through several drills; the bits would outlast the motors. Drilling even a small hole would take days.

The School of Turin couldn't afford to spend a day or more drilling through the vault door. In fact, they couldn't spend any time at all drilling, as the vault was equipped with seismic alarms. These sophisticated detectors intended to sense vibrations in the physical fabric of a building or room are designed to recognize the unique repetitive vibrations of drilling, sawing, and hammering but can be programmed to ignore other frequencies like those produced by slamming doors or the passing rumble of a dump truck. But even if there hadn't been any such sensors, drilling presented the danger of creating enough noise that a concierge could hear it if they were unlucky.

It was possible to learn the combination without drilling, but it would probably take just as long. The stereotypical image depicted in the movies of a safecracker using a stethoscope to hear tiny clicks and clacks is not far from reality. What he's listening for are the telltale sounds of the fence making contact with the edges of the notches in the wheels as they rotate. Unlike in the movies, however, this isn't done in minutes. The safecracker uses a graph to plot the "locations" of the clicks on the dial for each wheel, eventually coming up with the numbers that correspond with them. Then it's a matter of trying every combination of those four numbers until the door opens. While it might be the most elegant way to crack a safe, it's also the most difficult, with a high probability of failure.

Automatic safe dialers are available to do this job with the aid of computers—a robotic hand can be connected to the wheel to quickly dial through the combination possibilities—but they aren't significantly quicker than a human safecracker spending days with his ear pressed to the door. In fact, the automatic dialing method can likely take days, if not weeks.

The last hurdle posed by the door was its magnetic alarm. The magnets—one bolted to the outside of the door, the other to the jamb—were the size of bricks. When the door was closed, they lined up side by side and created a magnetic field between them. A ten-digit keypad on the wall armed and disarmed the alarm (along with all the other sensors in the room), and the cables connecting the contraption to Securilink were housed in a flexible steel tube that snaked into the ceiling. The control mechanisms were tamper-proof; if the alarms were turned off with the keypad, or if the cables were severed with a power saw, the security company would know it.

The thieves could bypass the magnetic alarm, in theory, if they used a plasma cutting torch or thermal lance to cut a man-sized hole in the door itself, leaving the alarm attached and intact. A plasma torch is like a gas welder, but far more powerful, capable of cutting steel like butter. But since they would have to cut entirely through the door, the shower of sparks that would arc into the safe room would set off the motion detector, the light detector, and the heat detector.

Blowing it up with C-4 was out of the question. The amount needed would probably threaten to collapse the building on top of them and even if it didn't, every alarm in the Diamond District would go off.

The thieves needed a quick way through the door, one that wouldn't take days to accomplish or require they bring with them a hardware store's worth of tools and machinery. Months of brainstorming brought them many ideas, but these were all discarded as quickly as they'd come up, deemed unsuitable, implausible, or dangerous—or all three. The unavoidable truth was that there was no quick way through the door without the key and the combination. Finding a way to get both became Notarbartolo's new primary mission.

◆ ◆ ◆

Of all the people who worked at the Diamond Center, the person who knew the vault door the best was also the person most likely to be overlooked by the diamantaires hustling through its hallways.

Paul De Vos was in his mid-fifties, and, without his billiard-ball eyeglasses, he was all but blind. His fingernails were cracked and yellow, thick as seashells from years of working with tiny mechanical parts. He cut a frail figure shuffling through the streets of the Diamond District, but on days when it was warm enough for him to ride to work on the back of his gleaming Harley-Davidson Electra Glide, it was hard to remember that he was going to retire in a few years. It seemed incongruous for such a slight half-blind man to ride such a huge motorcycle, but the bike fit perfectly with his love for all things mechanical. In his view, the Electra Glide was the perfect machine.

De Vos hardly minded that he didn't share in the glitz and glamour of the diamond industry. He was simply pleased to work in a field that he loved—not diamonds, but locks. De Vos worked for Hillaert BVBA, an independent locksmith company founded in 1921 that most diamond businesses knew to call when they needed work done on their vaults, or the locks changed on an office door. No one knew the workings of a lock like De Vos.

De Vos lived in a small cottage home he had built himself near the town of Heist-op-den-Berg, about a forty-minute drive from Antwerp. Although it looked like it was made of gingerbread, he could rest assured that no one would break into this house in his absence. The windows were barred, their frames made of reinforced steel. The locks on every portal were top of the line. Most impressive was the front door, certainly the only one of its kind among the small cluster of forest homes nearby, and perhaps even in all of Europe.

It was a twelve-inch thick Ribeauville vault door with a custom glass panel on the inside showing its clockwork gears and locking pistons. The door opened with a deadbolt connected to a combination dial and four twists of a long forged metal key. It was as strong and impenetrable as could be found in any Diamond District bourse or bank. If the house burned to the ground, the door would remain standing. Primarily a novelty, this custom-built door was homage to De Vos's life's work with locks and sprockets and keys and flywheels.

While the house was tidy, the attached workshop was a rat's nest of tools, spare parts, and gizmos. Four or five thousand-pound safes anchored the workshop to the ground; some were functional, others eviscerated. A *Playboy* calendar hung on a wall behind an array of different sized crowbars. Piled in the corners were boxes full of locks and parts from around the world; return addresses were from Tann, Sargent & Greenleaf, and Fichet.

De Vos literally knew the LIPS door in the Diamond Center inside and out. He had installed it when the building was first constructed, along with the rows of safe deposit boxes that it protected. Over the years since, he had been called many times to change its combination. That required opening a panel in the back of the door, loosening its innards, and averting his eyes while Grünberger or Boost set the new four-number combination. With the numbers from zero to ninety-nine for a hundred possibilities on each turn, that equaled 100-million possibilities.

De Vos did similar work on the safe deposit boxes. Although the boxes came in various sizes—Diamond Center tenants could rent boxes that ranged in size from three-inch tall letterbox safes to ones that were nearly two feet tall and could fit a small suitcase—the doors were all designed the same. The hinges were on the right and located inside the safe itself so they couldn't be dismantled from the outside when the door was closed. The brass deadbolt, two inches tall and a half-inch thick, locked into a slot an inch deep on the left side of the safe box opening. When the doors were shut and locked, their edges were flush with the housing, machined to within millimeters of the opening they covered so that not even the blade of a pocketknife could be jimmied between the door and the jamb.

Tenants may not have given the locks' mechanism much thought so long as they did what they were supposed to, but, like a soldier with his rifle, De Vos could take them apart and put them back together again with his eyes closed. Their mechanics were produced in modern factories, but their principles were at least forty centuries old. As locks go, they were simple, but highly effective.

Everyone who rented a safe deposit box was given a short silver key with an oval bow, or handle, which was etched with the LIPS logo and the box number. The key was inserted in a horizontal slot in a round steel plug on the left side of the safe deposit box door. The grooves cut into the stamp corresponded with metal wards, or barriers, in the keyway. When the correct key was inserted, all of the grooves lined up opposite the wards so that the key could be rotated clockwise inside the lock, engaging levers that moved the deadbolt horizontally to disengage it from the slot in the doorway. Importantly for Notarbartolo and his gang, only the key and the internal levers moved; the horizontal slot into which the key was inserted did not.

But nothing would move—no matter how much force was applied—if the right combination of letters wasn't first dialed on the gold wheels lined up to the right of the keyhole. Each dial controlled another lever mechanism that locked the deadbolt into place through a tongue-and-groove system. The lever disengaged the tongue only when the dial was in the right position. With twenty-six positions on each, the three dials added up to 17,576 possible combinations. The deadbolt, the levers, and all the metal innards of the mechanism were attached to the inside of the door and covered with a faceplate.

One of De Vos's jobs at the Diamond Center was to set new combinations for safe deposit box owners, as he had done upon Notarbartolo's arrival. When tenants moved out of the Diamond Center, they were required to either leave their boxes open or provide the combination so that De Vos could access the lock mechanism on the inside of the little doors. He would remove the faceplate with a screwdriver and then loosen a catch on the dials so that, from the other side, the new owner could choose a three-character code. When the new combination was set, De Vos would tighten the catches and replace the faceplate.

The operation took only a few minutes and was much easier than another of his responsibilities, which was opening the safes when tenants forgot their combination. That was far more arduous and required a few hours. The only way to open the safes without the combination was to drill through the door. The process ruined the door, and he would then have to replace it with a new one.

In the decades since he had first installed the bank of safes, he had replaced about a dozen or so of their doors, although he knew all of them needed to be replaced. The original design had a flaw: the inner faceplate covering the brass deadbolt and the guts of the lock was made of thin gray plastic, a weak point. In the years since the Diamond Center had been constructed, LIPS had upgraded its design to include steel faceplates, making the lock mechanism bolted inside the doors much sturdier overall.

But upgrading all the doors would have been a disruptive, time-consuming, and expensive endeavor. De Vos's suggestion to replace them, repeated to both Grünberger and Boost at various times during his tenure, was ignored.

Chapter Six

SAFEGUARDS

Always keep in mind why you are picking any particular lock, and realize that there is often a better way to bypass it, which may ignore the lock completely.

— *The Visual Guide to Lockpicking*

Whichever of the men figured out that Styrofoam and hair spray knocked out the motion detector surely earned himself a few rounds of drinks. Investigators don't know if it was Finotto, who had been faced with motion detectors many times during his illustrious career, Elio D'Onorio, an electronics and alarm system expert who was also a thief of some renown in Italy, or one of the other, never identified accomplices.

Whereas Finotto provided the muscle and Notarbartolo the charm, D'Onorio provided the brains. D'Onorio officially resided in Latina, a small town an hour south of Rome, but law officers called him "the Roman" just the same. He had been arrested and jailed in 1992 for his involvement in a string of robberies, including a heist of five kilos of drugs and weapons from an Italian courthouse, the theft of a billion lire from the Monte dei Paschi di Siena bank, and the robbery of the postal service of 5.8 billion lire. Altogether these netted him and his accomplices 8 billion in Italian lire, the equivalent of $6.15 million. Back out on the streets in 1996, D'Onorio wasted no time getting back in action.

Like the other members of the School of Turin, D'Onorio owned front companies that presented a veneer of respectability. He owned both a real estate company and an alarm business. An expert in computers and electronics, he had a way of thinking around problems that emphasized the simple approach.

The police don't know when or how D'Onorio first met the other members of the School of Turin or when he joined their crew—in fact, when Marco Martino learned of his involvement, he was surprised the gang went outside of Turin to recruit an accomplice.

It's plausible that they were stumped by how to get around the LIPS door and put out word at one of the smoky cafés on the fringes of the city that they needed an alarm expert. It's just as likely that he was an acquaintance of one of the men. Whatever the circumstances, D'Onorio's reputation preceded him when he joined in the plan to rob the Diamond Center. Given his skills and the hurdles they faced, it was a natural partnership. Like the others, D'Onorio had a flair for exploiting obvious loopholes.

A fine example of this skill was the way they figured out how to get around the motion detector. It was genius in its simplicity, a hallmark of the School of Turin's operations.

The motion detector in the safe room was actually two in one, equipped with both passive infrared technology (called PIR) and microwave Doppler radar. This dual-technology unit was small, a white box about the size of a large computer mouse with an opaque curved lens dominating half of it, but it was more than enough to cover the whole safe room from its location to the left of the entryway.

The PIR detector worked by noting sudden changes in the amount of infrared heat energy in the room. Because temperature can change frequently in a space, such as when the lights are turned on and off, it was calibrated to notice changes in the frequency range emitted by the human body. This is common among household motion detectors as well, which ignore minor heat changes so they don't sound an alarm every time the family pet walks in front of them. Theoretically, it's possible to trick this kind of motion detector by moving extremely slowly into and through a room, slowly enough that the change in temperature is gradual and minute. But that was hardly plausible for the School of Turin's purposes.

The second sensor, the Doppler radar, emitted microwaves and "mapped" the room based on the pattern that resulted from their being reflected off the walls and furniture. If something or someone moved through the room, the reflection pattern would be disrupted.

Either of these measures was daunting, but, critically, the device was set with a fail-safe meant to minimize false alarms: both the infrared sensor and the microwave sensor had to register changes at the same time before the alarm would be triggered. A book falling off a shelf wouldn't provoke the alarm because it wouldn't change the amount of infrared in the room. Likewise, turning on the light would spike the temperature, but it wouldn't set off the alarm because the microwave pattern wouldn't be disrupted. Someone entering the room, however, would both create motion and emit body heat, thereby triggering the alarm.

Police believe it's almost certain that the School of Turin bought a motion detector, or several of them, for practice. Based on Notarbartolo's photographs and description of the one in the Diamond Center's safe room, they could have easily purchased a similar model, if not the exact one, in most hardware stores or ordered online from security companies. They would disassemble the motion detector in order to understand exactly how it worked and then work toward defeating it.

Since walking in super slow motion was impractical, the preferred solution was to cover the sensor with something. Infrared rays are easy to detect, but they also are easy to block. In fact, infrared rays can't even penetrate glass. If Notarbartolo could knock out the PIR sensor in the daytime, when the device was turned off, the thieves could place a shield in front of it during the break-in and disable it for good.

The demonstration of how this could work was probably done with everyone involved in the heist present. Even if not everyone was going into the vault on the night of the heist, the practice session would be an educational opportunity for them all.

First, the detector would have been turned off, as it was during the day at the Diamond Center. Then, someone produced a product intended to obscure the lens. It would take just a few sprays from an aerosol can of hair spray to create a sticky opaque film over the lens of the motion detector. They could also have used Vaseline smeared across the lens in a thick coating, but applying it would have been trickier than with a spray can since the person doing it would have to use both hands. Once the film was applied, it would be all but impossible to notice with just a casual glance that the infrared lenses were now masked. Even if the film across the detector didn't completely prevent it from picking up infrared rays, it would have at least greatly reduced the distance at which it could detect changes.

Most modern motion detectors use a technology that renders this sort of trick obsolete. Detectors are programmed to sense when they've been masked based on a specific pattern of responses from both the infrared and microwave signals. In fact, Belgian law requires that any motion detectors installed as of 2002 in the Diamond District be anti-masking. However, as with much else at the Diamond Center, such as the VCR-reliant surveillance system, the motion detector was never upgraded as new technology became available.

With the heat sensors masked, the next step in the demonstration would have been to disable the microwave sensor. For this, they used a large Styrofoam panel three inches thick and attached to an extra-long broom handle. It looked like the world's largest and ugliest sponge mop, but, with a rectangular recess cutout on one side meant to fit perfectly over the unit on the wall, it would completely cover the motion detector. The material would also help block some body heat while it was being maneuvered into place, just in case the masking film didn't work as well as expected.

Their next challenge was the second alarm in the vault—the light detector. Based on Notarbartolo's surreptitiously recorded videotape, they knew it was attached to the ceiling roughly in the center of the room. According to the blueprints, that placed it about twelve to fourteen feet from the motion detector. The light sensor itself was a small rectangular box about the size of a tube of lipstick. A tiny lens exposed a photoresistor, a high-resistance semiconductor connected to a simple circuit board. When light waves of a certain frequency came into contact with the semiconductor, they caused a small atomic reaction—the loosening of electrons—that created an electrical current; the current triggered the alarm. This was the same technology used in cameras to automatically prompt the flash in low-light conditions.

Since the concierge turned off the lights in the vault each weeknight, the thieves would have to remember to turn out the lights in the foyer before opening the LIPS door, if they figured out how to open the door at all. Any light spilling into the vault from the foyer would set off the alarm; therefore, they needed a way to subvert the sensor.

They devised a way to defeat the light sensor that was as simple as the methods that took out the motion detector. They needed only to cover its lens with black rubber electrical tape. The ceiling was low enough that a man Finotto's size could reach up and touch it.

Once they knew how to disable the alarms, the big question at hand was which to disarm first, the motion detector or the light sensor. If the motion detector were masked in advance with a film spray, as was the plan, it was likely that the PIR sensor would be sufficiently blinded that it wouldn't notice someone like Finotto creeping inside to tape over the light detector twelve feet away.

When the tape was in place, they could use low-energy LED headlamps or red-lens flashlights to see as they moved the Styrofoam into its final place over the motion detector. Then they could turn on the lights and move freely, the expensive technology rendered impotent by about €20 worth of material from a hardware store.

◆ ◆ ◆

Returning to Antwerp, Notarbartolo dutifully paid the rent on his office and his apartment three months in advance each quarter. As the months stretched on, the warm and sunny summer of 2001 turned again to winter. Ragged clouds were pulled off the Scheldt River by piercing winds and dragged through the streets of the city, bringing with them maddeningly alternating periods of snow and rain, then cold sunshine. And then, before long, it was springtime, then summer again.

If the change of seasons leading to summer 2002 seemed fast to Notarbartolo as he watched from his apartment's seventh-floor window, the plot itself moved forward slowly. Whenever it seemed they'd ground to a halt, when they began to think that maybe the Diamond Center's vault was indeed impenetrable, another part of the puzzle fell into place and kick-started their enthusiasm all over again.

One such moment came when Notarbartolo discovered that gaining access to the long key that opened the LIPS door would probably be the easiest part of the entire operation. As a clever security measure—and because it was about a foot long—the key was fashioned so that it could be broken down into two pieces: the stamp on the end that operated the locking mechanism and the long pipe that comprised the body of the key. Notarbartolo had known for some time that the concierges kept the pipe in a small lock box on the far wall of the storage room which was just to the left of the vault's heavy door. He must have assumed that they put the stamp in their pocket during the day and that it was locked with them in their apartments overnight.

He'd run through dozens of scenarios for getting hold of the stamp. They could infiltrate the building on the night of the heist, break into one of the apartments while the concierge was sleeping, and remove it by force, but they had ruled out the use of violence from the plan's inception. They could also break into the concierge's apartment during the day when he was occupied or out of the building, but they wouldn't be able to do so without being spotted by a video camera. If the concierge carried the stamp with him, they could pick his pocket, make a cast of the key stamp in a clay block, and slip it back, but it would be risky.

With other locks, a thief could have inserted a soft metal key blank and twisted it back and forth with enough force that the metal wards would mark the blade. Those marks would show the locksmiths where to cut the key so that it would work in the lock. That, however, was impossible with the LIPS door since it was left wide open during the day, and to get to the keyhole, Notarbartolo would have to at least partially close the door, which would immediately make him look suspicious to the man watching the video camera in the control booth. Even if he were able to escape notice, such an effort would be useless anyway; the lock was deep inside the heart of the door and the steel plates were too wide to leave an impression on a blank.

All of those sundry ideas fell to the wayside one day when Notarbartolo noticed that he wouldn't have to look far and wide for the stamp at all because it was never removed from the pipe. The concierges kept the two pieces attached together in the lock box just yards away from the vault door. It was another eureka moment, a fabulous piece of luck that fell into line with his earlier observation that the staff had fallen woefully complacent.

Notarbartolo didn't question why they would leave the entire key in a room directly next to the vault. Maybe they were astoundingly lazy, or maybe someone had lost the stamp in the past and they didn't want to take the chance of its happening again. He was just happy to note that it was kept in a room with a flimsy plywood door and in a lockbox that would come apart with one twist of a crowbar. And so, an integral part of the door's formidable defense had been overcome, through a combination of the concierges' slack habits and Notarbartolo's highly tuned powers of observation.

Of course the key was useless without the combination to the door. Learning that magic number would take some serious finesse.

Or another stroke of amazing luck.

♦ ♦ ♦

While Notarbartolo worked on discovering the combination, Elio D'Onorio tackled the magnetic alarm. He stared at freeze-framed video images and diagrams Notarbartolo had drawn and admired the alarm's simple ingenuity. It consisted of two identical rectangular pieces, each about four inches wide and twelve inches long. The first piece, the receiver, was bolted vertically to the jamb on the upper right side of the doorframe. The second piece was bolted to the door itself so that when the door was closed, the two pieces were aligned side by side. A keypad to the right of the door armed and disarmed all of the alarms inside the vault and the magnetic alarm on the door. When the magnetic alarm was armed, it sent a constant signal through wires, which were encased in a flexible steel pipe, to a round-the-clock security switchboard at Securilink. This confirmed that the magnets were connected and the moment they were separated and the magnetic field broken, Securilink would know.

Unlike the solid steel tubes that anchored the door to the doorway when it was closed and locked, the magnets didn't physically prevent the door from opening. But they ensured that whoever opened the vault door when he wasn't supposed to would go to prison. Securilink wasn't even located in Antwerp, but it would take only a phone call on a dedicated line to the police to have the building surrounded in minutes.

D'Onorio didn't bother wondering how to figure out the keypad code to turn off the alarm. Even if they obtained the code, the fact that the alarm had been turned off would have been evident to Securilink. Likewise, there was no point in figuring the quickest way to cut the wires. The vault door was never to be opened during off-hours, including the weekend. Any deviation from that rule would be immediately apparent to Securilink.

The magnets needed to stay together to keep the alarm quiet, but they needed to come apart if they were to open the door. D'Onorio stared at the video images and willed an idea to come to him. The magnets stared back at him, bolted firmly into place with a huge hex bolt in each of their four corners. He assumed they were locking bolts that would be impossible to unscrew, but even if they weren't, what then? The only thing that worked in his favor was that the magnetic alarm was installed on the outside of the vault. Had it been inside, as would have been logical, it would have been impossible to tamper with once the door was closed. According to a security expert, the only explanation for this security lapse was financial—the magnets presumably were installed after construction on the vault was already completed; retrofitting them on the inside of the door would have been more costly than simply affixing them to the outside.

It took time, but slowly, an idea formed. The more he thought about it, the more it seemed plausible. He ran the idea past the other men, and they agreed there was a good chance it could work. The trouble was that it was labor intensive and it required a dangerous mission to Antwerp. Undeterred, D'Onorio made a list of supplies for his own infiltration of the Diamond Center. As the alarms expert, he would need to do this himself.

◆ ◆ ◆

While D'Onorio dealt with the alarms, other members of the School of Turin carefully studied the images Notarbartolo provided of three important doors: the door accessing C Block from the parking garage, the door to the security control booth near the main entrance, and the door to the vault-level storage room that held the key to the LIPS door. They would all be locked, so they would need to make keys or at least reasonable facsimiles.

One thing the School of Turin knew well was that a few basic skills could open 80 to 90 percent of all the doors a person was likely to encounter, whether they had a key or not. Most locks are extremely simple, utilizing basic principles. If one knows these principles, lock picking can be extremely simple too.

The elegant method preferred by private eyes on television is to skillfully pick the lock using special tools that resemble something a dentist would use to probe for cavities. The difference between television and real life, however, is that in reality the work is tedious and delicate, utilizing a lock picker's refined sense of touch.

A somewhat faster method is called "raking." An L-shaped torque wrench is inserted into the bottom of a doorknob's keyway and a small amount of constant pressure is applied on the plug. A special pick with a number of small "teeth," or peaks, is inserted to the very back of the keyway, and the lock picker drags it quickly across the pins that bind the lock, like a pianist sweeping his fingers across the keys. The motion, combined with the torque on the plug, causes the pins to set one by one. It usually takes several sweeps of the rake to set all the pins. It's less elegant than the first method, but no less effective. And it's quicker.

The School of Turin had a great advantage in their quest to open the doors between themselves and the diamonds: The fact that one of their members ran a locksmith company meant they could order any lock they wanted to investigate without raising suspicions. Thanks to Notarbartolo's reconnaissance, they knew that the inner doors of the Diamond Center were equipped with LIPS-brand locks, consistent with the make of the vault door and the safe deposit boxes. So they ordered a few locks and opened them up to see what they were dealing with.

The School of Turin used an Allen wrench to make a rake and made a special key specifically for the door that opened into C Block from the garage.

The locks that protected the safe deposit boxes themselves were an entirely different story. Normally, locks like these would be drilled open, but doing so risked setting off the vibration detector in the vault. Picking them was impossible unless the men also knew each door's unique three-letter combination. They'd have to be forced open, but even that was going to be a challenge; they couldn't be pried from the edges because the space between the doors and the housing was far too tight to insert even a credit card between them, much less the tip of a crowbar. For this job, they would have to invent and manufacture a specialized tool, one that couldn't be bought at a hardware store because it didn't exist. This tool would need to pull the doors directly outward with enough force to bend the half-inch-thick brass deadbolts that were sunk at least an inch into steel-cased holes.

Ordinarily, this would be a tall order. Only two inches of the deadbolt jutted out of the lock mechanism; the rest of it was contained inside the housing bolted to the back of the doors. Physics alone would indicate that it would be impossible for three or four men to generate enough force to bend a small knuckle of brass to an angle of nearly 90 degrees.

But Notarbartolo knew that the deadbolt didn't need to be bent so steeply. Soon after he began casing the Diamond Center, he'd noticed a clue on his very own safe deposit box door as to how it might be forced open: the faceplate that kept the deadbolt in place within the lock was plastic. Once they started pulling, they theorized, the faceplate would crack and give way, exposing all eight inches of the deadbolt to the force they would be applying to it, not just the two inches on the end. That gave them a lot more to work with. They figured that, at most, the deadbolt would bend 45 degrees before the faceplate broke. Then the whole deadbolt would bow until it popped free of the slot in the doorjamb, opening the door.

The thieves sketched their special tool over and over while consulting Notarbartolo's measurements of the safe door and crunched numbers into a calculator until they felt they had it right. Then they started calling around to check on the price of heavy aluminum stock and ran through their mental Rolodexes to see if they knew anyone who was a machinist.

◆ ◆ ◆

By late 2002, the School of Turin had conducted nearly two years of research and espionage with Notarbartolo visiting Antwerp while the rest of its members worked from Italy. It was time for that to change. Research could only take them so far. To overcome the obstacles that remained, they needed to move their operation to Antwerp.

They held a status meeting to plan their next step. The room was filled with notepads, sketches, and maps, the material they needed to run through each part of the operation, to visualize every element of the break-in and make sure nothing was being overlooked.

They discussed the schedule in which the primary participants would relocate to Antwerp at least a week or two before the break-in. Their tasks during that period would include deciphering the garage door code, making a remote control to open the doors, ferreting D'Onorio into the Diamond

Center so that he could have a closer look at the magnetic alarm, making adjustments to the safe deposit box pulling contraption they'd invented, and figuring out the combination to the LIPS door. On that last point, Notarbartolo had an idea, but it would require D'Onorio's help.

They talked in detail about what they would find inside the safe deposit boxes and they strategized about what to take. Since they could carry only a limited amount of loot, they wanted to be certain they made off with the items most easily sold for the highest values. That meant focusing on diamonds in their certificate blister packs. Loose polished diamonds would be fine, too, along with large rough diamonds and any other gemstones they found. Smaller rocks would be left behind. Cash and anything that could be melted was fair game. They would leave anything truly unique or personalized because those items would be easier to trace.

By and large it was a good plan, but it still hinged on cracking the combination and thwarting the magnetic alarm. Once in Antwerp, they would know quickly whether their ideas would work or not. And if they would work, there was no reason not to execute the heist at the next opportunity.

In fact, there was every reason to move quickly. Although they'd gained invaluable information about the workings of the Diamond Center and its staff during their long planning process, two years was a long time to hope that nothing changed in the interim. For instance, one of the concierges might quit or be fired and be replaced by someone who insisted that the vault's key stamp be removed from the pipe every day, as it was designed to be or make other changes to the security routine. Marcel Grünberger might order Julie Boost to beef up the building's security measures, which meant the motion detector might be upgraded to an anti-masking model. The garage door opener might break, prompting the purchase of a new one whose code couldn't be stolen out of the air by an electronic scanner. The possibilities were endless, and their concerns weren't unfounded. In December 2002, the Diamond Center hired painters to freshen up the hallways, demonstrating that while the management might be lackadaisical about the building's upkeep, they didn't entirely ignore it. The School of Turin's worst nightmare was that Notarbartolo would one day trudge up to the building and find workers installing a new computer-based video surveillance system.

They had to move, and they had to move soon. Their plan was as ready as it would ever be from their remote location. The last item of business in Turin was to pick a date to attempt the heist. They decided on Saturday, February 15, 2003.

There were a few reasons that particular date was perfect. First, Antwerp was hosting two big events that weekend: the annual Proximus Diamond Games, a tennis tournament featuring American sensation Venus Williams for which the potential prize was a diamond-encrusted golden tennis racquet, and the February 14 wedding of Peter Meeus, the director general of the Diamond High Council, whose wedding reception was sure to segue into a night of partying. Either event would keep the few diamantaires who might otherwise be working over the weekend occupied. The School of Turin hoped the combination of the two would be enough to keep the district virtually deserted. Second, the men knew that Jacques was the concierge on duty that weekend. Since his apartment was on the fourth floor of C Block, they would run less risk of being overheard or encountered in a hallway than if it were Jorge, who lived one floor above the main level in B Block. Lastly, there was a De Beers Sight in London earlier that week, which meant that Antwerp would be bursting with diamonds.

That the date of their heist was scheduled for the day after Valentine's Day was a nice bit of coincidental timing. Notarbartolo would not get to spend this holiday with his wife, as she would stay in Italy when he went to Antwerp. But if all went according to plan, it would be worth it. He would be able to give her more diamonds than a lifetime's worth of Valentine's Days.

Chapter Seven

MY STOLEN VALENTINE

No pressure, no diamonds.

— Proverb

Elio D'Onorio strode toward the Diamond Center on Monday, February 10, 2003. In his pocket was a work order, a single sheet of paper indicating that his security company had been hired by Leonardo Notarbartolo's diamond firm to install a Sony video surveillance system in his office on the fifth floor of 9–11 Schupstraat.

In his workbag, D'Onorio carried a variety of wrenches, a hacksaw, a roll of strong double-sided tape, and a curiously shaped piece of metal. This metal plate was about eight inches square. One side was flat while the other had a two-inch lip on one of its edges and another two-inch-tall ridge welded across its middle, forming a T shape with the lip. It looked vaguely like a large trowel that would be used to smooth out wet cement.

Visitors to the Diamond Center were required to stop at the guard booth inside the front doors to announce their arrival. The company expecting them was required to confirm the appointment. Only then would the visitor exchange a photo ID for a temporary badge, enabling him to swipe through the turnstiles and access the rest of the building. Just as with tenants, a computer recorded the time visitors went in and out of the building.

Upon his arrival that morning, D'Onorio skipped this step. Instead, he breezed by the guard booth without pausing. Police believe there was no elaborate subterfuge. Instead, they think it's most likely that Notarbartolo had simply lent D'Onorio his badge. Acting as if he'd been a longtime tenant, D'Onorio badged confidently through the turnstile and headed to the fifth floor. Had anyone stopped him because he was unfamiliar, he would have said he had borrowed Notarbartolo's badge in order to get to work on the security system. He had the invoice in his pocket to back up his story. But no one stopped him.

The computer records from that day indicate Notarbartolo's badge was used to enter and exit the building, with enough time between the two to indicate nothing but a normal day's business for the Italian jeweler. D'Onorio, however, never left, although he somehow used the badge to make it seem like he did. This was easy enough to fake; maybe he had acted like he was on his way out of the building, swiped the card, and then pretended to take an urgent call on his cell phone that stopped him in his tracks. He could then have slowly edged his way back toward the elevators without anyone noticing he'd badged out for the sake of creating a computer record, but hadn't actually left the building. Whatever the ploy, it would have been caught on videotape. But as long as the guard on duty didn't notice it at the moment, D'Onorio didn't care. He planned to steal the videotape later.

D'Onorio spent that day sitting in Notarbartolo's office waiting until the sky turned dark, and with it, the room around him. He waited for hours, until he was sure that any late-working tenants had gone home for the night and that Jacques, the concierge on duty that week, was safely in his apartment in C Block. As he waited, D'Onorio thought about the details of his mission, pushing out of his head the knowledge that if something went wrong, he would be immediately sent to prison and the heist plot would be scuttled.

When he was sure the building was settled in for the evening, he slipped on a pair of thin rubber gloves and shouldered his workbag. He crept quietly out of the office, locking the door behind him. It was only a few paces to the elevator foyer and he was soon in the stairwell, gliding quickly down seven flights of stairs, listening for the sound of anyone else moving through the dark building.

When he opened the stairwell door into the vault foyer, D'Onorio found himself opposite the elevator doors, just as Notarbartolo had described. The large white Siemens video camera, dutifully recording the dark foyer, hung from the ceiling in front of the stairwell door. The room was not quite pitch dark; the red light on the video camera cast a faint pink glow into the silent space. Even though he counted on no one ever watching the videotape of what he was about to do, D'Onorio would have hooded the video camera with a plastic bag or some other material to obscure its view. There was always the chance that something would go wrong before he could remove the tape from the Diamond Center. D'Onorio didn't want to take any unnecessary risks.

With the camera obscured, he flicked on the light switch and winced while his eyes adjusted to the stark fluorescent lighting. The LIPS door was locked tight for the night, a deceptively passive-looking barrier that he knew had the power to land him in prison if he made any mistakes. Seeing the magnetic alarm in person, after having studied it so intensely from videotape must have been gratifying. He examined its components from all angles for a few minutes to be sure there were no surprises.

From his workbag, he took the strange metal plate. It may have looked odd, but it was a central component of the heist. It was designed to fit perfectly across both magnets, positioned precisely between the upper and lower bolts that held the magnet to the door. It was a custom-made piece of metal that would keep both pieces of the alarm together while he worked to unbolt them. With a satisfying metallic clank, it stuck in place perfectly.

Next, D'Onorio produced a wrench from the bag and carefully unbolted each of the eight bolts that held the contraption in place. It was hard work. His arms were over his head and the bolts were old. He had to be very careful not to yank too hard and risk dislodging one of the magnets, which would set off the alarm.

If his work wiggled the magnets enough to break the connection and set off the alarm, D'Onorio wouldn't have known it. There wouldn't have been clanging bells or flashing lights, just an interruption of the signals transmitted to Securilink that D'Onorio wouldn't be able to detect. He would know that he failed only if the stairwell door or the elevators opened and heavily armed cops spilled into the foyer. D'Onorio was used to dealing with the tension such work generated; deep in the bowels of the Diamond Center, subverting an alarm in the middle of the night, D'Onorio was in his element.

One by one, the long and sturdy bolts came out. When the last bolt came free, so did the entire contraption. But, though separated from where they'd been anchored to the door and the jamb, the magnets stayed connected to each other, thanks to the metal plate. They dangled from the flexible steel pipe that led into the ceiling. This apparatus could be moved a few inches to the side, far enough to allow the door to open when the time came to do so. The magnets still had to be handled with care, though, to ensure that the connection between them wasn't jostled in even the slightest way, or Securilink would be notified immediately.

He had been successful in his first task, but D'Onorio was far from finished. So that the thieves wouldn't have to repeat the laborious job of unbolting the magnets on the night of the heist, he used the hacksaw to shorten each bolt so that it would screw only into the magnets, and not their anchors in the door and the jamb. He then used heavy-duty double-sided tape to stick the magnets back into place where the bolts once held them. When he screwed in the shortened bolts and removed the metal plate, it was impossible to tell that tape, and not steel bolts, held the alarm in place. He'd been in the vault foyer for a long time, but he was satisfied knowing they wouldn't have to take nearly as much time during the heist to get around the magnetic alarm.

D'Onorio took another look at his handiwork to be sure that nothing out of the ordinary would be noticed when the concierge came to open the vault for the day's business in a few hours. Because they'd tested the holding strength of the tape, he wasn't worried that the weight of the magnets would cause them to fall off from where they were anchored, but Notarbartolo would check nonetheless throughout the week to be sure they hadn't moved. D'Onorio flipped off the lights, retrieved the shrouding material from the video camera, and slipped into the stairwell like a phantom. Only a careful inspection would reveal that he had not left everything behind him as he had found it.

Still, his long night wasn't finished. D'Onorio exited the stairwell on the main level, sticking his head cautiously out into the hallway opposite the elevators, scanning for any sign of the concierge. Nothing. The video cameras recorded him as he slipped across the hall and peered down the corridor that led to C Block. Again, the coast was clear, so he tiptoed silently to the door leading to the parking garage.

As D'Onorio prepared to exit the Diamond Center through the garage, investigators would later theorize, he took a few moments to check some final details. He tested that the special key made in Turin specifically to open the C Block door from the parking deck worked properly. He confirmed Notarbartolo's earlier observation that the key used to open and close the garage doors was permanently left in the opening mechanism.

And, according to one theory, he also removed from his workbag a frequency scanner. This simple battery-powered transmitter was connected to a circuit board and used to test all possible radio frequencies for the garage door until it hit on the correct one. Because the frequency was based upon the on or off positions of twelve toggle switches inside the garage door's circuitry housing, there were 1,024 possible combinations. D'Onorio would know he'd found the right one when the garage door opened; he would then keep track of the code so that they could use it again to open the door remotely on the night of the heist. He had only to sit where he couldn't be seen if the concierge made an unexpected visit to the garage, and let the scanner do all the work.

As much as he'd anticipated the noise the garage door would make, it was still a startling burst of sound; whether it was triggered by the scanner hitting on the right frequency or by the key opening it manually—the chain and pulley mechanism jolted to a start and the door began lumbering upward with a great metallic racket that ricocheted throughout the cavernous garage.

D'Onorio grabbed his workbag and hustled to the garage door. He looked around to be sure no one was watching, then turned left on Lange Herentalsestraat and walked swiftly down the sidewalk away from where the police kiosk stood just around the corner to the right.

Back at the apartment, D'Onorio was elated. His mission was a success on every front. While giving his report to the others, he tore the work order in his pocket into little pieces, along with a business card with his name on it. He'd been carrying both of these items in case he had been stopped while in the Diamond Center. He threw the remnants of both documents into the kitchen trash, where they scattered amid used coffee grounds and other household refuse.

♦ ♦ ♦

There were other preparations afoot in Antwerp that week. Most of the gang members had arrived in the city the weekend before the heist. They came to Antwerp in separate groups, just as they would leave. Notarbartolo had flown to Brussels as he normally did, but some of the others drove, coming over Brenner Pass through the Alps between Italy and Austria on Sunday, February 9. In all, detectives believe at least seven people, and maybe more, were directly involved in the plot to rob the Diamond Center. Each had a different responsibility, from lookout to getaway driver. Not all of them have been identified.

They took care to arrive at Notarbartolo's Charlottalei apartment without attracting attention; for more than two years, he had been a nearly anonymous tenant who was quiet as a mouse. The men were careful not to draw unnecessary attention to themselves as they crowded into the miniscule elevator and trudged down the cramped hallways, burdened with their bags of clothes, food, and equipment.

Police believe that some of the School of Turin members were tasked with perfecting their specialized safe deposit box tool in the days leading to the heist. They went to a few industrial areas on the outskirts of the city that were home to welding companies, machine shops, and scrap yards. Notarbartolo rented a car—not a flashy model like an Alfa, but a forgettable silver Peugeot sedan—because he planned that his baggage for the return trip to Italy would be far too valuable to risk bringing through airport security.

Otherwise, his job was simply to report to work in the Diamond Center as usual, and visit the vault daily to ensure that D'Onorio's modifications to the magnetic alarm hadn't been discovered. Had anyone at the Diamond Center been paying attention to his habits, they would have noted this as a huge change in Notarbartolo's behavior. He'd visited the vault sporadically during the last two years, but in the week leading up to the heist he went to the vault twice daily. Notarbartolo was delighted to find that the Roman had done an excellent job; it was impossible even for him to tell that the bolts had been shortened and that simple tape kept the magnets in their place on the door and the doorframe.

During one of his later trips to the vault, Notarbartolo waited until all the other tenants had left and he was alone. Standing outside the range of the video camera, he removed an aerosol bottle from his attaché case and sprayed the lens of the motion detector. He gave it a good thick coating that went on clear and hardened into a sticky, opaque film, and then slid the can back into his case. Masking the motion detector had taken only a few seconds.

On subsequent trips to the vault, he examined the masked motion detector in addition to checking the magnets. He was relatively confident that it would go undetected, since neither the concierges nor the guards actually came into the vault, and the tenants were focused only on what was inside their safe deposit boxes. Still, he needed to be certain no one had noticed the film and scrubbed it off.

Additionally, most diamantaires had other things on their minds that week. Valentine's Day was the biggest romantic holiday of the year and retailers around the world had spent months marketing diamonds as the perfect gift to demonstrate one's love. Although the wholesalers in the Diamond Square Mile were no busier that week than usual—retailers stocked up on diamonds and diamond jewelry starting in October for both Christmas and Valentine's Day—the industry took the occasion of the holiday to showcase Antwerp as the center of the diamond trading world.

Between the Proximus tennis tournament, Peter Meeus's wedding reception at the Beurs voor Diamanthandel, and the early winter start to Friday prayers for the district's substantial Jewish population—not to mention the fact that it was Valentine's Day, meaning that anyone with a significant other would have plans—the Diamond Center would be all but deserted for the last few hours of the workweek.

While Antwerp's diamantaires used Valentine's Day to celebrate the Diamond District's place in the world of diamonds, Notarbartolo, D'Onorio, and the others spent that Friday preparing to pull the rug out from under it the next evening.

◆ ◆ ◆

For at least one of the thieves, Friday couldn't come soon enough. Ferdinando Finotto remained holed up in Notarbartolo's small apartment practically from the moment he arrived. Even though the attempted bank robbery charge for the 1997 failed KBC job in Antwerp had been settled as far as the courts in Italy were concerned, it was still a problem in Belgium. In fact, he'd been convicted in Belgium in absentia, and should he get caught anywhere in the country, he would go immediately to prison to begin serving his sentence. So he stayed inside, running over details, pacing the floor, and losing his patience.

Finally, on Thursday, Finotto decided that if he couldn't assist in the reconnaissance he could at least cook his colleagues a proper Italian meal before their big night. He thought it worth the risk to go to the Delhaize grocery store around the corner on Plantin en Moretuslei.

Delhaize, a spacious and modern store, was about a ten-minute walk away. Once there, Finotto took his time wandering its aisles and filling his cart with mozzarella cheese, tomatoes, packages of pre-tossed salad, pasta, loaves of bread, and Italian meats. He also grabbed a bottle of wine and some beer. His early afternoon shopping trip cost just over €53; he paid with a 100-euro note. As trained as he was to notice security features, he couldn't have failed to note the video camera that recorded customers as they entered the store.

If anyone was upset that Finotto went out in public, the anger couldn't have lasted long considering the spread he prepared. With at least four people shoehorned inside an apartment made for one for the better part of the week, Finotto's meal was one of the few times they could relax and enjoy themselves while indulging in the tastes of home.

The School of Turin sprawled out on the low black vinyl sofas or at the tiny dining table. As in Italy, the food was laid out on plates and spread out on the coffee table buffet style; the wine was poured and beer bottles opened. It was a few moments of enjoyment before they inevitably scrounged for space to sleep, whether on the floor in sleeping bags or curled uncomfortably on the small sofas; only one of them enjoyed the relative comfort of the apartment's single narrow bed.

The next day, Friday, would be their last chance at surveillance before the heist. They needed as much rest as they could get.

◆ ◆ ◆

Perhaps because the hardware store was located twenty minutes away, in Mechelen, or perhaps because his foray to the grocery store hadn't resulted in police sirens and handcuffs, Finotto was confident enough to again venture out of the apartment in order to accompany D'Onorio on a supply run late

Friday afternoon. They pulled into the parking lot of Brico, a well-stocked home improvement chain store, and made their way slowly through the tight aisles, equipped with a detailed list of provisions. They loaded the cart with tool sets, a two-foot-long crowbar, an emergency battery similar in size to one that would fit in a car or a boat, an AC/DC power inverter for running power tools off the battery, drills, a pipe wrench, bolt cutters, and other tools. In the insulation section, they found several different-sized Styrofoam panels, and in the cleaning section, they found a dust mop on a long telescoping handle designed to reach cobwebs high in the corners of a vaulted ceiling.

This expedition cost €570. Again the men paid with big bills, a 500-euro note and a 100-euro note. The receipt showed that they paid at exactly 5:30 p.m.

Meanwhile, back in Antwerp, Notarbartolo was at the Diamond Center, one of just a handful of people still working that late in the day. Jewish Sabbath services had begun and the Shabbat prayers had started at the Sephardic Synagogue on Hoveniersstraat. Notarbartolo sat in his office and ran through everything in his mind, visualizing the plot over and over. He waited as the building emptied of the last few tenants who were finishing business ahead of a romantic night on the town.

Around half past six, Notarbartolo stood and looked around. The room was as empty as the day he had rented it. There wasn't a single trace of what he'd plotted there over the past two years. He grabbed his attaché case, locked the door, and headed for the elevator, where he pushed the button for the bottom level.

By now, his third time there that day, he'd grown accustomed to the cavernous hush of the vault and its bright white walls. He stepped to the day gate, eyeing the magnetic lock intently for any sign that D'Onorio's modifications had been detected. As far as he could tell, they hadn't. When the day gate buzzed open, he walked the few familiar steps to his safe deposit box and opened it. It too was as empty as ever of anything valuable, but he lingered over it, noting once again the features of its locking mechanism. He turned to look at the motion detector; it was still covered with a thin filmy crust of dried aerosol spray. Nothing had been discovered.

The video cameras recorded him as the last tenant in the vault that day. After he made his final inspection, he then exited the building at 6:44 p.m., just sixteen minutes before the staff locked up the building for the weekend. If the concierges followed the same patterns as they had for the past two years, once they closed the vault, they wouldn't even think about it until it needed to be opened sixty hours later.

As Notarbartolo walked to his apartment that night, he passed diamantaires headed in the other direction, toward the reception at the Beurs voor Diamanthandel and one of the weekend's many displays of lavish excess. Only Notarbartolo knew that the biggest show of all would take place far from the public's eye, two levels underground.

♦ ♦ ♦

If ever any place looked like a den of thieves, it was Notarbartolo's living room on Saturday, February 15, 2003. The floor was covered with tools and equipment laid out in orderly rows so that everything could be accounted for, checked, and double-checked. The bolt cutters, the pipe wrench, the power inverter, the emergency battery, and the big crowbar were arranged in a group. Scattered about were numerous pairs of rubber gloves, plastic water bottles, rolls of duct tape, electronic gadgets, power cords, and duffel bags. They had fake keys, lock-picking tools, fabricated aluminum parts, headlamps, spare batteries, and small bags of nuts and screws.

It was a lot to keep track of, and one way the men stayed organized was by fastidiously throwing away what wasn't needed in order to reduce clutter. In the kitchen, the household trash was already bursting with everyday waste. Added to that were boxes, packaging material, receipts, shopping bags, price tags, and other material stuffed into numerous garbage bags, as if parents had been cleaning up after their children's Christmas Day gift-opening frenzy.

The late hours of the afternoon were for sleeping and for completing whatever personal pre-heist ritual the men might have had. History is rife with examples of strange superstitions held by criminals, from the Highland bandits of Central India who would pour a little liquor on the ground before committing a crime to appease the demons of mischief to nineteenth-century European thieves who believed the hand of a dead man was an invaluably lucky talisman. Professional British burglars were said to carry pieces of coal or chalk in their pockets for good luck, and a study of two hundred Italian murderers done in 1892 found every one of them to be a devoutly religious person who considered the practice of his faith to be a potent source of good luck. In more modern times, thieves in Turin have been known to snort cocaine before a big job to give them stamina and courage.

For those fitfully trying to rest in Notarbartolo's apartment, rituals probably consisted of a few quiet prayers and maybe a vaguely worded phone call to a loved one. Calls were placed on specific cell phones; each man carried two—a personal phone used to conduct legitimate business or to call his wife or girlfriend, and one used only to call the other members of the job. This closed-circuit phone network was a trademark of Italian gangs like the School of Turin. For each job, the men bought prepaid cell phones with new SIM cards and limited their calls only to each other. When the job was over, they destroyed the phones and the cards.

Late in the evening, the men donned clothing that was dark but not sinister. They wanted to blend into the shadows without raising suspicion. They traded their treasured leather Italian loafers for soft-soled athletic shoes that wouldn't echo on the hard tile floors. The gear was zipped into backpacks and tote bags. Along with the tools were several empty bags that they planned to have bursting with stolen treasure in a few hours' time. They pocketed their cell phones, used the restroom, and passed small words of quiet assurance among themselves.

They staggered their departures from the apartment, meeting up a few minutes apart from each other at one of the cars parked outside. They wouldn't want to be spotted leaving en masse in dark clothes with a load of heavy baggage, but there was a practical reason for this as well: the building's elevator couldn't fit all of them at once.

The heist went into effect just before midnight.

Chapter Eight

THE HEIST OF THE CENTURY

Linus: *Smash-and-grab job, huh?*
Rusty: *Slightly more complicated than that.*

—*Ocean's Eleven* (2001)

Near midnight on Saturday, the lookout gave the all-clear. The only people walking the streets of the Diamond District were those taking a shortcut to the bars and restaurants on the plaza outside the central train station. The police were stationed inside their small kiosk at the corner of Schupstraat and Lange Herentalsestraat, but they may well have been watching the tennis match on a small portable television for all the interest they were showing the light foot traffic on the district's streets.

It was too risky to walk to the Diamond District with all their gear, so the thieves piled in a car and left the apartment on Charlottalei at 11:47 p.m. Detectives believe the infiltration crew consisted of at least Notarbartolo, Finotto, and D'Onorio, but they never ruled out that there was perhaps one more person they couldn't identify.

Pietro Tavano drove the thieves to the Diamond Center. Compared to the others, he didn't possess any well-honed burglary skill but was instead a trusted friend and a reliable "job man," someone who could be counted on to keep his head and hold down the fort. That was precisely the driver's job on that night.

The trip took about three minutes. The route followed the one Notarbartolo had taken on foot for the past two years. They must have passed the local police station with a bit of extra trepidation; they were all well aware that, if anything went wrong, they'd be in police custody before long. Someone would have been on the phone with the lookout posted somewhere within view of both the police kiosk and the Diamond Center's garage doors. As the car, filled with burglary tools and adrenaline, approached the intersection of Schupstraat and Lange Herentalsestraat, the men snapped rubber gloves over hands that were damp with nervous perspiration.

The garage door rolled open as the car was still cruising past the police kiosk. Because the police were stationed only a few dozen paces from the side entrance to the Diamond Center, the lookout watched to make sure that the police didn't react to the sound of the door opening. Tavano pulled to the curb and seamlessly delivered the thieves like a special forces operation inserting soldiers behind enemy lines. They shouldered their bags and ducked under the garage door as the car pulled away. It took only a moment or two. Then, the car's taillights turned a far corner and the garage door rolled down once again.

Inside, the booming echo of the door faded into the recesses of the empty garage. They paused for a few moments as complete silence returned. The lookout whispered through the phone that their entry into the Diamond Center had gone unnoticed; the street outside was as quiet and sleepy as it had been before.

Meanwhile, after dropping off his associates, Tavano drove the three-quarters of a mile back to Charlottalei 33. He parked near the apartment and went inside to monitor a police radio. If the men on the inside accidentally set off an alarm, he'd know it as soon as the police did. Tavano could then call his colleagues to give them at least a few minutes' warning that the mission was blown and the cops were on the way.

If that happened, the thieves would have to make an on-the-spot decision to either bolt out of the building through the garage and hope to slip through what would be a rapidly tightening noose of heavily armed law enforcement, or to flee to the fifth floor and hide in Notarbartolo's office. Either option was a desperate move. Attempting escape through the garage would almost certainly mean running squarely into the arms of the police, while running upstairs only delayed the inevitable. The building's security cameras would lead the police directly to office number 516. Now that they were inside the

Diamond Center, there would be no escape if things went wrong.

They didn't linger in the garage. Of all the places in the Diamond Center, it was here that they had the greatest risk of encountering one of the concierges or some workaholic diamantaire who simply couldn't stay away from his office, even on Valentine's Day weekend. As it turned out, as much as two years of meticulous planning was meant to minimize every risk, blind luck was also on their side: They missed running into Jacques Plompteux by a matter of minutes. Although he was supposed to be on duty around the clock that weekend, he later admitted to the police that he'd left the building around midnight to meet his brother-in-law for drinks on the plaza.

The thieves moved quickly to the C Block door. The time had come to use the key that they had fabricated especially for this lock. One of the thieves inserted it into the keyway and dragged it across the pins while light pressure was applied to the plug. The rest held their collective breaths. The door opened without a hitch; the custom-made key had worked flawlessly.

Had anyone been watching the Diamond Center's internal security cameras, they would have seen three or four shadowy figures lugging heavy bags through the darkened hallways. Fortunately for the thieves, no one watched the live feeds at night or on the weekend. The guard booths were empty, the monitors turned off.

Notarbartolo led the others through the Diamond Center's dark and silent corridors since he was most familiar with the building. Having long tailored his actions to the knowledge that the video cameras were watching his every move, it was a new sensation for him to be freely walking within their sight while overtly committing a crime. The thieves made as little noise as possible as they moved swiftly to the stairwell door in the main corridor, opening it carefully to reduce the noise the latch would make in the echoey confines of the stairwell shaft. When they were all through the door, they closed it just as gently.

At 12:14 a.m., Notarbartolo spoke to Tavano on the phone, updating him on their progress and learning that the police radio traffic gave no indication that anyone knew they were inside the building. The bottom of the stairwell outside the vault foyer was a good place to take a quick breather; there were no cameras there and the stairs reaching fifteen floors above them were silent. So far, so good.

Like D'Onorio had done earlier that week, the men entered the dark foyer and shrouded the video camera before turning on the lights. They dropped their equipment and began unzipping bags. D'Onorio withdrew the metal plate and delicately placed it over the two magnets composing the alarm. He grasped the magnets and pulled them straight outward from where the tape anchored them to the door and the door frame. As they came off, there was the harsh sound of peeling tape, but the magnets never broke contact with each other. Just as on Monday night, the alarm was kept intact, but it now dangled from the wiring out of the way so that the vault door could be opened without sounding the alarm.

Next, the men moved to the corner of the room to the left of the door. The ceiling was composed of thin white slats that created a false ceiling to accommodate wiring and ventilation equipment above them. They bent one of these slats to the side, presumably to remove something that may have been placed there by D'Onorio on the night of February 10. If that was the case, D'Onorio had apparently been much more careful about placing it than they were about removing it; the ceiling slats weren't damaged until the break-in. That it was a video camera in the ceiling was the investigators' best theory. There was nothing else above these slats that would have interested the thieves, such as alarm wiring or video cables. One theory was that the camera might have been used to record the combination dial on the vault door. This would explain the mystery of how the thieves obtained the combination.

This theory has its detractors. The most convincing argument against it is that an outer cover encircled the combination dial and shielded the numbers from view; the concierge had to stand directly over the dial to peer down through a small window in the top of the cover to see the numbers as he entered the code; the numbers were visible only through this window. This would almost certainly have obscured the view from overhead since the concierge's head would have been between the hidden camera and the dial.

However, because the video camera would have been to the left rather than directly above the combination dial, it might be possible that it was angled perfectly to see the numbers. It would have been easier to achieve the right angle using a flexible fiber-optic lens no wider in diameter than one's pinky than a standard off-the-shelf video camera.

Thieves associated with the School of Turin have been known to use such technology. For example, during a jewelry store robbery in Turin only a few months before the Diamond Center heist, the perpetrators drilled through a safe door's keyhole to insert a fiber-optic camera that allowed them to read the combination off the back of the lock mechanism. By connecting such a camera to a laptop computer, D'Onorio may have been able to calibrate the view precisely.

A further problem, though, was that even if the camera had somehow been positioned so that the concierge's head didn't block its view of the top of the dial, the window of the dial used a distorted lens so that the numbers were only visible at a precise distance. Any camera that captured the image from a distance would be distorted beyond recognition. As Paul De Vos, the locksmith who had worked with the vault since its installation three decades before, later explained, "In my opinion, there is no way that a camera was installed somewhere to see the number combination when someone [dialed] it in. It is just impossible to see it when not holding your eye exactly in front of it."

Another possibility was that Notarbartolo had discovered the combination some other way and the video camera was a means of making sure that nothing had changed prior to the night of the heist. Only four people knew the combination to the door—Jorge Dias De Sousa, Jacques Plompteux, Julie Boost, and Marcel Grünberger, although Grünberger later told police he'd forgotten it. According to Detective Agim De Bruycker, one concierge (De Bruycker did not indicate which) admitted that he kept the combination written down on a piece of paper he kept in his wallet. Police also considered the possibility that Notarbartolo discovered this and obtained the combination by having someone pick the concierge's pocket.

Perhaps the most intriguing hypothesis—suggested by insurance investigator Denice Oliver and admitted as possible by police detectives—was that the combination was never erased from the wheel. For the combination lock to be of any use at all, the concierges should have given the wheel numerous spins to clear the code each night when the door was locked. It would only open again once the code was dialed correctly—four twists to the right, three to the left, two to the right, and one more to the left. If the door was shut and locked with the key, but the combination not erased, then it would only take the key to open it again.

Unlike other vault doors, the Diamond Center's LIPS door did not automatically clear the code when it was closed. Known as "auto scramble," such a feature would have forced the concierges to enter the combination each time they opened the vault door. Pieter De Vlaam, the manager of testing and certification for LIPS, explained that "the auto-scramble function is rarely used as it requires a complicated link between the lock and the bolt work. Mechanical combination locks require disciplined use—procedures ensuring that the lock is closed; the code is frequently changed. This explains the emergence of electronic locks that can impose all of this. In other words, it is quite possible that the guards relied on the key only. A combination in that case is [as] effective as a safety belt [that is] not strapped on."

If the concierges did not use the combination, it would have been obvious on those occasions when Notarbartolo stayed late in the vault to observe the door-locking procedure. It also would have been another eureka moment when watching any hidden video of the vault door.

And so, whether by high-tech means of fiber-optic espionage, low-tech means of copying the combination from someone who had carelessly written it down, or the lax habits of complacent concierges who didn't deem it necessary to fully lock the door, the combination dial had the correct code on it when the LIPS door was opened in the early morning hours of Sunday, February 16.

It was only then that police believe the School of Turin ran into a roadblock, albeit a minor one: a fabricated key the men hoped would unlock the storage room to the left of the vault door didn't work. But that was the beauty of having a two-foot crowbar as backup; investigators later surmised that it was simpler for them to break the door down than to pick the lock by hand, which would have wasted precious time. The flimsy door cracked easily around the lock, the sound of splintering wood like rifle fire in the tiled foyer. The men forced the door open, sidestepping the water bottles and paint cans strewn about the storage room to apply the crowbar again to the lock box on the wall. The entire key, pipe and stamp combined, hung inside, just as Notarbartolo said it would.

The key slid into the door, and with a few twists of the handle, the large bolts anchoring it into the doorframe retracted from their moorings. The LIPS vault door was unlocked.

The next moments must have been ones of deep breathing and focus. One of the men likely kept his hands on the sabotaged magnetic alarm to ensure that it was out of the way of the opening door. Another had the crowbar in his hands, ready to force open the day gate. All wore headlamps, although they were turned off. With everyone in place and ready, the lights were switched off and the foyer plunged into pure darkness.

Despite the enormous expense, the untold man-hours, and the centuries of technological advancement intended to keep men like the School of Turin out of the vault room, the foot-thick door swung open smoothly on its hinges. A bomb couldn't have breached that door without destroying the whole building, but they had managed to open it with a combination of patience, ingenuity, and determination. The door worked exactly as it had been designed; it was the human security surrounding it that had failed.

For the men who had never been in the vault before, it would have been a weird sensation knowing that the treasure room lay just ahead in the darkness, maddeningly out of sight until they could ensure that its alarms were disabled.

No one but the thieves themselves knows for sure if the darkness was total. Because of the light sensor, using flashlights or headlamps was out of the question. But they may have used a red-lens flashlight; red is at one extreme of the visible spectrum of light, the closest to infrared, which is invisible to the human eye. Having practiced with light sensors in the months leading to the heist, they might have discovered that the sensors wouldn't detect the lower frequency of red light, or that, even if they did, the red light took longer to provoke the electrical reaction that would set off the alarm. They may also have used one or more night vision devices, expensive high-tech goggles used by hunters and soldiers to see in the dark.

The latch on the day gate was pried loose with a loud clang, and the gate was pushed into the room. The thieves used a can of paint from the storage room to prop it open so that the pneumatic hinges couldn't close it again. The rubber electrical tape in hand before the lights went out, one of them—Finotto would have been the obvious choice because of his height—walked to the center of the room, reached to the ceiling, and masked the light sensor with two or three overlapping strips of tape.

They were now free to turn on the lights. As their eyes adjusted to the sudden stark assault of the fluorescent tubes, it was the first time any of the thieves besides Notarbartolo had seen the inside of the vault in person. Everything they knew of this room came from Notarbartolo's surreptitious handheld video recordings. Now here they were, crouched on the threshold like stormtroopers prepared to assault an enemy stronghold.

They were still for a long moment, listening intently for any faint echoes of pounding footsteps from the floors above. Nothing happened. The thieves realized that they were still safe and went back to work, this time with the Styrofoam panel and its handle. The handle was from a glorified dust mop of comic proportions, used to clean cobwebs from the distant corners of vaulted ceilings. The dust mop part had been discarded long ago; now its telescoping handle was attached to the Styrofoam.

Holding the panel before him toward the motion detector, one of the men crept into the safe room like a hunter wielding a spear at a lion. Even though the motion detector had been masked with the aerosol spray to reduce its ability to detect the infrared energy of their body heat, he reduced his movements to slow motion. The movement of the panel would have triggered the sensor's microwave radar as it was inched forward, but the alarm wouldn't sound unless the infrared detector also went off. They both had to be triggered simultaneously for the alarm to go off.

The panel fit perfectly over the small white device. A few dollars' worth of expanded polystyrene foam, a ten-dollar duster, a scrap of metal, some strips of black tape, and a can of aerosol spray had neutralized the Diamond Center's alarms. The total spent on these materials was less than it would cost for all the thieves to have lunch at one of the restaurants on the nearby plaza.

Notarbartolo called Tavano at 12:33 a.m. to report that they were inside the vault. From what Tavano could tell of the police radio chatter, the thieves were still undetected.

Before the thieves got down to the untested business of opening the safe deposit boxes, there was one more task. During his many trips to the vault, Notarbartolo had noticed a mass of wires running above the ceiling slats just inside the door of the vault and was worried that they led to some other alarm that was too well hidden to notice.

They dismantled part of the ceiling and took a look. The bundle of multicolored wires was pulled partially out of the ceiling, and, as Peys later said, "tampered with." The thieves spent little time with them, however, perhaps quickly discerning what the detectives would later learn from the building staff and the security company: that the wires were not part of the alarm system. In fact, during the investigation, no one could remember what they were for.

"We asked everybody what the meaning of that was and nobody knew," Peys explained. "Nobody could tell us. That tampering had no use at all, it had nothing with the alarm, nothing with the light, nothing with any detector." Satisfied that the wires posed no threat, the thieves left the wires hanging loose and didn't bother replacing the ceiling slat.

Time was ticking away and the bulk of their effort was still ahead of them. They carried their heavy bags from the foyer into the vault and began unpacking their supplies. Soon, the floor was scattered with duffel bags, backpacks, water bottles, and all manner of tools.

Since each box required a key and a combination to open, the thieves had long ago rejected the subtle approach; there was simply no way to crack the code and pick the locks on almost two hundred individual safes in just a few hours. Drilling would be time consuming and risk creating vibrations that could be sensed by the seismic detector. Just in case their device didn't work, however, they also had the power inverter, the heavy battery, drills, and an arc welder to cut through the safe deposit box doors. But their invented tool was their best bet.

In the middle of the vault floor, they assembled their specially designed pulling device. The device consisted of a long square aluminum rod about a foot long, which was fitted with two rectangular metal legs each about four or five inches long. When placed on the ground, this frame looked like a crude toy bridge.

Through a slot in the center of the bridge between the two legs, the thieves inserted a long steel bolt with a flat metal tip on the end with a hole through it. Then another piece of metal shaped like a clamp was attached to the flat end of the bolt with a hinge that allowed the clamp to rotate independently on the end of the bolt.

To the other end of the bolt—the part that protruded through the top of the bridge—they screwed a stout metal plug about the size and shape of a large flashlight battery. On opposite sides of this, they attached two slim metal tubes parallel to the bridge. These tubes created a handle; twisted to the right, the clamp attached to the bolt was pushed away from the bridge, and twisted to the left, the clamp was pulled toward it. The final attachment was a steel prong with a small lip that was inserted into the clamp. The prong was modeled after Notarbartolo's safe deposit box key and worked as a hook that would pull the door open.

The tool resembled an oversized corkscrew, and it worked on the same principle. Once fully assembled, it was aligned over one of the safe deposit box doors, with the legs bracing it above and below the door. Although the doors were different heights, the legs were adjustable, meaning the device would be able to open the tall safes as easily as the letterbox-sized ones. The prong was inserted into the keyhole and twisted so that the lip rotated inside the keyway behind the plug. The handle was turned to the left and the bolt slowly drew back the clamp holding the prong, causing it to pull outward on the key plug. Once it bound tightly against the key plug and the handle became more and more difficult to turn, the tension was enough that they could let go of the contraption and it stayed attached to the door, with the "bridge" design now perpendicular to the floor. At that point, it was just a matter of applying enough force to the handle to bend the deadbolt as the door was pulled outward.

Since he was by far the most muscular of the men, Finotto was the likely choice to crank on the handle, twisting it mightily as if he were tightening rusty lug nuts on a car. The door didn't warp, but it began opening, pulled by the steel pin inserted into the plug. There was the sound of wrenching metal as the deadbolt bent and scraped against its housing. Then came the loud crack of plastic from inside the box as the faceplate gave way.

Finally—*BANG*. The box popped open with the sound of a firecracker, but they did not worry too much about the noise. The seismic sensors wouldn't be triggered by isolated thumps, otherwise they would go off every time someone dropped a gold bar. And Jacques' apartment was six stories up from the vault level and in a different building, so it was impossible for him to hear. Although Jorge Dias De Sousa was off duty, there was a chance he was in his own apartment, but his was four stories from where the heist was taking place, on the second floor of B Block.

The group of eager thieves crowded forward to see what the box contained. After lovingly unfolding white diamond papers, the School of Turin finally held diamonds in their gloved hands. The polished ones refracted the dull white light of the vault into a disco ball–like assortment of rainbow colors.

As they forced open each new box, the loot began to pile up. One box contained seventeen stones, all of them just under two carats except for a larger one that was closer to three carats. The same box also held a small container with a white gold chain, a silk Chinese bag containing old heirloom jewelry, a bracelet, a few ladies' watches, a pair of diamond earrings, two Bulgari watches (both a man's and a woman's), a diamond-studded bracelet in a plastic bag, and another bag with a variety of white and yellow gold rings studded with diamonds. Finally, it contained a wad of U.S. currency totaling \$8,000.

They moved the tool to another box and broke it open with another loud bang. There they found a brooch with marquise-cut diamonds, a brick of pure gold, a gold medallion inscribed with the name "Frans," gold earrings, gold cufflinks, and a gold men's Rolex. There were also two other gold watches (one decorated with twenty diamonds), gold pendants embedded with amethyst and pearls, and gold coins, some imprinted with the seal of Baudouin of Belgium, the king from 1951 to 1993. This box also contained a treasure of gemstones, many in their certification blister packs from the HRD and the GIA. Carefully wrapped diamond papers contained dozens of loose stones as well, in marquise, heart, pear, and brilliant cuts, ranging in size from a half carat to more than four carats. Part of this collection included a rare hexagonal one-carat black diamond as well as numerous industrial diamonds.

The thieves quickly settled into a well-organized routine. One of them opened the safe deposit boxes as quickly as he could while the others sorted the loot, their work punctuated by the loud popping of the doors springing open. Diamonds were thrown together into the same bag; watches, jewelry, and cash went into their own bags. They knew they had to be selective, so Notarbartolo took on the role of impromptu gem evaluator, deciding quickly which stones to take and which to discard. There was no point in wasting space with industrial diamonds when they had their pick of the far more precious gemstones.

If the adrenaline had waned in the time it took them to get down to the business of opening the boxes, it was now surely surging again. For the School of Turin, this was the Christmas morning of a lifetime, each newly opened box investigated with held breath and wide eyes.

One box contained nothing but diamonds—one hundred and forty of them. They were poured into the canvas tote bag like gravel into a sandbag. Another box was stuffed with fat bundles of dollars and euros, twenty Napoleonic gold coins, a matching set of men's and women's gold watches and bracelets, several gold chains with gold pendants, a long string of pearls, and three heavy bars of solid gold. A third box held stock certificates, gold European Currency Units—the predecessor to the euro—a gold tie pin, a brooch with rubies, a brooch with diamonds, a diamond armband, and a matching diamond bracelet and earring set. There were gold necklaces, bracelets, and rings in several small boxes. There was also an envelope with the name "Estelle" printed on the outside that contained several gold pieces.

The thieves emptied this envelope and tossed it on the floor in the middle of the room, as they did with all the other containers found inside the safe deposit boxes, from cardboard cigar boxes to expensive velvet jewelry cases. The vault was soon littered with empty silk bags, felt-covered ring boxes, metal fireproof drawers, leather handbags, canvas shoulder bags, briefcases, and even Tupperware containers. To this growing pile, the thieves added pictures, letters, business invoices, transaction ledgers, company documents, cheap jewelry, personal items, credit cards, at least one passport and even a load of bullets. Though valuable enough to the tenant to store in a subterranean vault, these items were of little value to the thieves when compared to the diamonds and cash they were gathering.

Unless the safe deposit boxes contained business information, the thieves didn't know from whom they were stealing. Their victims included individuals as well as large companies. They stole a gold cigarette box, a wedding ring, a tourmaline clip with embedded emeralds, and a cache of diamonds weighing about ten carats, among other items, from a box owned by Fay Vidal, the IDH Diamonds employee who was nearing retirement. They even plundered the box owned by Julie Boost, the building's manager, who stored valuable jewelry, including a white gold watch with diamonds, gold necklaces, three diamond rings, and a gold brooch.

As frequently as the School of Turin hit upon personal boxes, they also cracked those belonging to the big diamond companies. These were virtually spilling over with glittering, dazzling stones, which often represented the entire assets of the company that owned them. The thieves stole every carat.

One such box held one hundred and twelve huge rough diamonds, the size of skipping stones. They were the De Beers specials from the most recent Sight, found in a box belonging to Pluczenik Diamond Company, one of the biggest De Beers Sightholders. Exclusive Diamonds lost three hundred and eighty-one carats' worth of loose stones while another company, Emrusadiam, lost nearly three thousand carats. The thieves stole from Diabel a package of nine diamonds worth $31,000, another box of seventeen diamonds worth $68,000, and a cornucopia of loose colored stones known as fancies, ranging from brown cognacs to yellow canaries. Capital Diamonds later estimated it lost more than a half-million dollars' worth of diamonds. The bags in which the thieves poured these diamonds began filling quickly because many of the polished stones were in their blister packs, which took up space but which were valuable because they proved authenticity.

Just as the thieves could guess when they were stealing from a wholesaler, it was also obvious when they opened a box owned by a jewelry firm, as these overflowed with gleaming rings, necklaces, and bracelets. One box produced a 100-gram gold Cartier bracelet that, in the value of the gold alone, was worth about $10,000; a gold necklace with a pendant spelling "Sony"; and a ring with the initials "J.H." In another box, they found a custom diamond-studded cigarette lighter, a gold Star of David, and a package of Israeli bonds. Another box stored a stash of about a million U.S. dollars.

The School of Turin opened forty boxes, then fifty, then sixty. The thieves stopped only to switch off the duty of cranking the boxes open with the pulling tool, which required a lot of exertion. They drank bottled water they had brought with them, throwing the empties on the pile of discarded bags and boxes. Their work surely raised the temperature in the vault, but, so long as the Styrofoam stayed in place on the motion detector to mask their movement, they didn't worry about setting off the alarm. Regular phone calls to their colleagues on the outside confirmed that the streets of Antwerp were as quiet and sleepy as ever. No one had any idea what they were up to in the subterranean vault.

The only sign of movement at the building occurred around two in the morning when Jacques Plompteux returned to the Diamond Center with his brother-in-law after their night out drinking. As they entered, they virtually traced the School of Turin's footsteps through the garage and through the door leading to C Block. Jacques later told police that they went straight to his apartment and then to bed while the biggest heist in history was taking place several floors below. Half an hour later, Jorge—who was not on duty and who had been having dinner at his parents' house, followed by drinks with a friend—also returned to the Diamond Center. He later reported to the police that he didn't see or hear anything unusual when he returned to his apartment that night.

Down on the vault level, there was a sudden snag in the plan: the pulling tool broke with the unmistakable high-pitched ping of shearing metal. The steel prong used to pull the doors outward from the keyhole had broken in half without so much as budging the door they were attempting to pry open. It was only a momentary problem; the School of Turin wasn't to be outdone by equipment failure, and, from one of their bags, they pulled out another metal prong. They'd had several made just in case the tool wore down and broke after enough use.

What they didn't know was that stressed steel had nothing to do with the prong's wearing down. The safe deposit box on which their tool broke was one of several that locksmith Paul De Vos had upgraded over the years—this newer door did not have a plastic faceplate covering the internal lock mechanism, but a reinforced steel faceplate. Had the Diamond Center acted on De Vos's earlier suggestion that all the safe doors be replaced with sturdier ones, the pulling tool wouldn't have worked at all.

For the thieves, it was a mystery. While most doors opened with relatively little resistance, a few didn't budge at all. They discarded the prongs that snapped in half in the pile of empty boxes on the vault floor and moved on to try other safe deposit box doors. Although they were quickly amassing an enormous fortune in the bags at their feet, they had no intention of stopping until they opened every door they could before it was time to leave.

Some of the boxes had contents worth as much as any jewelry store they'd ever robbed in Turin. Some had more. From one, they grabbed a platinum ring with more than seven carats of stones, a four-carat marquise diamond, a pearl necklace, gold bracelets, gold necklaces, an envelope with €22,000, packages of uncut diamonds weighing about two hundred carats, and a creatively designed brooch depicting a bird in its nest made of gold and diamonds.

The vault looked like a bomb had gone off, with shrapnel made of gems and gold. Safe deposit box doors stood agape around the room. On the floor was a riot of empty bags and boxes, in addition to bracelets, rings, gold ingots, and loose diamonds. As their bags were crammed with ever more treasure, they needed to be selective about what they could take with them. To make room for the most valuable items, they had to sacrifice some that were worth less.

A metal prong broke off in the keyhole for box number 25. This may well have been the last of their backups. It was shortly before dawn and they had been working hard in a state of heightened anxiety for many hours. They had broken into one hundred and nine of the Diamond Center's one hundred and eighty-nine deposit boxes. Notarbartolo's own safe deposit box was among those that were not breached, part of a large section of still-locked doors that the School of Turin hadn't gotten around to breaking open.

The thieves had been awake since whatever fitful sleep they'd been able to get Friday night. Adrenaline—and the euphoria of stealing as yet uncounted millions of dollars in diamonds—could only last so long. They were approaching the giddiness of full-blown fatigue, and there were many risks ahead. They needed to make their escape while it was still dark outside. They didn't want to risk there being any traffic on the street or any early risers walking their dogs before church. Besides, it was best to exit while the concierges were likely to be sound asleep; neither of them was likely to get up early on a Sunday morning.

Leaving, however, was easier said than done. They had a heavy load of tools and treasure to sneak out of the building. Some tools were sacrificed to make space for more loot; they left the crowbar, for example, amid the debris from the boxes. That was a surprising deviation from the discipline they'd honed throughout every other aspect of the heist. On a normal job, they would carry out with them everything they had brought in. The School of Turin knew that investigators would carefully examine anything left behind for clues, and its standard mode of operation was to give the police as little as possible to go on. The men had been careful to ensure that the items they planned to leave behind—such as the Styrofoam and the tape on the light detector—had been thoroughly cleaned to eliminate fingerprints or other clues.

But after several hours of looting, they had a true embarrassment of riches on their hands: they'd stolen more than they could carry. They only wanted to make one trip out of the building in order to minimize their exposure and they wanted to do it while it was still early. And there was so much worth stealing that, in the end, they had to make tough decisions; should they take the crowbar or leave it behind so they could steal another brick of gold?

The bags were zipped closed and arranged at the door to the stairwell. They took a last look around at their handiwork, surely with a tinge of regret at the millions of dollars' worth of gems and jewels scattered on the floor that they simply couldn't take with them. Then they called their friends on the outside to tell them they were coming out.

At the Charlottalei apartment, Tavano put on his coat, grabbed the car keys, and took the elevator to the ground floor. The lookout on the street near the Diamond District reported that the coast was clear. The thieves had the go-ahead to vacate the vault. They didn't even attempt to cover their tracks; they left the doors wide open and the lights on. There was no point wasting time trying to disguise the crime since it was going to be apparent to the first person who came down to the vault Monday morning.

The thieves retraced their steps as carefully and quietly as they could with the loads they carried. The bag of diamonds alone weighed at least forty-four pounds, as much as a microwave oven. On the way to the garage, one of the men ducked off toward the Schupstraat entrance and, using another fabricated key, opened the door to the security control room. He ejected the tapes that had recorded their crime from the two VCRs, placing them in his backpack, and replaced them with blanks. He looked through the archive of the previous month's tapes and stole the four tapes that had recorded the happenings of February 10, the day D'Onorio snuck into the building and sabotaged the magnetic alarm. They were not hard to find as the tapes were labeled by date and organized accordingly. He exited the control room quickly, locked the door behind him, and rejoined the others.

The final task was a coordinated, smooth withdrawal from the Diamond Center. Again, the thieves were on the phone with both Tavano and the lookout. As the car pulled to the curb, the lookout gave the green light and they opened the garage door. After the sweaty work in the vault, the predawn winter air was bitingly cold as the men swiftly left the building. The car sagged on its springs as heavy bags of stolen diamonds, cash, gold, and jewels were dumped in the trunk, no more than fifty feet from where police officers pulling the graveyard shift sat bundled in heavy coats in the police kiosk around the corner on Schupstraat.

The thieves piled into the car and disappeared down the street.

◆ ◆ ◆

The temptation to shout in exhilaration must have been overwhelming. But considering that it was dawn on a Sunday, they wisely refrained from waking Notarbartolo's neighbors. Exhaustion was creeping in, but it couldn't overcome the powerful, otherworldly high that made them lightheaded. The thrill of having gotten away with the heist of the century was better than falling in love. It was better than every holiday and birthday they'd ever had.

The men beamed at each other, the intense focus of the past several hours bleeding off into a faint awe that they had pulled it off. They wasted little time pouring the king's ransom of treasure onto the large, reddish rug in the middle of the floor to tally their ill-gotten gains and divide the loot into parcels that would be taken separately back to Italy. No one seemed to mind this part of the job.

Like the winners in a game of Monopoly, they sorted and counted stacks of multicolored cash. Most of it was American currency, because diamond prices are set to the U.S. dollar throughout the world. There were also euros, Swiss francs, British pounds, Indian rupees, Australian dollars, outdated Belgian francs, and Israeli new sheqalim. They decided that they should throw away the more obscure currencies that would be hard to redeem without risking questions. The rupees were tossed into a large garbage bag that was already being filled with the equipment from the job, including the dismantled pulling tool that had served them so well, the alligator clips they used to test the wires in the ceiling, rolls of duct tape, and other material that could tie them to the heist.

They sorted the government bonds and stock certificates which came from around the world, most from Belgium but a few from as far away as

Israel. The watches took up a lot of space because most were stolen with their original packages so as to make them easier to sell. The diamond earrings were piled so high they looked like a glittering snowdrift on the rug. The men passed jewelry back and forth to one another, admiring the settings in a ring or studying the emeralds, rubies, and sapphires in the bracelets and necklaces.

What surely entranced them the most, however, was the staggering cache of diamonds they'd stolen, so many that their weight strained the seams of the bag. They were poured carefully onto the rug. There were thousands of rough and polished diamonds—many of the latter were in their blister packs while others were wrapped in diamond papers. The men hadn't taken the time in the vault to open these paper packages, so they peeled apart the folds on the living room floor to discover what they contained. Some had great stones, which were added to the pile of diamonds on the carpet.

Others contained comparatively worthless pebbles, such as a package that was filled with hundreds of emerald pointers, tiny green rocks in a marquise shape that were four or five hundredths of a carat. Static caused them to pop off the surface of the inner layer when the package was opened and a few jumped onto the rug; this was a common problem with tiny stones and merchants often took special care when opening such packages of pointers.

The members of the School of Turin weren't as delicate. They didn't even notice the little emerald stones that were quickly lost in the fibers of the rug. All they cared about was that the package's contents were worthless compared to the other items they'd stolen. The paper was crumpled up—pointers and all—and tossed in one of the trash bags. "Even though this little collection of emeralds still had some value," as Peys later explained, "at that moment, in comparison to what else they had, it was rubbish. It's like having an envelope with tens of thousands of dollars and one with small coins."

It took a few hours to account for all that they'd stolen and to repack it into several bags that would be divided for the trip back to Italy. Notarbartolo marveled at everything they had to take from the apartment. Not only were there several bags of priceless loot, but he'd packed most of his personal belongings as well. He made himself a sandwich from the bread and salami left over from Finotto's shopping trip, ate all but a few bites of his sandwich and threw the rest in the kitchen trash can.

They faced a long drive back to Italy; Notarbartolo was going southwest through France, while other thieves were heading east through Germany, and some toward Brussels and the airport. Since no one in Antwerp knew where Notarbartolo lived (his apartment wasn't listed on his lease at the Diamond Center and he paid his rent in cash), they could have rested for a bit before heading out.

When they were ready to go, the little elevator in the Charlottalei apartment building made numerous trips to and from the seventh floor that day as the men emptied the apartment of anything related to the heist and loaded it into their cars. Transporting the luggage to the cars was no problem, but it looked a little suspicious when they began filling one of the cars with teeming garbage bags.

The heist had produced a lot of waste. They threw away the tools and equipment along with the loot they didn't want to take with them, including diamonds that they deemed not worth trying to sell, the emerald pointers, and the obscure currencies. They also threw their rubber gloves and the stolen security tapes (all of them dismantled with their tape unspooled) into garbage bags to be brought to the cars.

As an afterthought, on the way out the door, someone also grabbed the household garbage in the kitchen trash can. They had reused the bag from Finotto's trip to the Delhaize supermarket, still containing the receipt, as a trash bag. He stuffed that bag, a white plastic shopping bag emblazoned with the Delhaize logo, a black and red design featuring the stylized image of a lion, into one of the larger bags. In all, there were four large black plastic bags that filled the trunk and back seat of one of the cars.

They said their farewells without a hint of mistrust that one of them would be tempted to vanish before they could properly divide the loot, a task they would do Monday in a location far removed from their usual haunts around Turin. In a movie, this would be the point where a conniving double-cross would occur, but many of these men knew each other from childhood. They knew each other's wives and children. And as much as they were thieves, they considered themselves men of honor. It's true that they had just wiped out scores of businesses and destroyed the livelihoods of innocent strangers, but there was nothing personal about it. Stealing from faceless strangers was one thing; stealing from a trusted colleague was quite another.

They went their separate ways, knowing all they needed to do was drive cautiously and arrive at the rendezvous point on time before they could say that they'd gotten away with the biggest job they—or anyone—had ever pulled.

Only one of them needed to make a final stop before he was free to escape from Belgium: the driver heading toward the Brussels airport, about thirty minutes to the south, had to find a place to dump the garbage where it would never be found. Just a few exits from the airport, with the jets clearly visible as they took off and banked over the Belgian capital, he found what looked to be the perfect place.

Chapter Nine

ONE MAN'S TRASH IS ANOTHER MAN'S TREASURE

"They always call it 'the crime of the century,' but it never is."

— Lodovico Poletto, *La Stampa* reporter

At a quarter past six on Monday morning, Jorge Dias De Sousa began his weeklong shift as the caretaker on duty. Though the previous night had been a late one—he'd returned to his apartment in the Diamond Center at three a.m.—he didn't have the luxury of sleeping in. His duties began a bit earlier than usual, as he had to open the garage to let in maintenance men who were there to do some work on the building. Thirty-five minutes later, he got into the elevator and pushed the button for -2 to unlock the vault for the day, just as he'd done countless times before.

Expecting darkness in the foyer, he was instead surprised to find the lights on. That was easy enough to dismiss as an oversight by Jacques Plompteux, who could have forgotten to turn them off when he locked the vault on Friday night. "The lights were on," Jorge recalled later. "Normally the lights are turned off in the evenings. I was thinking Jacques was there first [so] I called him, I called his name."

There was no answer, but as soon as he turned to face the vault, Jorge knew Jacques had nothing to do with the lights being left on. "The safe was open," Jorge said. "When I walked in the safe, I saw everything on the floor."

The room was a disaster of open deposit boxes and discarded bags, jewelry pouches, and attaché cases. The storage room door was cracked and ajar; the magnetic alarm that was supposed to be attached to the vault door instead dangled freely from its wiring.

Like all of the School of Turin's victims before him, Jorge understood what it was like to not believe his own eyes. As puzzlement turned to panic, he could not comprehend how what he was seeing was possible. No one should have been able to break into the building's impregnable vault, but that it had happened he couldn't deny. The Diamond Center had been robbed. Jorge called the police and the building manager, Julie Boost.

Phones began ringing from one end of Antwerp to the other, a chain reaction that soon had the entire Diamond District buzzing. The first to react were the uniformed police, who ran from their nearby substations, and the sight of cops zeroing in on the Diamond Center sent word rippling outward from every diamantaire they passed along the way that something big had happened. News of a heist was like word of a neighborhood fire: Everyone scrambled to see if they or someone they knew was affected. Before long, the street outside the Diamond Center was clogged with a mob of policemen, journalists, traders, Diamond Center tenants, and curious onlookers.

Philip Claes, a lawyer for the Antwerp World Diamond Centre who would go on to become its secretary general in 2008, found the area in front of 9–11 Schupstraat mired in chaos and confusion. "People were making gestures, they were surprised and astonished by what happened," he said. "A lot of people were in shock because their safes were opened. For a lot of people all of their belongings were in the safes . . . Yeah, it was gone. It had disappeared and people just couldn't understand what happened, how it was possible."

The Diamond District police immediately called the federal detectives on the diamond squad, who were just starting their day. A heist trumped any other plans they had; like firemen responding to a five-alarm blaze, they dropped what they were doing, grabbed their coats and car keys, and sped through the streets with blue lights flashing and sirens wailing. They covered the short distance from their headquarters to the Diamond Center in record time.

Insurance investigator Denice Oliver was also among the first to get an urgent phone call about the heist. She arrived shortly after the initial pandemonium, and quickly learned from tenants that Jorge was distraught.

Since neither Julie Boost nor Marcel Grünberger had been at the building when the heist was discovered, Jorge was the senior staff member on site. He was so upset that he let several tenants into the vault to see for themselves what had happened—a misstep for a crime scene that should have been cordoned off. A rumor circulated quickly among the tenants, putting at least part of the blame on the shoulders of Jorge, who wasn't even on duty the weekend the crime took place. When she arrived at the Diamond Center, Oliver heard from some of the tenants that Jorge admitted keeping the key stamp attached to the pipe and not clearing the code from the combination dial. "Apparently, he had memory problems, and he would go in and lock up the vault room door," Oliver said, "but he didn't enter the code and [he] put the key in a box off in the side room . . . He was like a headless chicken down there."

Though it sounded hard to believe, such practices were more common than might be imagined. According to safe makers, it was not unusual for safe owners to pick codes that were easy for them to remember, like birthdays or to mutter the combination out loud as they dialed it in, even in the presence of strangers. And it wasn't unheard of for them to skip clearing the code from the dial for the sake of speed and convenience.

Fay Vidal, one of the tenants whose box had been broken into and robbed, heard the same thing from one of the police detectives. She was shocked at how carelessly her treasures—and those of the other tenants—had been guarded. "Our dear Jorge, being one lazy S.O.B., decided that it was much too much work to put in that combination every morning," she said. "So [when locking the door for the night], he just turned the key and left the combination . . . I don't know if he did it always, I wasn't there, it's not me, but that's what I heard from the inspector."

What these accusations fail to take into account was that it was Jacques, not Jorge, who last locked the vault before the heist, something Jorge himself was quick to point out when discussing this accusation years later. "Not me," he said, "because that week I was not on duty. It was my colleague that closed the safe, do you understand? I never, in fourteen years that I am here, forgot to clear the combination . . . You're used to doing that, it's automatic."

As for whether Jacques was as careful, Jorge couldn't say. "Jacques, I don't know," he said. "I can't speak about that . . . That's possible of course [that he didn't clear the combination], but I don't know that."

Tenants' ire may have been directed at Jorge because he was the head caretaker and so was responsible for setting the standards for those he supervised or perhaps simply because he was there that morning. If there were an unwritten policy that it was acceptable to only partially secure the door, it would have applied to Jacques as well as to Jorge.

By the time the diamond detectives arrived, they found a crime scene that was being explored by dumbstruck civilians and a hysterical concierge. Only when Boost arrived did Jorge get hold of himself, and he did so by following his boss's orders to keep his mouth shut.

The detectives, led by Agim De Bruycker and Patrick Peys, took control. They cleared everyone out of the vault and began their investigation. It would take a while before they learned the scope of the heist—their first task was to figure out what the building's security features and policies were, as only then could they understand what measures the thieves had bypassed—but they could tell from a glance that it was a professional job. They couldn't help but admire the simple ingenuity of the Styrofoam on the motion detector and the tape on the light sensor.

Given that the vault door had been opened without being damaged, the detectives first thought this had to be an inside job. They called for Paul De Vos, the locksmith who had installed the vault more than thirty years before, to examine the door and explain how it worked.

♦ ♦ ♦

The vault buzzed with activity. Two forensic technicians dressed in white head-to-toe Tyvek outfits like those used to handle hazardous waste dusted for fingerprints. They gingerly picked through the debris on the floor, changing rubber gloves after handling each item to avoid accidentally transferring any DNA that might be on one to another. They collected bits of adhesive tape, the shrouding material blinding the cameras, the tools left behind by the thieves, and the discarded water bottles. Among the many items from the safe deposit boxes littering the floor of the vault were ledgers of diamond transactions. Since the detectives were trained to spot schemes to trade diamonds on the black market, they quickly realized these could hold the key to more crimes than just the heist. Considering the scale of the robbery, however, the detectives decided to ignore any evidence of black diamond transactions they found. Their priority was to try to solve the heist, not add a further layer of misery to those who'd been robbed by looking into whether they'd evaded taxes. "We spoke about it with [the investigating judge assigned to the case, similar to a district attorney] and he agreed with us that it wasn't the appropriate time to take advantage of what happened," Peys recalled. "So we didn't."

Besides potentially incriminating ledgers, the vault floor contained numerous treasures. "I can assure you that whatever was left regarding valuables, if it would have been ours, the six of us, we didn't have to work anymore," Peys said. "At that moment it was very difficult and very important that we could return all of those belongings to the right owner. To retrieve them wasn't the problem, they were lying there on the ground, but who is the owner? That was a major difficulty at that moment. You have some diamonds or jewelry that are easily recognizable and nobody's going to discuss about it, but some kind of diamonds or money or whatever, there might be a very serious discussion about [who owned] it. We found for example a bar of gold. Just like that. A bar of gold. No name on it, of course, so who is the owner of the bar of gold?"

To help sort it out, the detectives ordered a desk be set up in the foyer. They allowed tenants to descend to the vault level in groups to speak to investigators.

"The landing was full of people," Vidal said of the scene outside the vault. "You had to come and give your name, safe number, and all that. Then there were three policemen inside the vault, each taking care of one person. We were queuing up outside after we'd given our name and one by one, they let somebody in and that person would then go to their own safe to see if it was opened or not."

Those waiting for their turn in the vault were "decimated, destroyed," according to Vidal's description of the crowd that day. When she herself was led into the vault, she found that her small letterbox safe was open and empty except for some envelopes that contained nothing of value to the thieves. Everything else—gold trinkets from when her daughters were children, jewelry she'd inherited from her mother—was gone. She saw that the deadbolt was bent at about a 45-degree angle.

The detectives asked her to look around on the floor and see if there was anything she recognized as hers. It was an arduous task, like sifting through a landfill.

"The floor was littered that high, from one side to the other, with what they didn't take," Vidal said, gesturing with her hands to illustrate the clutter on the floor. "There were bags: plastic bags, travel bags, linen bags. People just put things into their safe with a bag. Then there were coupons, bonds, papers like that . . . There was jewelry on the floor as well." She found nothing that was hers.

Tenants who were able to identify their belongings weren't allowed to leave with them. The valuables were still considered evidence, so the police placed them in clear plastic bags, wrote the tenant's name on the outside, and kept the property to sort out later, after the forensic team had a chance to examine the items.

Denice Oliver set up her own triage operation to begin the Herculean task of processing insurance claims and assembling a list of stolen goods. When she had heard that there had been "an incident," as she called it, at the Diamond Center, she hadn't been greatly surprised. She'd been in the building numerous times to visit clients, and although she had never been allowed to closely inspect its security measures, she hadn't been impressed with what she saw. She had long ago dismissed the staff as inadequate; in fact, she didn't consider the concierges who checked visitors in and out of the building to be legitimate security guards. On previous visits to the Diamond Center, she was amazed that she could take as much time as she liked wandering its halls, no questions asked. "Everything in that building was just so lax," she said later.

While Oliver interviewed her clients and the police puzzled over how the thieves had penetrated the vault, Paul De Vos explained to detectives how the LIPS door operated. He had to draw a verbal picture of the two-part key because it couldn't be found amid the debris on the floor. The detectives assumed the thieves had taken it with them. De Vos explained that he didn't know the combination to the safe because he always averted his eyes when it was being reset, but he told them who did. Those people went to the top of the detectives' list of suspects.

De Vos was also asked to examine the safe deposit box doors. Like the detectives, he couldn't understand how the thieves had opened the safes. He knew that the faceplates were a weak point, but he didn't think it was possible to pry the doors open. He took his time moving from one broken door to the next, examining each carefully. Then he noticed something strange about one of the unopened boxes, number 25: there was a sheered-off prong of metal protruding from the keyhole. He pointed it out to the detectives. They had their first clue as to how the thieves had opened the safe doors.

◆ ◆ ◆

When August "Gust" Van Camp woke up Monday morning, he couldn't remember whether or not he'd locked the heavy green metal gate on the service road leading into the Floordambos forest the day before. If he had forgotten, it was out of character. Well into his sixties and retired from a career as a grocer, Van Camp was meticulous about the care of this picturesque stand of woods on the outskirts of Brussels. He patrolled them nearly every day as a member of the conservation organization Jacht en Natuurbeheer, or Hunting and Nature.

It was Van Camp's self-imposed duty to keep trespassers off the land, a wildlife and nature preserve, and it was a never-ending job. He treated the responsibility as if he were guarding a nuclear missile site; if he wasn't at home or helping a friend tend his nearby pumpkin patch, he could be found walking the paths of the green forest or the cornfield that abutted its edge, shotgun on his shoulder and his trusty English Springer Spaniel bounding along beside him.

Van Camp was perpetually on the lookout for dirt bikers who tore along the area's wooded paths on loud motorbikes, and for other trespassers who treated the forest like a garbage dump. It never failed that Van Camp discovered beer bottles and cigarette butts deep in the glades, the telltale signs of some late-night teen party. People even dumped household appliances and old furniture in the underbrush. Once, he discovered a pile of dozens of old tires that had been tossed in the middle of the rutted dirt road separating the field from the trees. Years before, he'd even found a dead body in a wooded ditch, a victim of foul play.

Van Camp hated that fact that so few people seemed to share his devotion to preserving the natural beauty of the woods. Over the years, his mission to protect the Floordambos from litterbugs began to look less like a job to enjoy in retirement and more like an obsession. Anyone encountering Van Camp on his regular foot patrols wouldn't think of him as the friendly neighborhood woodsman but as the tyrannical guardian of the forest who was best not encountered twice. He'd gotten so frustrated at the endless stream of litter that he took to calling the police on a regular basis. His name and his gruff voice became well known at the local police station. In fact, they considered him something of a nuisance. In most cases, his calls went unheeded and there was nothing for him to do but gripe to his dog and clean it up himself.

Although it rarely helped, Van Camp always locked the gate on the dirt road that led from the cornfield into the forest. Waking up that Monday morning, he was troubled by the thought that he might have forgotten to do so the day before. He dressed in his standard outfit (a camouflage T-shirt under his overcoat, a faded green baseball cap, and grubby blue work pants tucked into thick rubber boots that came halfway to his knees), kissed his wife good-bye, and grabbed his keys. As always, he brought along his shotgun in case he spotted a rabbit or a pheasant.

Van Camp drove his dusty white Volkswagen van the few miles from his tidy home on a suburban street in Vilvoorde, a village just a few miles from Brussels and its international airport, to the forest. Originally part of an eighteenth-century estate, the Floordambos was divided into two by the E19 highway that connected Brussels to Antwerp. The local government had placed seventeen acres of it under protection in 1991. Van Camp owned some of the land he patrolled, but acted as if he owned the whole forest.

Van Camp turned on to a wooded road where a tongue of dirt emerged between the trees on the right and led into the cornfield. He trundled the van down the pitted track until he reached the end of the field at the steep berm leading up to the highway. Where the path curved left into the dense trees, the dark green gate stood wide open. Annoyed he'd forgotten, Van Camp parked, grabbed his shotgun, and decided to take a stroll into the forest before coming back to lock the gate.

Approaching a fork in the road, Van Camp started to turn left, away from the sound of speeding traffic on the highway, when he stopped in his tracks, his attention caught by something in the path straight ahead. He muttered a string of colorful Flemish curses, his pleasant morning walk ruined by the sight of empty champagne bottles in the middle of the wide path. As he walked closer, he saw that the bottles were only the tip of the iceberg.

In the underbrush to the right of the path was what looked like a Dumpster's worth of large gray garbage bags, some spilled open. They hadn't been there as recently as late afternoon the day before, when he'd last patrolled the area. They were littered over an area ten to twenty feet from the path and scattered around the bases of small trees. If it hadn't been for the champagne bottles lying in the open, he might have walked past the mess without noticing; despite the lack of leaves on the bare trees in February, the branches of the undergrowth formed a screen that was hard to see through from the path. Van Camp propped his rifle against a tree and began rooting through the trash bags, determined to find something—a discarded piece of mail, perhaps—that would identify whoever was too lazy to find a proper rubbish bin. He fully intended to file another police report.

Within one of the bags, Van Camp found a smaller white trash bag from a Delhaize grocery store that was filled with kitchen waste, including used coffee grounds, a half-eaten sandwich, and some torn-up pieces of paper. He pulled out the shreds of paper and examined them closely, noting that he could make out part of an Antwerp address. He pawed deeper into the larger bag and found brown paper envelopes and other documents from the Diamond District, including what seemed to him to be certificates or invoices for individual diamonds. He knew for certain there was something odd about the trash when he discovered one of the bags contained Indian rupees.

At the same time that Van Camp was fuming in the forest over yet another brazen example of disrespect to his precious forest, his wife Annie was at home watching the news. The story dominating the broadcast wasn't that Venus Williams had won the singles match in the Proximus Games and come one step closer to winning the diamond-encrusted tennis racquet. Instead, the lead story was about a spectacular burglary that had occurred over the weekend in Antwerp's Diamond Square Mile. A vault in one of the big diamond office buildings had been looted and the thieves had gotten away with untold millions of dollars' worth of diamonds. Though no one had yet calculated the amount of the loss, reporters were already calling it "the heist of the century."

The Van Camps would disagree for years over which of them connected the dots to realize that the garbage strewn in the Floordambos was from the great heist in Antwerp. According to Gust Van Camp, he realized right away that the refuse was connected to a diamond robbery, although he had yet to hear the news that the Diamond Center had been looted. His wife, however, tells a slightly different story. According to her version, Van Camp returned from the forest livid at the desecration, intending to call the police to report yet another incidence of littering. When he described some of the odd contents of the garbage bags, it was she who made the connection to the Diamond Center heist.

It was indisputable, however, that Gust Van Camp had discovered a treasure trove of valuable clues. He called the local police, and they, in turn, called the investigators in Antwerp. The local officers cordoned off the area and awaited the arrival of the federal detectives, who wasted no time speeding south along the E19 highway. Before it was even noon on Monday, the forest was crawling with investigators, who photographed the scene, gathered the trash, and walked for miles through the underbrush looking for additional evidence. For the police, it was an astonishing break early in the case; the heist had been discovered only a few hours before.

The trash had been discarded in a flat area between the path and the steep slope leading up to the highway that was about thirty yards wide. From the forest floor, it was another twenty yards or so up to the shoulder of the road. It was too far for the thieves to have heaved the garbage over the guardrail. The trees between the highway and the location of the trash would have made that impossible anyway. Investigators surmised that the thieves had driven past the forest on the highway, taken the exit to Vilvoorde, and circled back until they found the dirt access road leading into the cornfield. The champagne bottles suggested they had spent some time toasting the discovery of what they thought was the perfect place to lose the trash forever.

Indeed, it would have been perfect if anyone but Van Camp had been in charge of keeping an eye on things. As they drove out of Antwerp, the thieves would have been anxious to get rid of the garbage as soon as they were a reasonable distance away from the city. They didn't want to risk driving with it for too long. Large teeming bags of refuse filling the trunk and the back seat would be hard to explain to a highway cop should they be pulled over for a traffic violation. Cruising down the open highway, it was easy for them to think they'd have their choice of dump locations before getting to Brussels. There was no shortage of places they could have gotten rid of the evidence—including gas stations, rest areas, and the refuse bins outside of restaurants near the highway—but they probably didn't want to take the chance of being caught dumping so many bags. Business owners in Belgium were serious about preventing the unauthorized use of their garbage cans. Many were locked and some were even monitored by security cameras. That was especially true of businesses along the highways.

"On every highway you have gasoline stations. Everywhere there are signs that it is forbidden to throw [away] personal belongings," Peys explained. "It's forbidden. There are cameras in those petrol stations. I can imagine if I had that garbage, I wouldn't throw it away in an official garbage bin that is standing next to the public way as you never know who is going to collect it."

By the time the thieves could see airplanes leaving from the Brussels airport, the little stand of trees seemed like their last opportunity. After dumping the trash, they did nothing to destroy its evidentiary value, such as burning it. Doing so would have risked drawing unwanted attention. Smoke rising from a fire in a forest so close to the highway would have been hard for authorities to ignore. While not burning the trash can be seen as a huge mistake in retrospect, at the time it made perfect sense just to leave it where it seemed well hidden. The thieves drove out of the Floordambos confident that their stash of garbage would never be found.

But thanks to Van Camp, the hiding place lasted only half a day. It was the first time the School of Turin's luck went against it, and detectives were well aware that it was only by pure chance that the garbage was discovered so soon after the heist.

"We're talking about a highway that has miles of forest and green next to it," Peys said. "I'm talking about thirty or forty kilometers [from Antwerp]. Now, on thirty-eight of those kilometers, nobody would ever bother about trash, and after months it would be taken by public services and thrown away . . . For one reason or another, it's written in the stars, they threw the garbage right on that spot, where that guy is coming every day and annoying himself every day about rubbish that's thrown away by people."

The champagne bottles, the unopened bags, the emptied shells of Sony videocassette tapes from the CCTV system, and the material Van Camp had handled were carefully packaged up and transported back to Antwerp. Police technicians made plaster casts of tire treads found in the softer soil. Officers searching the underbrush found long ribbons of videotape strung through the foliage a few dozen yards from the trash dump that presumably belonged to the dismantled videocassettes they'd already found.

The videotape was carefully gathered up, and one of the investigators organized a search party to scour the shoulders of the highway for miles in both directions to see if they could find additional clues. It seemed to pay off: searchers found numerous strands of videotape all along the road, as if someone had held one end of the tape and tossed the spool out the window so that it would unwind in the hope that it would degrade from exposure to the elements. Police thought that these bits of tape could also be from the dismantled CCTV videocassettes. Eventually, all of the recovered tape was sent to the Belgian headquarters of Sony for expert reconstruction.

The heart of the investigation moved to the diamond detectives' offices at the federal police building and to the Antwerp Forensics Laboratory, a plain building just across the street. Peys and the others who'd been in the vault returned after sundown with their load of evidence at the same time that detectives who'd gone to the Floordambos returned with the garbage bags. The bags were opened and their contents carefully sorted and logged.

"It was the day after that colleagues tried to reconstruct what was in those garbage bags," Peys said. "It came surely from the heist, but finding clues toward the suspects is something different. It wasn't obvious, I assure you."

The bags contained rubber gloves, rolls of tape, wrenches, pliers, spools of wire, alligator clips, and several metal components that confounded the police at first. It would take weeks before a police technician was able to put it together properly, and surmise that this was the device used for pulling open the safe deposit boxes. Investigators also found both parts of the vault door key and several other fabricated keys that were used to pick locks inside the Diamond Center. There were discarded documents, envelopes, and diamond papers, one of which was uncrumpled to reveal tiny emerald pointers.

The discovery of the garbage put the investigation on a fast track. Several inquiries were going on at once, and the diamond detectives' offices became the round-the-clock command center for the investigation. Every detective on the squad was assigned to the case, and detectives from neighboring cities were temporarily reassigned to help.

The pressure to solve the crime was phenomenal. The heist had made news around the world. Estimates of the thieves' haul ranged from more than €100 million to more than €400 million. It was difficult to quantify the losses, especially early on. One way was based on what was claimed as lost to insurance companies; another way, which produced a much higher number, was admittedly a guess based on the fact that not all of the victims were able to calculate their losses.

Many of the companies that were robbed had no idea what was in their safe deposit boxes that weekend. There was also the widely held belief that not all tenants reported the true value of their losses, afraid that claiming staggering amounts would reveal their participation in black market diamond trading.

The bare fact was that, even without knowing the true amount of what the School of Turin made off with, the documented losses alone meant that it was unparalleled in the annals of crime, in Belgium or anywhere else. Any way you counted, it was the largest heist in history.

The news was a crippling blow to the image Antwerp had been trying to project as a safe place to do business. As far as most diamantaires knew, the Diamond Center was as secure a building as any in the Diamond District. The thieves and the investigators knew differently, of course, but the average merchant found himself feeling very nervous in the days immediately after the heist.

"It was no good for the [city's] reputation. It never is," said Claes, of the Antwerp World Diamond Centre. "People weren't particularly feeling secure anymore because the Diamond Center was known for having a good security system. Everything was in place there. Everything was in order there like in the other buildings. There were television cameras . . . Of course the room itself with all the safes, it was protected. So when you then see that none of it worked, then of course you don't know who to trust anymore."

Anxious to prove that Antwerp could protect her assets—or could at least bring the perpetrators to justice swiftly when that failed—the detectives worked under tremendous pressure. The clock was ticking: if any of the stolen goods were to be recovered, police needed to find them as soon as possible. Even hundreds of millions of dollars' worth of diamonds can be sold quickly, at which point the chance of recovering them falls to near zero.

◆ ◆ ◆

The discovery of the trash put the detectives on the scent immediately and led them in many different directions. The Delhaize bag with the household garbage contained beer bottles, a wine bottle, empty plastic yogurt pots, and half of a partially eaten salami sandwich, all of which the police analyzed for DNA. They found two toll receipts in the garbage as well: one was for passage over the Brenner Pass from Italy on Sunday, February 9, 2003, and one for a toll highway through Innsbruck, Austria, on the same day. It was the first clue that their suspects were Italians.

The bag also contained receipts for items bought at a Brico hardware store in Mechelen on Valentine's Day and at a local Delhaize supermarket the day before that. The items on the receipts matched what was found in the garbage as well as in the vault, including the crowbar, the Styrofoam, and the duster handle. Detectives were eventually dispatched to both stores, to see if anyone remembered who had made these purchases and, if they were lucky, to get CCTV video. They purchased all the items from both receipts so they could compare them with items found during their investigation.

Detectives also recovered thirty-five torn squares of paper stained by used coffee grounds from the Delhaize bag. "My colleagues started to puzzle that document together, not knowing whether it would be an invoice or somebody's account," said Peys. "You never know what you're going to find."

Many of these clues paid off quickly.

At the Brico store, for instance, detectives showed the receipt to the staff and a cashier remembered the purchase. It stuck in her mind, she said, because the men had paid with a 500-euro note, which was a rarity. Only one other customer that day had paid with a bill that large. The store hadn't deposited the bills yet, and the police collected them to test for fingerprints. They found none.

The store didn't have security cameras, but the employee described the men in detail. The detectives would later match those descriptions to D'Onorio and Finotto.

If there was any group of people who were as good as thieves at remembering the details of past heists, it was the police detectives who investigated them. As soon as the heist was discovered, they ran a catalog of comparable crimes from the past through their minds. One stood out as similar: the botched job at the KBC bank on Pelikaanstraat in 1997. During that attempt, men posing as bank clients had tried to access the vault area after hours but had set off an alarm in the process of trying to disable it. The thieves got away, and the police were able to identify one of them, but only long after he had fled the country. Detectives remembered that he had rented an office in the Diamond Center from which to organize the bank heist.

The man who'd been convicted in absentia in Belgium and arrested in Italy—but who'd never served time for the crime in Belgium—was Ferdinando Finotto of Turin. They dug out an old picture of Finotto from the case file and stuck it to a white dry-erase board in one of the conference rooms that became the detectives' main theater of operations.

Finotto became the first person they suspected of being involved in the heist.

Others were soon to follow. Investigators piecing together the shredded document from the trash discovered it was a work order for video surveillance equipment to be installed at a business called Damoros Preziosi. They also found a ripped-up business card for Elio D'Onorio, a security expert whose business name matched that on the work order. Peys looked up Damoros Preziosi on the list of Diamond Center tenants and discovered that its owner—Leonardo Notarbartolo—had suffered no loss in the heist. His safe deposit box was among those that weren't breached. "We saw that it was under the name of Notarbartolo, which at that moment didn't mean anything," Peys said. "But we knew that his safe hadn't been opened."

That in itself wasn't suspicious, but if Notarbartolo's box hadn't been looted, then how did the work order get mixed up with the discarded items from the heist?

The diamond detectives obtained a search warrant for Notarbartolo's office and returned to the Diamond Center on Wednesday, two days after the heist had been discovered. They were escorted to the fifth floor by Julie Boost, who was relieved to learn that the police had their sights set on someone other than an employee of the building. She and the three others who knew the code to the vault door had been grilled at the federal police building since Monday. That the police had found a copy of the building's blueprints with a Post-it note with Notarbartolo's name on it hadn't helped divert suspicion away from the staff.

Boost opened office number 516 with her master key. Notarbartolo's office was empty. Even the wastebaskets were barren. It was obvious to Peys that this was not an office used for legitimate business. They opened all the desk drawers and all the filing cabinets, finding nothing of value. Notarbartolo had done his job well, leaving not a clue as to his whereabouts.

The next stop was the vault, a surreal visit if only because the same LIPS door that the thieves had so smoothly bypassed still stood guarding the entryway. It worked perfectly fine, after all; replacing it would have been a foolish and time-consuming waste of money. After the police left the crime scene Monday night, the door had simply been relocked, this time with a spare key Marcel Grünberger kept in his private safe and with a new combination. It was a sure bet that the key stamp would no longer be kept in the storage room with the pipe. Likewise, the magnetic lock was perfectly functional and required only a new set of bolts to reattach it to the door and the door frame.

Inside the vault, the safes that had been cracked were in the process of receiving new doors. Paul De Vos finally had the opportunity to replace the old ones with the sturdier new ones with steel faceplates. In fact, it was De Vos who the detectives were there to meet. After dusting door number 149 for fingerprints, the detectives watched as he drilled through the lock and popped the door to Notarbartolo's safe. Like the office had been, it was empty of anything worthwhile.

Upstairs in the security control room, the detectives checked Notarbartolo's badge traffic and learned he was among the last people to leave the building Friday night before it was robbed. Back at headquarters, they watched countless hours of security videotape for their first glimpse of their latest suspect. They saw the handsome Italian go in and out of the vault every day the week before the heist and three times on Friday.

In some frames, he carried a little purse under his arm that, when one was paying close attention, obviously was used to film through a hole in the side. The camera wasn't visible, but the hole was. It was easy to miss such a detail if one wasn't specifically studying Notarbartolo's actions. Notarbartolo had apparently done some last-minute filming to satisfy the others that all systems were go.

The detectives had no doubt that he was the inside man. They were duly impressed with the patience he'd displayed in meticulously orchestrating the heist of the century over the course of more than two years.

Notarbartolo would have been proud to know that none of the staff members interviewed by the detectives remembered anything useful about him, much less an address for where he lived in Antwerp. He hadn't listed a residence on his office lease.

Peys knew that because the thieves shopped at a grocery store just around the corner from the Diamond District, Notarbartolo's apartment was likely nearby. He also knew that, because of the level of professionalism he'd come to expect from Notarbartolo and his team, it would be empty too. He was sure the thieves were in Italy, but they might as well have been on the moon. Although Italy was in the European Union, it would be very difficult to extradite any of its citizens for this crime, something that Peys was certain the thieves were well aware of. That didn't mean he was about to give up, though; the next step was to contact the local authorities in Turin.

In Turin, Marco Martino's phone rang.

Chapter Ten

BEEN CAUGHT STEALING

"If you want to steal, steal a little cleverly, in a nice way. Only if you steal so much as to become rich overnight, you will be caught."

— Mobutu Sésé Seko, president of Zaire

While Belgian police ran their names, photos, and criminal histories through Interpol, the School of Turin congratulated themselves on pulling off the perfect caper, one that they were certain would leave investigators baffled for years.

After a long but uneventful escape through Europe, they gathered again on Monday, February 17, 2003, immediately upon their return to Italy. The meeting was not in Turin, but instead at a rendezvous point that they had agreed upon in advance. Investigators have never disclosed the exact location of the meeting point, but based on mobile phone records obtained later, they believe it was a villa in the Lake District northeast of Milan, near Lake Iseo, a slender finger of water surrounded by steep rocky hills and with a stunning Alpine backdrop.

Red-tiled villas and mansions sprinkled the lake's shores, the rooftop landscape punctuated generously with brick church bell towers. The lake itself was dotted with islands that were home to Gothic castles and Baroque mansions accessible only by boat. In the summer, wealthy vacationers overran the place, with even a few Hollywood stars escaping to the seclusion of its craggy foothills; in the winter, it was virtually deserted. Instead of swarms of tourists, a handful of locals remained in town to live in the picturesque snow and ice of a summer town in the heart of winter.

It was a perfect remote location in which to divide their loot in luxury. They could certainly have afforded to rent the most expensive villa available, even without an off-season discount. It was here that the School of Turin had their first chance to truly relax and bask in the glory of a job that made them all richer than they could have imagined.

The men ate, drank, and relived the heist instant by instant while the money was sorted and the diamonds admired.

Notarbartolo now had enough to buy any model sports car he wished, and he could devote as much time as he liked to designing a private line of custom jewelry. He certainly had no shortage of material. But most important, his children—and his children's children—could live in financial security for the rest of their lives.

All of the men had reason to celebrate. They toasted themselves for having gotten away with the heist of the century. None of them knew that Gust Van Camp had made a discovery that same morning that put them squarely in detectives' sights.

They spent Monday night there and when they left Lake Iseo on Tuesday, Elio D'Onorio headed south toward his home in Latina, outside of Rome. Finotto and Tavano headed back to Turin. Notarbartolo headed toward Turin as well, but he didn't follow the thieves' protocol of destroying the cell phone and SIM card he had used to communicate with the others on the closed telephone network established for the heist. The hard part of the heist was finished, but, for Notarbartolo, the job wasn't quite over yet.

His final task was to return to Antwerp to tie up loose ends.

♦ ♦ ♦

Marco Martino was momentarily speechless. The head of Turin's Mobile Squadron had already heard of the heist in Antwerp—it was all over the news—but he never imagined that the plot had originated in his backyard, and certainly not with Leonardo Notarbartolo at the center of it. In Martino's mind, Notarbartolo was a small-time criminal, a pilot fish to Turin's more storied crooks. Martino simply didn't think it was in Notarbartolo to pull off a job of this caliber.

It was a sentiment that was later shared by reporters who covered crime in the city. Turin was overpopulated with flamboyant thieves. Lodovico Poletto, a reporter for the daily newspaper, *La Stampa*, didn't even put Notarbartolo in the same league as the other criminals he covered.

Pancrazio Chiruzzi, for example, had earned the nickname "the Soloist with the Kalashnikov" for single-handedly holding up an armored car in 1988. Chiruzzi had a long history of bank robberies, stickups, and burglaries under his belt and was eventually sent to prison for twenty years on a murder charge. He was reported to have $25 million in assets, even though Poletto said he "never worked a day in his life," meaning, of course, at a legitimate job. Though men like Chiruzzi made for more interesting newspaper articles, Poletto knew that Notarbartolo, who took great pains—albeit in vain—to keep his name unconnected to what would be his greatest criminal exploit, had aspirations that were no less grand than Chiruzzi's. "He was a man with a dream," Poletto said with a shrug years after the heist, going on to say that since Notarbartolo was identified so soon after the crime, the thief was still an amateur at heart.

Martino, though, was taking Notarbartolo very seriously.

The call had come to Martino on Thursday, February 20, 2003, from the Central Operations Service in Rome, similar to the U.S. Federal Bureau of Investigation. The agency had received a request from the Belgian federal police seeking assistance in gathering evidence to connect Notarbartolo to the heist, and, to do so, they needed help from Martino and his unit.

Martino's Mobile Squadron occupied a series of offices on the first and third floors of an ancient stone police building on a broad, stately boulevard in central Turin. Whereas the Antwerp diamond detectives enjoyed modern facilities with glass-walled offices and modular cubicles, their Italian counterparts made do with drafty windows, wheezing radiators, and out-of-plumb doorways. The only adornments were what cops the world over decorated their walls with: totems and symbols that were important to them. For Peys and De Bruycker, those were the photographs of all the locations their team had conducted investigations around the world. For Martino, it was the religious icons of his faith, including a crucifix and two huge renditions of St. Michael, the patron saint of police officers, driving a spear into Satan writhing underfoot.

After the phone call alerting him to a Turin connection to the Antwerp diamond heist, Martino met with his detectives around their beat-up desks and aging PCs to devise a strategy for finally driving a spear into the School of Turin.

Barging into Notarbartolo's house in Trana wasn't as easy as one might think, regardless of the compelling evidence against him in Belgium. Searching for diamonds or anything else connected to the heist would require a judicial warrant issued by an Italian court, which could only be considered after the Belgian courts made a formal request—a process that would take time.

However, since Notarbartolo was a previous offender, Italian law allowed the Mobile Squadron to search Notarbartolo's residence for two particular sorts of contraband without the need for a warrant: weapons or drugs. Martino's officers hit the streets and, according to the official version of events, quickly located informants who told them that Notarbartolo kept illegal weapons in his house. In fact, the weapons search was nothing but a ruse.

On Friday, February 21, when the caravan of police cars wound through the mountainous subalpine roads toward Trana and arrived at Notarbartolo's well-kept property, neither Notarbartolo nor his wife was home, but his adult sons Francesco and Marco were there. Francesco, the younger brother, was handsome and athletic, with the physique of a soccer player. Marco was his brother's opposite, with more than a passing resemblance to actor John Belushi in his *Animal House* years. What they had in common, however, was a contempt for police veiled by an impassivity they had clearly inherited from their unflappable father.

The brothers opened the door without a fight, and soon investigators were scouring the bedrooms, the living room, the billiard room, and even Notarbartolo's detached workshop. In the backyard, they attempted to search a two-thousand-gallon tank of heating oil, but they had no comparably sized container in which to transfer the oil, and emptying it onto the ground to see if there was a cache of diamonds inside would have been an unforgivable act of pollution if it yielded no evidence. They tried a different tactic to see if it was worth the effort: with Francesco and Marco Notarbartolo standing nearby, several officers put on a loud and exuberant show, pretending they'd found the mother lode. But the brothers didn't so much as twitch at the bait.

Of course the officers found no weapons, but, when they ordered one of the sons to open the family safe, they found cash (euros, dollars, and British pounds amounting to about $97,000), jewelry, and seventeen diamonds. At the moment, the detectives had no idea if they were connected to the heist. Although some of the diamonds were in certification blister packs, that wasn't necessarily suspicious; it was to be expected in the home of a jeweler with an office in Antwerp.

Since the Italian detectives didn't have a list of goods stolen from the Diamond Center, the best they could do was catalog and photograph their discovery. Officially, they were there looking for weapons, not diamonds, and so had no authority to seize them. The packaged diamonds, including an unusual 70-point cognac, were carefully photographed so that their certificate numbers and accompanying information were clear. Pieces of jewelry were removed from the plastic Ziploc bags they were stored in and individually photographed.

All the goods went back into the safe, and Martino placed Marco Notarbartolo in charge of safeguarding all of the items. It was a binding order, effectively making him legally responsible for the safekeeping of the gems and jewels they'd inventoried and photographed. Such orders were usually reserved for property that was unreasonable for the police to take physical possession of, such as livestock, boats, and other such items. Although it seemed like a case of ordering the fox to protect the hens, there was nothing else they could do except threaten Marco Notarbartolo with the full severity of the law if he failed to comply. He accepted the edict stoically.

Empty-handed except for what was on their cameras, the police drove the forty-five minutes back to Turin to e-mail the photos to their colleagues in Antwerp.

♦ ♦ ♦

While the Italian police were busy searching their home in Trana that Friday, Notarbartolo and Crudo were in the rented Peugeot driving over the Alps toward the one place where they were least expected to go: back to Antwerp. He'd had several days to bask in the afterglow of pulling off the greatest heist in history. As far as he was concerned, they'd executed it perfectly and left no trace of themselves behind.

It was important to return to Antwerp for several reasons. He had to return the rental car he'd driven after the heist to Italy. He also had to thoroughly clean the Charlottalei apartment, since they had left in a hurry and didn't have the time to do a proper job of eliminating any trace of a connection to the heist. He also had to return to the Diamond Center so that he could badge in and out one final time; he knew the police would be watching the computerized traffic to see if any of the tenants failed to return to work after the heist.

It seemed like a suicide mission to return to the scene of the crime, but Notarbartolo was bloated with confidence, even after newspapers reported that the trash had been discovered in the thieves' supposedly impossible-to-find dump location. He had no idea anything in the garbage could be connected to him—he didn't know the household trash with D'Onorio's work order had also been tossed into the forest—or that the police had already searched his office and his safe deposit box.

Notarbartolo knew from two long years of experience that the Diamond District would be practically deserted late Friday afternoon due to the Jewish Sabbath, so he planned to slip in and out of the Diamond Center just before closing time, when the fewest number of diamantaires would be around to see him.

He was so sure that he could charm his way in and out of the Diamond Center that he called his old friend Antonino Falleti, who lived in the Netherlands, and asked him to bring his family to Antwerp for dinner on his last weekend in town. He was done with Belgium, he told his friend; after this last trip, he would no longer have an apartment or a business office in Antwerp, so this was their last chance to see each other until their paths crossed again. He arranged for Falleti to meet him and Crudo at the Charlottalei apartment around 6:00 p.m. Notarbartolo and Crudo planned to leave Antwerp the next day, Saturday, on a Ryanair flight from Brussels to Milan he'd booked over the Internet.

Once they returned to Italy, they would be home free.

◆ ◆ ◆

Antonino Falleti, who bore an uncanny resemblance to a younger Robert De Niro, was notoriously bad with directions. He'd made the trip from Haarlem in the Netherlands to Antwerp with time to spare, arriving in the city by 5:30 p.m. on Friday, February 21. Once there, however, he had trouble getting to Notarbartolo's apartment. So he called his friend's cell phone to ask for directions and Notarbartolo answered after just one ring. It took another half an hour for Falleti to find his way through Antwerp's network of winding streets before he arrived outside Charlottalei 33. Falleti was excited to see his friend again.

"Tonino," as Antonino Falleti was called, had known Notarbartolo almost his entire life. Their dads had both worked as truck drivers; they also lived in the same building growing up. His older brother Mimmo was Notarbartolo's best friend since childhood. While Tonino was eight years younger than Mimmo and Notarbartolo, that came to matter less and less as they got older. Like all of Notarbartolo's friends, Falleti called him "Leo," but also "Pino," a nickname from childhood, or "Tarrun," referring to his southern Italian roots.

Falleti had brought along his wife, Judith Zwiep, and their eight- and eleven-year-old daughters, as well as a feast of home-cooked Italian food in Tupperware containers. While their wives took the food and the children up to the apartment, Falleti followed Notarbartolo to the car rental company to return the Peugeot.

After returning the car, Notarbartolo got in Falleti's car and instructed him to drive to the Empire Shopping Center, where they parked on Appelmansstraat, a narrow boulevard connected to the streets of the Diamond District by the mall. The indoor shopping center was filled with luxury retailers as well as service businesses for the diamond industry, such as a beauty salon, a small kosher food market, and several diamond supply companies. It was also filled with a wide variety of ethnic restaurants where diamantaires could find something resembling the food of their heritage regardless of their ethnicity. The two Italians settled in to drink a beer and catch up.

Falleti worked in Haarlem as a parking enforcement officer, and, although he'd been in the Netherlands for nearly twenty years, he remained constantly homesick for Italy. He cherished his visits with a fellow Turinese, and, during the time of Notarbartolo's long reconnaissance, he'd come to

Antwerp from time to time to visit his friend. He later told police he knew little more about Notarbartolo's activities than what Notarbartolo told him: that he worked in Antwerp to buy stones for his Italian businesses and to supply his jewelry design hobby. Notarbartolo had also once told Falleti that all of his transactions were off the books; he bought diamonds on the black market because they were cheaper and avoided the hassle and expense of Belgian taxes, he said.

If that were true, it might explain what the police already knew by that point: Damoros Preziosi hadn't recorded a single diamond transaction with the diamond industry authorities in all the time it was in Antwerp. To the detectives, it was yet more proof that Notarbartolo rented an office in the Diamond Center purely to case it for the heist.

What Notarbartolo told his friend, however, wasn't impossible, just highly unlikely. Diamond companies importing or exporting diamonds outside the European Union were required to have their parcels examined by experts from the Belgian customs agencies, the Federal Public Service's Economy and Finance departments. This was called the "Diamond Office" for short, and it oversaw several important functions. It estimated a parcel's value to ensure that it conformed with what the importer or exporter claimed, then it confirmed the type of diamonds being transported and their weight, and, in the case of rough diamonds, it checked that the parcel was accompanied by a Kimberley Process certificate guaranteeing that the stones weren't from conflict zones. The documents were important to the government for tax reasons, but they were also important to the diamantaire in that they provided some measure of independent proof of the value of their stocks. Diamond Office documents were used by banks to verify the value of goods they were being asked to finance, and by insurance companies as proof of a company's assets.

That was the official procedure, but everyone in Antwerp knew transactions regularly happened off the books for a variety of reasons, such as convenience, tax avoidance, money laundering, cost, or uncertainty over a diamond's origins. Still, Philip Claes of the Antwerp World Diamond Centre considered it "ridiculous" that a diamond company in operation for more than two years would never show up on the Diamond Office's registry, not even peripherally as a customer of another company.

Over their beers, Notarbartolo told Falleti that he'd already cleared out his space at the Diamond Center and was shutting down his Antwerp office to focus his attention in Turin. Though both men were eager to get back to the apartment for dinner, Notarbartolo told Falleti he needed to drop by the Diamond Center first, to check his mail. They might as well walk over since they were so close, he said. Notarbartolo knew that he needed to swipe his badge through the turnstiles at the Diamond Center at least one more time, and there were only a few minutes left before the building was locked for the night. This seemed like the perfect opportunity.

Falleti, like most people in Europe who followed the news, was well aware of the heist. In fact, there had been a bulletin on the radio during his drive from the Netherlands. He had even clipped newspaper articles about the robbery, thinking he'd save them for Notarbartolo, but had forgotten them at home in the Netherlands. Falleti was no stranger to Notarbartolo's past, and he suspected his friend might have had some involvement. He didn't want to get involved, so he didn't ask any questions, at least not as they sat over beers just a few hundred yards from the scene of the crime.

They walked through the mall and exited onto the Diamond District at the junction of Hoveniersstraat and Rijfstraat. It was cold, so Notarbartolo wore a heavy parka over his dark sweater, white button-down shirt, and dark casual pants.

Just as he'd hoped, there were hardly any people strolling the district at that time of day.

◆ ◆ ◆

Notarbartolo envisioned himself pushing through the plate glass doors into a nearly empty main hallway and breezing past the main guard with, at most, a "bonsoir" before swiping through the turnstiles and heading to the elevators. He needn't stay long; in fact, the sooner he could feign accomplishing some errand in his office, the sooner he could take the elevator back down to casually swipe out again. He didn't even bring the key to his office or his safe deposit box; his plan was to be in and out in a hurry. He didn't want to risk running into anyone who would delay him longer than was absolutely necessary to accomplish this final task and then vanish forever into the night.

Unfortunately for him, Notarbartolo did not know that he was no longer the most overlooked tenant at the Diamond Center. Instead, he was the most wanted man in Belgium. And everyone on the building's security staff knew it.

Julie Boost had assisted the police in executing the search warrant on Notarbartolo's office and safe deposit box. She had helped police get access to the hundreds of hours of the Diamond Center's surveillance tape they examined to see what he'd been doing in the days leading up to the heist. She'd also ordered all of the guards to keep an eye out for Notarbartolo, but, like the police, no one in the Diamond Center thought they'd ever see him again.

Kamiel, the guard in the front security booth, was as stunned as the day he'd learned the building had been robbed when he saw the jeweler approaching the front doors. Notarbartolo, who was with another man the guard did not recognize, sauntered in from the cold, smiling as pleasantly as ever, while his companion remained outside. Kamiel overcame his shock and discretely grabbed the phone to raise the alarm that Notarbartolo was back in the building. In quick succession, he dialed his boss (Julie Boost) and the diamond detectives. As with all the Diamond Center's staff members, these detectives had interrogated Kamiel frequently since Monday and he knew their direct number.

Boost had been through the wringer that week. As the building manager, she had initially been among the primary suspects since she was one of the few people who knew the code to the vault door. She had also been the subject of scathing criticism among the tenants for the slack level of security in the Diamond Center. Now, she saw her opportunity to redeem herself by helping apprehend the man who'd robbed her building, and she acted decisively.

Boost dropped what she had been doing and raced to the lobby. She intercepted Notarbartolo in the main hallway, turning on her own long-dormant charm to greet him as if he were a lost son. Speaking in French, she began a long recitation of the week's events, acting as if she assumed he was there to find out if his safe deposit box had been looted. Even though this was precisely the sort of encounter he had hoped to avoid, Notarbartolo listened politely; he didn't want to seem suspicious by dodging her questions. As Boost prattled on about news of the heist, Kamiel's phone call to the federal police headquarters had ignited a frenzy of activity.

♦ ♦ ♦

At the time their phone started ringing, the diamond detectives were at an impasse. Since Monday, when the robbery had been discovered, they'd been working twenty-hour days tracking down suspects. They were tired and frustrated.

Detective Peys remembers well that the downturn in morale after a swift few days of nailing down solid leads fizzled to the realization that the thieves might be gone for good. "It doesn't happen like in the States, where we take the airplane and go to Italy," Peys said. "It always has to go officially and it takes some time. It will take us, let's say, approximately a week or at least a few days to get there, which we were going to do, to get to Italy and to confront Notarbartolo with what was going on. But at that time, we couldn't go there, willing or not. We had the possibility, physically, but not the permission."

Even with permission, a trip to Italy still might not have resulted in an arrest. That would have been at the discretion of the Italian authorities, and even then, the possibility of extradition to Belgium to stand trial was remote. At the time, it was very difficult to get Italy to extradite one of its citizens for a nonviolent crime, no matter how dramatic the financial impact.

With Notarbartolo apparently slipping from their grasp, the detectives decided early Friday evening to relieve the tension of the week and take a few personal hours for themselves. Agim De Bruycker, the unit commander, went with a few of the visiting investigators to a nearby pub to unwind over a few glasses of beer. Peys was on his way to pick up his wife for dinner at a restaurant. The only detectives still working in the office when Kamiel called were Kris De Bot and Gerry Vanderkelen, who were interviewing Marcel Grünberger.

"The interview with Mr. Grünberger just at that moment ended," De Bot later recalled, "and he was reading his declaration again. At that moment the call came in, I immediately took contact with the local police because they have a station not so far from the building of the Diamond Center . . . They have patrol cars and policemen in the neighborhood, so when there's something very urgent, they go first."

This was a delicate moment. De Bot and Vanderkelen were ten minutes away, even if they sped there with lights and sirens wailing. The Diamond

District was filled with cops, but the last thing the diamond detectives wanted was for the district police, who would be there first, to arrest Notarbartolo.

"We needed guys [on the scene] who knew the importance of Notarbartolo, but who also knew that it was as important to know where he stayed," Peys said. "Arresting somebody, throwing him to the ground, and then saying 'Okay, you're the suspect, we have every evidence and now we want to know where you live,' that's where it stops."

The diamond detectives needed Notarbartolo to think he was nothing more than an important witness and to volunteer his address as part of a routine interview. If they could get to him before he slipped away, it was possible that any associates of his who might have been watching could retreat to frantically clean out his apartment and scour it of vital clues. Since Kamiel had noticed that another man had accompanied Notarbartolo, this was a real possibility in the minds of the detectives. The ticking clock they faced was the possibility that someone connected to Notarbartolo would notice his detention and then quickly react by destroying potential evidence. The detectives would not learn where Notarbartolo's apartment was in time if the district police stormed into the Diamond Center and slapped handcuffs on him. Once Notarbartolo was placed under arrest, the detectives anticipated that, as a professional criminal, he wouldn't tell them anything.

De Bot called the district police, described what was going on at the Diamond Center, and gave strict instructions to keep Notarbartolo at the Diamond Center but not arrest him or say anything about his being a suspect.

As De Bot peeled out of the parking lot, Vanderkelen sat in the passenger seat frantically calling the other detectives. While they had planned on joining everyone at the bar and had only been in the office to finish their interview with Grünberger, the other detectives would now join them instead. Across town, the eight investigators drinking with De Bruycker put their beers aside and rushed to the Diamond District. Peys did a U-turn and called his wife to tell her he would be going back to the office again.

Meanwhile, at the Diamond Center, Notarbartolo was growing increasingly impatient with Boost's inane chatter. It was very out of character for the manager to be so gabby. Peys later complimented her performance. "I'm not always in the best way of dealing with Julie Boost," he said, "but she did an excellent job by stalling him."

Outside the building, several police officers slowly gravitated toward the Diamond Center, and a few went inside. The appearance of the police in the main lobby was more than Notarbartolo could bear and he began edging his way toward the front door and freedom.

Boost, on the other hand, was relieved that law enforcement had finally arrived, but she couldn't understand why Notarbartolo wasn't being taken into custody. The scene fell apart into one of sheer confusion—Notarbartolo tried to talk his way toward the exit, Boost argued in hushed tones with one of the officers to arrest him immediately, and the officers grappled with what, exactly, they should do to contain the situation until the detectives arrived. One thing they were not willing to do was to arrest someone just because Julie Boost told them to.

Fortunately, they didn't have to wait long. De Bot later commented that it felt like he made the ten-minute trip from headquarters in "ten seconds." They'd turned off the emergency lights and sirens as they maneuvered through the vehicle barricade on Schupstraat and parked in front of the Diamond Center. Though their hearts were racing, they strolled inside trying to appear friendly and casual. It wasn't hard to pull off. Vanderkelen looked like a wholesome college athlete and De Bot could have been his balding father.

As disarming as they may have been, Notarbartolo knew he was in for a dangerous game of cat and mouse as they took him to the side in the hallway to speak with him. "Notarbartolo, because he's quite intelligent, knew something was going on," Peys explained, "but he couldn't afford to act suspicious. If he'd said 'No, I'm not going to say anything,' he would have burned his last bridge."

The questioning was easy at first, but the detectives soon got to the point: And where do you live in Antwerp? Suddenly, Notarbartolo's French wasn't so good and, as politely as ever, he explained that he didn't understand. "Mr. Notarbartolo said that he speaks only Italian, that he doesn't understand English or French," De Bot recalled. But it was such a bald-faced lie—Notarbartolo had been speaking French perfectly well when they arrived—that the detectives patiently but firmly repeated the question. Notarbartolo now did the stalling, his mind racing for a way out of the jam in which he found himself.

◆ ◆ ◆

Unaware of the tense drama unfolding on the main floor, Fay Vidal finished her work at IDH Diamonds on the third floor and took the elevator to the -1 parking level. As she tried to exit, she found the garage doors shuttered. The guard steadfastly refused to let her, or anyone else, leave the building. Orders of the police, he said.

For Vidal, it was the last straw of a long and exhausting week. From Rijfstraat to Schupstraat, there had been only one topic of conversation: the heist. Like many other victims, she'd filed her insurance claim, and there was nothing more to do now except try to get back to a normal routine. At the end of this very long week, she was eager to get home and try to put it all behind her. Now this.

But Vidal wasn't easily told what to do. "That's not one of my characteristics," she later explained. At that moment, she resolved to herself, "I'm going to leave this building."

She marched down the main corridor toward the Schupstraat entrance, intent only on finding Julie Boost and demanding that she be allowed to leave through the garage. Like most tenants of the Diamond Center, she had no clue who Leonardo Notarbartolo was and, in fact, had never even heard his name. It was clear that the man she passed in the hallway was being questioned in relation to the heist, but so had many people in the previous five days. She had no idea that he was the one who had stolen her precious jewels, diamonds, and family heirlooms.

"I see a man standing there with a little jacket on, and there are three other men, very tall, and they're looking at his papers, and they're obviously talking to him," she recalled. "I hear him say, because he's Italian, '*Questo non è possibile*' ['This isn't possible']. Here's this man who doesn't understand what they want of him and why they want his papers and [he's like] a little virgin, 'What do you want?'"

At the time, Notarbartolo was "absolutely nobody" to her, but when she found out later that she could have reached out and punched the man who robbed her, his name was forever pronounced as if she were spitting gristle from her mouth. *No-tar-BAR-tolo.*

♦ ♦ ♦

Shortly before the police arrived, Tonino Falleti realized he had to go to the bathroom.

It was freezing outside, and Notarbartolo, stuck in conversation with Boost, was taking a lot longer than the few minutes he'd promised. Falleti paced under the Diamond Center's concrete awning and eyed the empty street for a convenient place to use the facilities, but there was none. Schupstraat was filled with diamond businesses and banks, all of which were either closed this late on a Friday or required security badges to enter.

His need finally became too much to bear, and he walked around the corner to a nearby tavern. Rather than return to the Diamond Center right away, he decided to drink a beer and wait for his friend from the warmth of a barstool. Falleti became slightly concerned when he tried calling Notarbartolo on his cell phone to tell him where he was and while the phone was answered, whoever answered didn't say anything. So he decided to walk past the Diamond Center again in the hope of running into Notarbartolo on the street. What he saw when he turned the corner baffled and alarmed him.

Schupstraat was filled with police outside the Diamond Center, with more arriving every minute. There seemed to be a lot of excitement and confusion on the street. Falleti had a sinking feeling that Notarbartolo was in some sort of trouble and that it had to do with the heist. He called Crudo and asked her what he should do; she told him to return to the apartment immediately.

As calmly as possible, Falleti walked away from the mob of police toward his car and managed to find his way back to Charlottalei without getting lost. During the drive back, he tried calling Notarbartolo but this time there was no answer at all. He was extremely worried about Notarbartolo and the depressing little apartment did nothing to help. He drank a shot of grappa to help clear his head. It was getting on in the evening and the dinner he and Zwiep had brought from the Netherlands was still untouched. Crudo was tense and filled with dread, unsure what to do.

Crudo was worried that Notarbartolo was in trouble because of his extensive criminal history. She and Falleti agreed to drive back to the

Diamond Center so that she could speak to the police about where he was and what was happening to him, but then they changed their minds in the car. It wasn't like Notarbartolo not to answer his phone; they took his silence as a signal that he was in trouble.

Falleti decided he'd rather not leave his wife and kids at the apartment and risk them getting caught up in a police investigation, so he and Crudo returned to the apartment, where they gathered Falleti's family for the drive back to their home in the Netherlands. They packed up the items in the apartment in a hurry. There was the sense that they were trying to flee ahead of some calamity. The uneaten food was repacked, the girls bundled back into their overcoats, and the suitcases arranged by the front door. Falleti helped Crudo organize everything she and Notarbartolo had planned to dispose of at their leisure later that weekend. Falleti would return to Antwerp the following day after he'd had some time to think of a plan.

Less than a half a mile away, Notarbartolo understood the pressure Crudo felt. He knew that the moment he told the detectives his apartment address, it would be overrun by police, so he stalled for as long as he could, giving his wife and friends time to clean up and clear out. He was aware he was playing a losing game; it was only a matter of time before the polite insistence of the questioning collapsed into pointed suspicion that he was being intentionally unhelpful.

Of course, for the detectives there was never any question that Notarbartolo was a suspect, but he didn't know that. He had no clue of the evidence the police had against him and he still hoped to be able to talk his way out of this by playing the confused, innocent victim. The detectives knew Notarbartolo was hiding something, but, by keeping their inquiries as friendly as possible, they gave him no reason to become indignant and uncooperative. "He was very confused," De Bot recalled. "He was very surprised. You saw that on his face and nonverbal behavior. I don't think he knew that we were looking for him."

Notarbartolo's only hope was to eat up enough time to give Crudo and the others time to abandon the apartment and hopefully leave nothing behind. And he had to be polite enough about it that it would be impossible later for the detectives to claim he'd hindered their investigation, which could have been another excuse to arrest him. Plus, as long as they continued talking in a friendly way, the police might let slip what they had on him.

Under questioning, he claimed he didn't know his apartment's address. He told De Bot he only knew how to walk there from the Diamond District. De Bot, as pleasant as ever, steered Notarbartolo toward his police car and said they'd be happy to drive the route back to his apartment. The Italian thief was like a determined chess player desperately moving his lonesome king from one square to the next while his opponent's rooks and knights patiently worked him into checkmate.

Eventually, Notarbartolo ran out of squares, and from the back seat of the squad car, he directed De Bot to the apartment.

"He was very afraid to say where his apartment was," De Bot recalled, "but when we say to him, 'Sir, when you are not involved in the criminal case, why are you afraid to say where you live, of where you stay?' he understood that when he doesn't cooperate on that matter, that it was difficult for us to believe him . . . So he understood that he must give an address or otherwise he had problems with the authorities."

Once the detectives drove him to Charlottalei, Notarbartolo pointed to his apartment, hoping he'd given his friends enough time to clear out. Without backup, De Bot and Vanderkelen decided not to get out of the car. They didn't want to walk into a trap if there was a lookout hidden on the street. They also didn't want to risk Notarbartolo's somehow making contact with the other suspects. Instead, they radioed for reinforcements and left to take Notarbartolo to police headquarters for further questioning.

For a few moments after they pulled away, there was no police presence outside of Charlottalei 33.

◆ ◆ ◆

The final leg of the attempted escape from the apartment would have been comical had the moods of the escapees not been so dire. Three adults and two small children were jammed like sardines into the puny elevator with a rolled up carpet, several bags, luggage, and a home-cooked Italian dinner. After a painfully slow descent from the seventh floor, the elevator reached the ground floor.

It was at that same moment that the first police car pulled to the curb. Depending on the perspective, the timing was either perfect or abysmal.

Falleti, his family, and Crudo exited the elevator directly into the arms of the police, caught red-handed with a wealth of damning evidence.

Falleti, Zwiep, and their two small children were put into one police car, and Crudo in another. Notarbartolo had already been driven away in a third. None of them were placed under arrest, but they were all driven to the federal police building for questioning.

Still, however, the detectives were not finished racing the clock. So far, they were lucky to have made it to the Diamond Center before Notarbartolo grew suspicious enough of Boost's stalling techniques to leave the building, and they'd captured Falleti and the others only moments before they would have vanished with valuable evidence. Now, however, they needed a warrant to search the apartment, and, if they didn't have it in hand by 9:00 p.m., Belgian law prevented them from entering the building until the following day.

It was already 8:30 p.m. when they called the investigating judge, who was at home in a community outside Antwerp. The judge, however, did not have a fax machine or a home computer. He would have to write the warrant out by hand and someone from the local police would have to pick it up at his house and then fax it to the diamond detectives. If they couldn't get the warrant in time, they would have to post guards outside the Charlottalei apartment overnight. But guards wouldn't be able to prevent anyone from entering the building. If there was another accomplice in town who knew his colleagues had been detained, nothing would prevent him from walking past the police, entering the apartment, and flushing any remaining trace evidence down the toilet.

The detectives' great fortune was still with them. De Bot's sister was an officer on the police force in the judge's community, and she was on duty that night. With blue lights flashing, she sped to his house to retrieve the warrant and then drove back to her police station. From there, she faxed the warrant to the diamond detectives.

While his sister was getting the warrant, De Bot revved his engine outside the police building, blue lights already flashing, ready to race off to deliver it to the apartment.

"The time was very short," he later said, "Agim [De Bruycker] was waiting by the fax machine and I was waiting with the car downstairs."

When the fax arrived, De Bruycker jumped in the elevator, ran out the glass doors of the police building, and stuffed the warrant into De Bot's hand. De Bot floored it.

The handwritten search warrant arrived on the doorstep of Charlottalei 33 at 8:58 p.m.

Chapter Eleven

CHECKMATE

"Whether we fall by ambition, blood, or lust,
Like diamonds, we are cut with our own dust."

—Duke Ferdinand, *The Duchess of Malfi* (1613–1614)

Leonardo Notarbartolo still thought he could talk his way free.

As far as he knew, it was possible that the detectives were simply being aggressive in their pursuit of additional witnesses. In Notarbartolo's mind, there was nothing that tied him to the heist. He'd worn gloves during the break-in, and they'd been vigilant about destroying the videotapes and not leaving behind any trace of themselves. He knew that the garbage had been found, but was unaware the garbage included household trash that had led police straight to him.

Sitting at a table in a quiet interrogation room, Notarbartolo continued playing the part of the befuddled jeweler who didn't understand why the police were interested in an innocent man such as himself. He needed to find the right combination of indignation and cooperation, if he was going to convince the detectives that they were making a big mistake.

This was precisely the demeanor Patrick Peys wanted him to adopt. As long as Notarbartolo felt there was an escape route, Peys could keep him talking—and, in talking, even about matters that might seem mundane, Notarbartolo might accidentally reveal something of importance.

"I first treated him not as a suspect, but more as a witness and somebody who might know some information," Peys explained while recounting the details of this interrogation years later. "He was telling everything about what he was doing those days [surrounding the heist]."

Notarbartolo had an answer for everything. He rented the car, he said, after oversleeping and missing his flight to Italy. He stayed a few extra days in Antwerp in the hope of doing a little extra business and chose to drive home rather than fly. It might have seemed an odd decision considering the distance, but it was far from criminal.

Peys asked Notarbartolo why there were no records of him or his company conducting any business in the two years Damoros Preziosi had been in Antwerp. The company didn't have a license application on file at the Ministry of Economy, a prerequisite to importing or exporting goods, or a record of any transactions through the Diamond Office. This, Peys said, seemed highly suspicious. Opting to take the fall for a small crime to avoid the larger one, Notarbartolo claimed that he dealt purely in black market diamonds to avoid taxes.

Peys switched gears, asking Notarbartolo why he was at the Diamond Center the night of his apprehension. "He [said he] had something to do in the office, which was bullshit because it was perfectly empty," Peys said later. Plus, Notarbartolo didn't have the keys to his office or his safe deposit box. The police had found those in his apartment.

That was correct, Notarbartolo countered when Peys pointed out the contradiction. He had only realized he'd left his keys behind once he'd stepped inside the front doors. It was then that he spotted Julie Boost and decided to ask about the heist. His explanation was a nimble maneuver in which he tried to turn Boost's trap to his advantage.

Peys embarked on a different tack next, pointing out that Notarbartolo had been the last person in the vault the night before the heist. Notarbartolo said there had been another man in the vault when he'd left the last time, an Indian. The police had already analyzed the videotapes of that visit carefully; Peys knew it was a lie. The detective then asked Notarbartolo why he had taken so long to return to the Diamond Center to inquire about the heist. Notarbartolo explained that he'd emptied his safe deposit box of all his cash on his final trip to the vault and knew there had been nothing to steal.

The Italian had a valid answer for all but one of the detective's probing questions: where he'd been on Saturday night, February 15. Notarbartolo said he'd made dinner alone in his apartment, watched some TV, and was in bed by midnight. As far as Peys was concerned, this was no alibi at all.

Hours ticked by as the detective took his time, drawing out their conversation in order to keep Notarbartolo talking. They were both polite and professional; this was part of their mutual façade to disarm each other, but for Peys it was practical as well.

"As a policeman you have to regard a person as neutrally as possible," he said later, explaining why he didn't simply confront Notarbartolo with the evidence against him. "You have to keep in mind that a person might be innocent. On the other hand, you have to be realistic. . . . If you have all kinds of evidence like that, and you have somebody who's saying 'I don't have anything to do with it, I'm an honest businessman who did one and a half years [of business] in Antwerp'—which we didn't find any [record] of—and who has a background of twenty years of burglary, well, we're not judges; we're just seeing what we have as evidence. And after a while, you realize that you are dealing with the right guy."

Peys had gotten as far as he was going to with this line of questioning. Notarbartolo was unusually self-possessed, so the detective decided to try to rattle him to elicit a reaction. Since it was clear to Peys that Notarbartolo had no idea the police had been looking for him when he was apprehended at the Diamond Center earlier that night, Peys figured that Notarbartolo did not know that the police were also onto some of his accomplices. And so, in the middle of some light banter, the detective dropped Finotto's old police mug shot in front of Notarbartolo. "Look, what do you think about that guy?" Peys asked as he planted the photo on the table. "Who is he?"

Even a detective as seasoned as Peys, who makes his living tracking down scam artists and con men, was surprised by Notarbartolo's reaction. "He didn't move a muscle," Peys recalled, still impressed by the Italian's poise years later. "He just acted as if he'd never seen the person. . . . Imagine that, a week after the burglary we show him a picture of one of the accomplices and say 'this is the guy.' I would really fall from my chair if you had that evidence during an interrogation. And he didn't do *anything*. I can remember it so well because afterwards it seems so illogical and so unreal."

In fact, Notarbartolo held his act together so well that Peys momentarily doubted that Finotto was involved. "We were absolutely not sure that Finotto was involved in that crime," Peys said. "Okay, Finotto was involved ten years ago [in the failed bank heist] and Finotto, according to the information from the Italians, knew Notarbartolo, but that doesn't mean anything. I mean, [the School of Turin] is perhaps fifteen, twenty, twenty-five people who only work together when it's necessary. Afterward, we knew Finotto was involved, but at that moment I didn't know."

After that, it was clear Notarbartolo wasn't going to slip up and accidentally divulge anything of importance. Peys played his last remaining move, telling Notarbartolo directly that the detectives believed he was involved in the crime. Just as Peys suspected, it brought the interrogation to an abrupt halt.

"He said very politely—because he was always very polite—he said, 'Okay, I'm not going to say anything anymore, you do whatever you like,'" Peys recalled. "And since then he hasn't spoken another word regarding the case with us."

◆ ◆ ◆

Investigators had more luck talking to Falleti, who was eager to convince police of his innocence so that he could take his wife and daughters home. Before his questioning, the detectives had allowed the family to share an awkward meal, finally eating the food they'd brought from the Netherlands in the police lunchroom under the watchful eyes of an officer. They were all nervous and scared and barely spoke. Falleti was then forced to leave his children in the cafeteria with a cop while he and his wife were taken away for questioning.

Interviewed separately, Falleti and Zwiep both maintained their innocence, telling the detectives they were only in Antwerp to enjoy a farewell meal with old friends. They claimed to know nothing of the heist beyond what they'd seen in the news; they said they knew nothing whatsoever about Notarbartolo's involvement in it.

The detectives weren't entirely clear on how this couple fit into the crime but assumed that at the very least they were accessories after-the-fact who were at the apartment specifically to rid it of evidence. Falleti had been caught holding the rug that, on close inspection back at the forensics lab, yielded the tiny emeralds the thieves had accidentally dropped while tallying the loot. And they had been accompanying Crudo, who was carrying a striped shopping bag and a large purse containing a cordless drill, three flashlights, the small purse with the hole cut out for Notarbartolo's video camera, and a used vacuum cleaner bag. This last item was filled with dirt, dust, and "very small 'glass fragments,'" according to Peter Kerkhof, the forensic technician who collected and examined evidence in the case. When he later examined these glass fragments more closely, he realized they weren't glass at all. Instead, he labeled them as "possible emeralds."

The detectives' real score was their discovery of two SIM cards in Crudo's purse, one labeled *mio* ("mine" in Italian), and the other labeled *non mio*. Detectives loved to find SIM cards on their suspects, since they were full of information, such as the dates, times, and phone numbers of calls sent and received, as well as where the cell phones had been used.

As if the possession of these items wasn't incriminating enough, Falleti had admitted to the police on the scene that he intended to throw the rug away, which suggested to them that he knew he was disposing of evidence.

If in fact Falleti and Zwiep were the cleaners, they were woefully unprepared for the job and incompetent to boot. While the suspects were being interrogated, De Bruycker and a team of forensic specialists were going over every inch of the dreary Charlottalei apartment. They found all sorts of valuable clues, but also evidence that the "cleaners" hadn't had time to clean a thing. Falleti and Zwiep had left their fingerprints all over the place, including Falleti's on a grappa bottle and a glass. Detectives also found a used tissue in the apartment that was later revealed to have his DNA. The couple had showed up in Antwerp to perform their alleged role in the heist without any bleach, gloves, disinfectants, or other cleaning supplies but with their young children in tow. It was an odd scenario, to be sure.

Falleti and Zwiep tried to convince the police that they were simply helping Crudo at a time when she was concerned about her husband's welfare. When she asked them to take out some trash on their way downstairs, it didn't occur to them to question her. "Everything went so fast, I was not curious why I was needed to help carry everything downstairs," Falleti told detectives.

It was a reasonable story, but the police weren't buying it. They decided to hold the couple, so their DNA could be compared with samples from items from the trash at the Floordambos and recovered from the vault. Plus, their statements to police differed in one critical way that made the detectives question the rest of their story: when asked where he was on Sunday night, February 16, Falleti said he had been at a friend's birthday party while Zwiep said they had been at home that night.

Crudo also had a lot to explain since her baggage was filled with suspicious items, and she admitted being the one who suggested gathering everything up and fleeing the apartment. She told the police that she had panicked when she learned from Falleti that police were questioning Notarbartolo, presumably in connection with the diamond heist.

It was no secret that her husband had a long history of problems with the police and she told the detectives she didn't want to risk leaving anything in the apartment that could give investigators the wrong impression of a man she described as honorable and law-abiding. She too was held over for additional questioning.

All four of the suspects were placed in solitary confinement cells in the basement of the federal police building. Zwiep was unable to reach a relative in the Netherlands to come for their children, so they ended up as prisoners of a sort as well. The police took them to Paola Kinderziekenhuis, a children's hospital. The girls spent the night standing at the window, hoping someone would appear to take them home.

♦ ♦ ♦

The next day—Saturday—the prisoners received a quick schooling in the arcane features of the Belgian judicial system. They were driven separately to the justice building—an imposing old brick and stone facility—for questioning by someone known as a Preliminary Investigations Judge, or an examining magistrate, who was part of the prosecutor's office.

Falleti later described the subterranean holding cell at the justice building as resembling something from feudal times, lacking only a hay mattress and shackles on the wall to perfect the image. There wasn't even a toilet. He spent four hours alone there before being led through a maze of narrow corridors to the magistrate's office where, in addition to the judge, there were a stenographer and two police officers.

Falleti sat and waited in silence, the only sound the ruffling of papers as the magistrate read the police reports of his initial interrogation. When he was questioned at last, it was along the same lines as before: Why was he in Antwerp? Why was he trying to throw away evidence? What did he know about the heist?

The other suspects were put through the same paces. Asked again why she had tried to empty out the apartment the night before, Crudo elaborated on her earlier statement, admitting that she had seen a small sparkling stone on the carpet. She said she was afraid that if the police searched the apartment, they might use the stone as a reason to implicate Notarbartolo in the heist, and so she had asked Zwiep to help her gather items to be removed from the apartment. When it was his turn before the magistrate, Notarbartolo said nothing.

The magistrate did not consider the explanations offered by Crudo or the other suspects to be credible. He ordered them all detained for an additional five days. Just as before, they were kept apart from one another to prevent them from sharing details of their interrogations or colluding on an alibi.

They were separately transported to the Prison of Antwerp, which looked like it had been designed by Edgar Allan Poe. Just like the Belgian justice system, the detention center was a holdover from Napoleonic times. As viewed from the street, it was a grimy brick and concrete edifice about three stories tall with arched parapets, flying buttresses, and tall narrow windows covered in iron bars. A tall brick wall around the building took up an entire city block. The prison complex consisted of several narrow interconnected cell blocks that enclosed separate outdoor areas where hundreds of prisoners awaited their days in court.

It was a notorious facility known for stark living conditions that not even the guards could endure. As such, the guards often went on strike to protest their working conditions. The prisoners had their own upheavals in order to bring attention to the facility's dangerous level of overcrowding. The summer before the heist, the Prison of Antwerp had been the scene of hunger strikes and other inmate actions to protest their living conditions.

For Notarbartolo, the booking process must have been especially humbling. Only twenty-four hours before, he could have had the best that Antwerp had to offer, with his near limitless proceeds from the robbery. He could have stayed at the finest hotel, drunk the best champagne, and shopped at the most exclusive clothing boutiques. Now, though, like any other new arrival, he was stripped, deloused, and hosed off before he was thoroughly searched. He was given prison-issue sneakers, plain blue pants, and a blue sweater with a wide white stripe. Tea or industrial drip coffee—a foreign concept to Italians—was the best libation available. His accommodation measured thirteen feet by six and was bare except for a bed and a bucket to be used as a toilet.

During the initial five days of their incarceration, the four suspects weren't allowed to speak with each other or to engage in any outside communication, except to try contacting lawyers. They were confined in their cells with no TV or radio and no access to the exercise yard. Notarbartolo did catch Falleti's eye across the room during their initial processing, but they didn't speak. Notarbartolo simply offered his old friend an apologetic shrug.

During his isolation, Notarbartolo puzzled over what the investigators might have against him. Throughout the interrogation, Peys had been careful not to tip his hand, though it was apparent that the detectives were convinced of Notarbartolo's involvement. The questions were pointed and showed that, while Notarbartolo had been in Italy reveling in a job well done, they'd been busy snooping into every corner of his life in Antwerp. Notarbartolo knew that even with all of the planning, he and his compatriots had made a grave mistake at some point. He just had no idea what it was.

The ultimate irony of Notarbartolo's situation was that the man who had stolen between €100 and €400 million worth of diamonds and cash had to appeal to the Office of Legal Assistance for a lawyer since he couldn't pay with his pilfered loot without confessing to the crime. The attorney assigned to the case in turn referred him to an experienced defense attorney, Walter Damen. Notarbartolo also contacted his Italian lawyer, Basilio Foti.

Falleti had more trouble finding legal representation. He knew no one in Belgium except Notarbartolo and a sister who lived in Brussels. He only knew that he was in big trouble and he was scared. When he was sixteen, his father had been jailed for extortion and served six years in an Italian prison, missing a large chunk of Falleti's life. He wanted to avoid anything like that happening to his own children, so Falleti had always lived a law-abiding existence with an honest job. He knew he was innocent, but being innocent wasn't enough; he needed a good lawyer.

Desperate, he stuck his head out his cell window and yelled to the prisoners lazing about on the exercise yard, pleading for someone to recommend an attorney. Amazingly, one of them responded. A prisoner sauntered over casually, so as not to alert the guards, and gave him the name and telephone number of an attorney named Jan De Man. Falleti scrawled down the information and banged on his cell door, asking the guard to contact the attorney for him. This unconventional shot in the dark worked: Falleti met the chain-smoking, dapper De Man three days later, and De Man in turn arranged to have one of his associates, Eric Boon, represent Zwiep.

Falleti tried yelling the names of his friends through his cell window to see if anyone could hear him, and Crudo eventually yelled back. She didn't yet have a lawyer, she yelled to Falleti in their crude form of communication, and so Falleti arranged for De Man to find a lawyer for Crudo as well.

When they appeared before the magistrate again on February 24, all of them had representation, but that didn't result in their freedom. They were ordered to be held for an additional two weeks while the detectives and prosecutors continued to collect evidence and build their cases.

Leen Nuyts, a spokesperson for the Antwerp Office of the Prosecutor, told reporters that the four defendants were "being held on suspicion of being co-authors in the theft."

◆ ◆ ◆

While the prisoners cooled their heels, police detectives crisscrossed Europe gathering evidence.

In Italy, it looked like the military had invaded Trana. Local uniformed police, detectives from the Turin Mobile Squadron, three of the Belgian diamond detectives, and platoons of forensic investigators overwhelmed the hillside village when Martino and his men went to collect the evidence from the Notarbartolo family safe and to thoroughly search the property for other clues.

The Belgian authorities had found proof positive of their primary suspect's involvement in the Antwerp heist from the pictures the Italian police had taken of the safe's contents. Of the seventeen diamonds found during the first search of Notarbartolo's home in Trana, nine were in blister packs from diamond grading labs. Of these, one was a sure match to a stolen stone: a brilliant-cut, deep brown (known as "cognac") diamond weighing 0.70476 carats. This stone was fatal to Notarbartolo's pleas of innocence, as its certificate number was found on the list of goods reported stolen. It was only one stone, but it was damning evidence of Notarbartolo's involvement.

When the authorities arrived to assume possession of the stone, the Notarbartolo sons were home—but the jewelry, cash, and diamonds Marco Notarbartolo had been ordered to keep were not. Marco Notarbartolo told Martino that two men, whom he hadn't recognized, had come to the door one night and said they had instructions from Notarbartolo to remove some items from the family safe. They took everything and vanished in minutes. Marco Notarbartolo said he didn't know where they had come from or where they went.

The detectives exploded at the discovery that the irrefutable proof of Notarbartolo's guilt was gone, but the brothers did little more than shrug at the investigators' bad luck. It would have been difficult for most people to remain composed in the face of the screaming red-faced tirade that ensued—first at the house and later in Turin at the police station while the men were relentlessly grilled—but Francesco and Marco Notarbartolo had spent their whole lives learning from their father's example how to deal with cops. They were like disciplined soldiers who'd fallen into enemy hands, resigned to the consequences.

Police practically disassembled the house, looking everywhere from the flower gardens to the attic rafters for signs of a hidden cache. They found nothing.

◆ ◆ ◆

Elsewhere, police were conducting a massive roundup of known School of Turin members in an effort to find out who else had been involved in the heist. Aware of the gang's modus operandi, they knew there had to be more actors in this plot than the people they'd identified.

From the wiretap inside Aniello Fontanella's Personal Chiavi locksmith shop—set up as part of a broader sting against the School of Turin code-named "Magic Moment"—Italian detectives heard Fontanella and alarms expert Giovanni Spurgo discussing the diamond heist and then mentioning the failed 1997 bank job in Antwerp that Finotto had been convicted for. Police immediately arrested both Fontanella—"the Wizard with the Keys"—and Spurgo. Both men denied their involvement in the Antwerp heist and volunteered to give DNA samples to prove their innocence. In fact, the fifty-three-year-old Spurgo had the perfect alibi: he had been in jail during the heist weekend, nabbed on suspicion of pulling a job at a Turinese jewelry store.

Giovanni Poliseri, the elderly "King of Thieves," was at the top of the list of suspects, according to newspaper reports. In his thirty-plus years as a criminal, Poliseri had figured out how to disable alarms using a technique similar to that used on the motion detector in the Diamond Center vault, by masking them with a cream or a gel. The police didn't have enough evidence to arrest Poliseri for the Antwerp heist. But just two months later, Belgian police arrested both the sixty-nine-year-old Poliseri and his apprentice Pasquale Scelza for trying to break into the Martens jewelry store in Sint-Niklaas, a town about twenty minutes outside of Antwerp.

The investigation into those already jailed continued. The Belgians had yet to decide exactly what role Crudo, Zwiep, and Falleti had played and how deeply involved they were, if at all. Although they associated with members of the School of Turin, they weren't believed to be members themselves. Crudo had never been implicated in Notarbartolo's schemes before, and Zwiep was Dutch, completely unknown to the Italian police.

Falleti was more complicated because he was Notarbartolo's childhood friend, and he knew many of the criminals who orbited around Notarbartolo. But he'd lived in Holland for eighteen years, worked for law enforcement, and had a clean record. His story about his presence in Antwerp and why he was caught holding incriminating evidence was possible but too full of coincidences and inconsistencies for detectives to rule him out.

At the request of Belgian investigators, Dutch police raided Falleti's home in Haarlem, spending hours going through drawers and cabinets, upending the mattresses, and poring through bills and documents. They found the newspaper clippings of the heist and a prepaid cell phone, which was suspicious since Falleti was arrested with a cell phone in his pocket. Police also confiscated white gloves and a roll of tape that they believed to be connected to the heist.

Falleti later laughed about how the searchers were not nearly as thorough as they might have been. For safekeeping, he'd hung a parcel of family jewels and heirlooms on a string behind the radiator in the living room, a discovery that would have been quite suspicious if it had been found. But investigators overlooked it entirely.

The cell phone, however, was not a laughing matter. On it, the police found evidence that Falleti had used it to call no one but Notarbartolo. Why use an untraceable phone to call him rather than his personal phone? Again, Falleti had what investigators took to be an all-too-convenient answer: He'd bought the phone for his older daughter, he said, but his wife balked, claiming that eleven was too young for a child to have her own cell phone. Rather than return it, he decided to use up the airtime on the phone for personal calls abroad.

It was another instance when the explanation barely passed muster, this time only because the phone's call history showed that he didn't use the prepaid phone to call Notarbartolo's number that corresponded to the SIM card found in Crudo's possession. Detectives were still analyzing data on the SIM cards, but suspected that one or both were used as part of a closed telephone network in which the thieves used untraceable prepaid phone numbers to communicate only with one another. The number Falleti had called was Notarbartolo's official mobile phone number, registered in his name, not one of the anonymous phone numbers that so interested the police.

The cell phone Falleti normally used yielded more clues. His list of contacts included a confusing number of multiple references to Notarbartolo, including one for *P* (an abbreviation of Notarbartolo's childhood nickname, Pino) and one for *Tarrun* (a reference to Notarbartolo's southern Italian roots). There was also a number for *Pie & Leo*, which Falleti told police was a number Notarbartolo asked him to use when calling him in Belgium. Investigators believed *Pie* was a reference to Pietro Tavano, another member of the School of Turin the Italians had identified as a friend of Notarbartolo's.

Falleti and Tavano had been friends for years, from the time Falleti lived in Turin. Tavano had a criminal history that included robbery, aiding and abetting prostitution, and other charges. When investigators questioned Tavano in Italy and confiscated a prepaid cell phone with a Belgian phone number, he professed his innocence and refused to give a DNA sample. Detectives kept him under surveillance and followed him to a café in Turin. When Tavano finished a cappuccino and left, the agents seized the coffee cup off the counter and sent it to a lab for DNA analysis.

The Italian police were happy to help the Belgians with their investigation in whatever way they could. But as much as police like Martino hoped to put the most skilled of these men behind bars, the School of Turin remained relatively safe from the consequences of crimes committed outside of Italy as long as its members remained in Italy; at that time, it was very difficult for foreign governments to extradite Italian citizens in a case such as this as long as they remained in Italy.

That didn't prevent Italian investigators from questioning the suspects. They paid Elio D'Onorio a visit at his home in Latina. The detectives found four cell phones among D'Onorio's possessions and, even though they didn't have a warrant, they confiscated a pair of underwear, a toothbrush, and a comb to use for DNA comparison.

When the Italian detectives confronted D'Onorio with a copy of the document that helped unravel the plot more than anything else—the work invoice found by Belgian detectives in the Floordambos—D'Onorio claimed he'd bid on a contract to install a video camera system in Notarbartolo's office and said he had driven to Antwerp to discuss it with him. In addition, he denied having anything to do with the robbery of the Diamond Center. He said he had no idea how the invoice wound up among tools and equipment related to the heist.

Finotto was also picked up for questioning. A week after the heist was discovered, Belgian detectives had visited the Delhaize grocery store that produced the receipt recovered from the household trash found in the Floordambos. Using the receipt's 1:16 p.m. time stamp as a starting point, they viewed the store's CCTV surveillance tapes for Thursday, February 13. It didn't take them long to find what they were looking for. There on the tape, striding into the store at 12:56, was Finotto's unmistakable figure. The image was grainy, he was wearing a heavy parka, and he was visible only from the chest up. But the cement-block shape of his head, the furrowed brow, and the sharp widow's peak were undeniably his.

Under questioning by Italian police in Turin, Finotto denied any involvement whatsoever, cagily pocketing the butts of the cigarettes he smoked during his interrogation so that he wouldn't leave DNA behind. Belgian detectives located Finotto's girlfriend in Nice, France, just on the other side of the Alps from Turin, and searched her apartment with the aid of French detectives. In her safe, they found a stack of U.S. currency in $100 bills, subtly marked with a highlighter, matching the description of stolen money submitted by one of the heist victims.

♦ ♦ ♦

Not every avenue the investigators followed led to solid evidence. Technicians at Sony, for example, could not coax an image out of the videotape that had been strewn through the trees of the Floordambos. It was simply too damaged. They were able to reconstitute eight strands of videotape found along the shoulder of the highway, but those had nothing to do with the crime; the recordings were of the news, a company meeting, and pornography, all of them discarded for one reason or another along the E19 highway.

The detectives also discovered just a few days too late that the gold company on Lange Herentalsestraat had a surveillance camera aimed at the Diamond Center's garage doors. But by the time they requested access to the tapes, the videocassettes had been recycled and taped over.

The detectives had better luck with the analysis of Notarbartolo's SIM card. These prepaid cards provided cell phone users with what was essentially a secret phone number that couldn't be traced to an account with a name and an address. As long as phone calls from these numbers were placed only to other prepaid cards, there was no way to track the identity of the callers.

But once police had Notarbartolo's prepaid card, they had access to the private numbers used by the other thieves. There were seven "entities," as Peys put it, communicating on this closed network. The call records showed the date, time, and duration of calls among the entities. It was also possible to pinpoint the locations where the phones were used by measuring the signal strength between the phone and stationary cell phone towers that relayed the calls. When a certain phone's signal showed up on more than two towers, simple geometry—performed by a computer—allowed investigators to zero in on a caller's specific location. The more points of reference there were, the more exact the location, so it was easier to track a cell phone in an urban area than in the countryside because there were more cell phone towers.

Using this triangulation technique, detectives could tell that Notarbartolo's phone was in use inside the Diamond Center at various times from just after midnight on February 16 until 4:44 a.m. The calls were placed to Tavano's prepaid cell, which was determined to be in use at the Charlottalei apartment. Other information from the days leading up to the crime showed cell phone activity among this group of conspirators in an industrial area on the outskirts of Antwerp, home to many machining and fabrication companies. This led detectives to believe the thieves went there to make modifications to their ingenious pulling device.

The phone traffic immediately after the crime allowed the detectives to track the flight of the thieves as they left Belgium: based on these records, they could tell Notarbartolo drove back to Italy through France, at least one other thief fled through Germany, and yet another went inside the Brussels-National airport, leading to the conclusion that at least one of them flew from Belgium. Detectives scoured the manifests of all flights to Italy on Sunday, February 16, but found no names they recognized. Whoever left Belgium from Brussels was either unknown to the police, used fake documents to buy the plane tickets, or flew to somewhere other than Italy for his getaway.

After the heist, five of the cell phones, including Notarbartolo's, reappeared on Monday, February 17, near Lake Iseo, before dispersing in different directions the following day. One went to Latina, and three others toward Turin. The fifth phone fell off the network and was never heard from again. It may well be at the bottom of Lake Iseo. The detectives deduced that the loot was divided near Lake Iseo, but they were unable to pinpoint the exact address from the cell phone data.

Though the call records brought into clearer focus the guilt of the men the investigators had identified, they also revealed that there were as many as three more people involved who had yet to be found.

But what sealed the suspects' fate were the results of the forensic analysis. A piece of tape used to secure the shrouding material over the CCTV camera in the vault foyer had DNA that matched samples taken from personal items at D'Onorio's house. The half-eaten salami sandwich found in the household trash at the Floordambos, which Notarbartolo had discarded at the apartment as they'd prepared the loot for transport to Italy, matched up with his DNA. Belgian police discovered Finotto's DNA on a Vittel brand water bottle they recovered from Notarbartolo's dorm-style refrigerator. Tavano's DNA was found on items recovered from both the Floordambos and the apartment. The police also discovered male DNA that did not match any of their known suspects, bolstering their theory that there were more as-yet-unidentified accomplices in the crime.

Other small details helped fill in the cracks. A gem expert in Valenza told police that two men—whom he identified from police photos as Notarbartolo and Finotto—came to him the week after the heist asking about the value of small yellow diamonds they brought with them. He said they both spoke in the lingo of the diamond industry and he took them for professionals. Notarbartolo did most of the talking while Finotto took notes on a laptop. He told investigators that the men didn't try to sell him the stones but inquired about getting estimates and having them certified.

A university professor in Turin performed a computer-aided facial analysis on the grainy image of Finotto shopping at Delhaize and compared it to his mug shot. He wrote in a report that the two pictures were of the same person.

A gemologist in Antwerp analyzed the tiny marquise-shaped emeralds found in the rug Falleti had been carrying and determined in her expert opinion that they were a match to the ones found in the heist trash.

These reports, combined with the photo of the certified cognac diamond from Notarbartolo's safe, provided more than enough evidence to charge Notarbartolo, Finotto, D'Onorio, Tavano, and an unidentified fifth person—in the United States, such unknown suspects are commonly identified as "John Doe"—in the robbery of the Diamond Center. Even if convicted, however, the men didn't face too daunting of a sentence: Belgian law provided for a maximum punishment of only five years imprisonment for a robbery, even if it was of hundreds of millions of dollars' worth of diamonds.

Prosecutors asked for five years for Notarbartolo's involvement in the

Diamond Center heist as well as an additional five years for being the alleged leader of this criminal organization, an enhancement that meant a potential of ten years total punishment for him.

Because no plea bargains were permitted in Belgium, the case would go to trial. And the trial against all the suspects would commence regardless of the fact that three of them were enjoying a life of ease in Italy since Belgian law allowed defendants to be tried in absentia. But even if they were convicted in Belgium, at the time the odds were that all they had to do was stay in Italy to avoid doing time. As a practical matter, before legal changes that were still two years away, it would have been next to impossible for Belgium to get Italy to extradite its citizens in a case such as this.

In terms of house arrests, there were worse options than being confined to Italy.

♦ ♦ ♦

The collection of evidence took weeks and the cooperation of law enforcement in four different countries. While almost every new discovery seemed to further implicate Notarbartolo, the investigation also cast doubt on the involvement of Crudo, Zwiep, and Falleti.

The police eventually learned that three of the four suspects they had in custody had airtight alibis for the time of the heist. Falleti's employer confirmed that at the time of the robbery, late Saturday night, he had been busy at his job as a parking enforcer in Haarlem. Since he worked for the local police there, this was a solid alibi. Zwiep was able to prove she had been in the Netherlands as well, and Crudo was confirmed to have been in Italy during the heist. The only person in custody without a meaningful alibi was Notarbartolo.

Still, strong alibis for the night of the heist did not equal freedom, as their roles in the crime may have come at a later time. The wheels of justice turned excruciatingly slowly and the suspects were caught up in the machinery of the Belgian criminal justice system.

For criminal matters, Belgium, with a justice system based on that of France, had four levels of court. The nature of the heist was such that the suspects bypassed the Tribunal de Police, which heard minor criminal matters.

The court of first instance—Tribunal de Première Instance—was known as the Correctional Court, but unlike in the United States, the defendants did not have the right to a jury trial; juries were used with only very serious offenses, and such cases were heard at the Cour d'Assises. Instead of a jury, a panel of three judges would decide their fates. Following the Correctional Court, there was an appellate court, the Court of Appeal of Antwerp. All that remained after that stage was the Supreme Court, the Cour de Cassation, which exclusively handled appeals of law, not of fact.

Getting to court, however, was an exercise in patience. Court dockets in Antwerp were notoriously overburdened. Each courtroom was regularly booked with as many as twenty cases a day even though judges rarely got through more than five, which led to interminable delays. The situation was further hampered by overly complex procedures, outdated information management systems, and a budget that failed to keep up with the demands of the justice system. *De Standaard* newspaper reporter Jean-Charles Verwaest once wrote that it seemed at times like Belgian politicians didn't want a functional court system since they consistently failed to address its flaws.

While waiting for the courtroom appearances, Falleti and Notarbartolo fell into the routines of prison life. Authorities assigned Falleti to outfit new prisoners with clothing, and Notarbartolo read stacks of books and prepared his case. They had been separated from each other only during their initial week of incarceration; since then, the two old friends were part of the general population, and they frequently sought each other out in the exercise yard. They played soccer or walked around the perimeter discussing their circumstances. Other inmates treated them with respect; their reputations as alleged master thieves who pulled off a major heist was bolstered by rumors that they were in the Mafia.

Notarbartolo was courteous toward the people he dealt with, whether they were guards or fellow prisoners. The only exception was the time Notarbartolo punched an inmate who was giving Falleti a hard time. The man was a new arrival and apparently didn't know the prison-yard status of the two Italians. As soon as he hit the prisoner, Notarbartolo was backed up by others and the fight was over quickly. Notarbartolo and Falleti had no further problems.

Once, while talking in the exercise yard, Notarbartolo apologized for the mess he'd gotten his friend into, explaining that he'd thought the apartment would be empty by the time the police arrived. Falleti was a man of good spirits, whose strong Italian values made him cherish friends and family. Given their long history, Notarbartolo was a bit of both to him; it was easy for him to forgive his friend.

Actually, Falleti found himself oddly relaxed in prison. Of course he worried about his family and wanted to clear his name, but he enjoyed the fact that, while behind bars, he didn't have to worry about bills, work, and other everyday stresses. Still, he continued to meet with the authorities to appear cooperative in his ongoing attempts to convince them that he wasn't a thief. Falleti met with investigators as often as twice a week, and he was asked the same questions over and over. Each time, the investigators were just as dissatisfied with his answers as they had been the time before. Falleti felt like he was on a merry-go-round. Meanwhile, Notarbartolo stuck by the last words he'd said to Peys and refused to speak to investigators.

The men and their wives went before a judge again on Friday, March 28, 2003, and Falleti hoped he and Zwiep would go free on bail pending their trials. All recent evidence pointed toward their innocence: tests showed that the gloves and tape found at their house did not match those used in the heist, DNA tests showed no connection between the couple and any items found in the vault or in the Floordambos, and SIM card analysis showed that none of Falleti's known telephone numbers was among those used on the closed phone network. The couple's wish was granted, and after they'd spent five weeks in jail, the court granted Falleti and Zwiep bail. Falleti had to pay €2,500 and agree to return to Antwerp upon request or risk arrest. Zwiep was released on her own recognizance. Her children were waiting for her in the Netherlands; a relative had retrieved them after they'd spent three days at Paola Kinderziekenhuis.

In early May, Crudo was released pending her trial. She had been in jail for more than two months.

◆ ◆ ◆

Falleti might have been out of jail, but he was far from resuming the life he'd left behind in February. As he fought to get his job back and worried about the effects of his imprisonment on his children, his relationship with his wife started to crumble under the perpetual fear they might lose their cases and end up serving five years in prison.

The police searched Falleti's sister's home in the Belgian capital of Brussels (cell phone records indicated at least one of the thieves had gone to that city), telling her that, if she refused to answer their questions, she would be arrested. On August 19, 2003, the diamond detectives contacted Falleti and demanded that he return to Antwerp to answer additional questions. He had no choice but to comply; if he refused, it would be a breach of his bail agreement and a new warrant would be issued for his arrest.

During this new round of interrogation, the police peppered Falleti with detailed questions about his phone calls with Notarbartolo. They found it suspicious that Notarbartolo was the only person Falleti had called on that prepaid phone even though he knew other people abroad, such as his sister. The explanation that Notarbartolo was the only person he regularly called abroad did not placate them.

Detectives also found it suspicious that Falleti had called Notarbartolo from both his prepaid and normal phones. Though this contradicted his prior statement that he only called Notarbartolo on the prepaid, it should have helped clear him. It was significant that Falleti called the same number from both phones; it showed he wasn't trying to hide his contacts with Notarbartolo in the way someone who had dialed to and from only the secret numbers would have. But instead of seeing it this way, the police interpreted this as Falleti's having lied to them before in an attempt to conceal the extent of his communication with Notarbartolo.

The diamond detectives also believed Falleti stored Notarbartolo's phone numbers under *P* and *Tarrun* as an attempt to conceal his friend's identity. Falleti's nickname explanations, repeated numerous times in the past, were ignored. Italian cultural habits did not translate well in Belgium.

Despite his cooperation, Falleti's bail was revoked and the police put him back in jail. Detectives felt that their case against him was strengthening and that, therefore, he might pose a flight risk. "This uncertainty is killing us," Falleti said about this back-and-forth legal process. "We got into this adventure by pure coincidence."

Back in jail, Falleti and Notarbartolo were soon reunited. They went back to their old routines and were even allowed to share a cell. Notarbartolo slept in the top bunk while Falleti had the bottom one. Falleti found his friend to be a fastidious cellmate, taking care to perfectly make his bed first thing in the morning. Together, they cooked Italian food using a hot plate in their cell and ingredients bought at the prison's store. All they missed was wine to go with it.

While the defendants awaited their day in court, detectives in Belgium and Italy continued to scour Europe for more than just additional suspects and clues. They were also looking, so far in vain, for any trace of the estimated €100 million to €400 million worth of diamonds, jewelry, and gold.

With every passing day, the chance of finding a single stolen carat diminished further. They were looking for the proverbial needle in a haystack.

Chapter Twelve

THE TRIAL

"Any time you take a chance, you better be sure the rewards are worth the risk because they can put you away just as fast for a ten dollar heist as they can for a million dollar job."

— *The Killing* (1956)

From the moment his name was tied to the biggest heist of all time, Leonardo Notarbartolo's carefully cultivated anonymity disappeared just like the loot he pilfered from the Diamond Center. The School of Turin soon became infamous around the world, as much for the genius of their crime as for the manner in which they were caught.

The long months leading up to the trial were marked by international media interest that only intensified as the thieves' day in court approached.

Turin's daily newspaper, *La Stampa*, couldn't seem to decide if Notarbartolo should be treated as a folk hero or a villain. One reporter christened Notarbartolo with the nickname "the Man of Gold," while another called the decision to leave the garbage in the Floordambos the mark of "amateurs" and "beginners." A third wrote a long feature about the School of Turin's background that made them sound like Robin Hood's Merry Men.

The tone of the coverage in Antwerp was markedly different. The press identified Notarbartolo and the other arrestees as belonging to the Mafia, describing Notarbartolo not only as a man involved with organized crime, but also as a gunrunner and a drug dealer, allegations that were never substantiated.

The heist had been both devastating and embarrassing for the Diamond District, and the press coverage reflected this. Not only had safe deposit box holders in a major building been victimized, but the city's most important industry had been threatened. A secure environment in which to trade was at the heart of the Diamond District's ability to keep traders.

Despite grave concerns about security, no one seriously questioned Antwerp's ability to secure diamonds. "Nobody left Antwerp because of what happened," Philip Claes of the Antwerp World Diamond Centre later claimed. "It had no effect at all on the figures in general, of the imports or the exports, or the place of Antwerp as being number one as a world diamond center. What was very important, of course, is that the police rather quickly identified the guys who did it, so that was a relief, a relief to everybody. Okay, maybe the security failed, but the police did a great job."

Perhaps it was a desire by law enforcement to highlight the success of their investigation that led them to the unprecedented decision to cooperate with *ABC News* on a story for *Primetime Live*. Immediately after the robbery was discovered, the story was reported around the world and widely covered in major American newspapers, but only superficially. As a policy, Belgian police never openly cooperated with journalists—and they had certainly never gone on a program with millions of viewers to discuss a case while the trial was still pending. The confidentiality of an investigation, in deference to the defendants' rights to privacy and to ensure the credibility of the case against them, was taken more seriously in Belgium than in many other countries.

Initially, unit commander Agim De Bruycker simply refused to speak to the ABC team. But the television show's tenacious producer, Simon Surowicz, did not take no for an answer. He was so persistent that he was "kicked out of many buildings," Surowicz later recalled, including the police department and the justice building. Authorities even threatened to kick him out of the country if he didn't stop trying to dig up details about the heist. Surowicz, however, was undeterred. He kept reaching up the chain of command, repeating his requests for access to information about the case until it finally paid off. Much to the detectives' surprise, they were directly ordered by their supervisors to cooperate with Surowicz and the show's on-air reporter, Jay Schadler. Though the reason for this about-face in policy was never explained, it was widely seen as a move to highlight the investigative skills employed by the Belgian government. Privately, the detectives knew they were lucky to have broken the case open so quickly; if it weren't for Gust Van Camp, Notarbartolo and the others might never have been caught.

The American TV producer soon won over the detectives and gained their trust, particularly when they received a phone call from the security guards at the Diamond Center reporting that Surowicz had been caught in the building's vault without permission. Surowicz had left ABC's hidden camera equipment in the United States because he presumed the Diamond Center's vault was as "impenetrable" as reported and he would have no use for it. But when he arrived in Belgium, he discovered that even after the heist of the century, the vault was far from impenetrable; it was accessible by anyone who pushed the correct button in the elevator.

Surowicz bought a small video camera and rigged a shoulder bag to conceal it, just as Notarbartolo had done. He entered the Diamond Center as the guest of one of the tenants and then, by himself, took the elevator to the bottom floor. Once there, he hung around in the foyer and filmed through the day gate at his leisure until finally—after several minutes had passed—a security guard arrived to question him. Surowicz was allowed to leave, but the incident was reported to the police.

The detectives were more amused than angry, Surowicz recalled, in part because he had single-handedly proven how slack the security continued to be less than a year after the biggest heist in history had occurred there. "I went to the place that was 'impenetrable' and at that time got the only footage that I know of," he said.

The hour-long show aired almost exactly a year after the heist and compared the perpetrators to the fictional thieves in the film *Ocean's Eleven*. It included Surowicz's clandestine footage of the vault, computer reconstructions of many elements of the crime, and interviews with some of the victims. But the part of the show that had the most impact in Belgium was the interviews with Peys and De Bruckyer, in which the detectives openly discussed the evidence against their main suspect: Leonardo Notarbartolo. It was unprecedented in Belgium for police officers to speak so candidly about a case that was still under investigation. The only thing the show lacked was an outcome, as the wheels of justice were still barely spinning even as the diamond heist marked its first anniversary.

Just days after that one-year milestone, on February 19, 2004, after he'd been imprisoned for nearly six months, the court granted Falleti bail for a second time. At €25,000, it was ten times the amount of his prior bail. His first bail had been revoked when the police found additional evidence they believed strengthened their case against him. But since that evidence was not as strong as it had first appeared, the court allowed Falleti to leave jail again, albeit with a higher bail amount.

There was more good news for Falleti in mid-September 2004 when charges were dropped against his wife, Judith Zwiep. Her lawyer, Eric Boon, convinced the prosecutor that there was not enough evidence against her to continue the case. Now she could remain in Holland with no fear of ending up in jail. With Zwiep freed, Falleti could focus his energy on the charges he faced, knowing that even in a worst-case scenario, should he be found guilty, his children would have at least one parent to raise them while he served his time.

While Notarbartolo paced his cell in the Prison of Antwerp, the case against him moved slowly forward, plagued by delays. He was now the only one of the remaining defendants in jail. The trial—for all of the defendants at once—was to start on October 25, 2004, but hit another delay because the Belgians hadn't properly summoned any defendants to court other than Notarbartolo. Falleti had received his court summons only the day before the court date, and some of the defendants who remained in Italy received no notice at all.

The court postponed the proceedings until late November. A week before the new trial date, the three-judge panel surprised many courtroom observers by agreeing to a motion by Walter Damen, Notarbartolo's attorney, to set bail for his client in the amount of €50,000. In an accomplishment of biblical proportions, Damen successfully argued there was "absolutely no reason to hold Notarbartolo any longer. [There was] no more danger for collusion and, with imposing a guarantor, one eliminates the risk that he will flee from these proceedings."

The collusion part made sense; the police had long ago finished their initial investigation. But Notarbartolo potentially faced eight more years in prison, and bail set at €50,000 was not nearly enough incentive to prevent him from fleeing. Notarbartolo kept that amount of money at home in cash and had just played a key role in successfully stealing well over a hundred million euros' worth of loot. He was the very definition of a flight risk—he had no ties to the community and if he fled to his native Italy, he might have been beyond the reach of the Belgian authorities.

The prosecutor immediately appealed this decision and the court agreed not to grant Notarbartolo bail until the appeal was resolved. The appeal went against Notarbartolo and his bail request was ultimately denied.

Notarbartolo wasn't the only member of the School of Turin the prosecutors needed to consider. In advance of the trial date, prosecutors were sure to get the proper paperwork into the hands of all the defendants—for instance, Falleti was served his summons in person after he got off a bus on his way home from work—but the summonses were written in Flemish.

The defendants' lawyers argued that the summons should have been written in a language the defendants could understand. While the judges were not pleased with what would be yet another delay, they agreed that the summonses needed to be translated into Italian so the defendants could fully understand what these critical legal documents said. They did not want to risk a claim on appeal that the defendants were not properly served with notice of the charges against them. The prosecutors were ordered to serve the defendants again, this time with documents properly translated into Italian.

The prosecution, led by Ben Theunis, initially agreed to this seemingly reasonable request, but then, in yet another surprising maneuver, decided to appeal, arguing that there was nothing in Belgian law that required them to send out summonses in Italian. Of course, when the prosecutor's office needed help from the Italian police, they had no problem translating long documents into Italian on those occasions.

The trial was put on hold for two months pending the outcome of the prosecutor's appeal. This caused a significantly longer delay than if the prosecutor had simply translated the summonses. The calendar slowly wound its way toward the second anniversary of the heist.

◆ ◆ ◆

While this seemingly farcical argument played out on the appellate level, Notarbartolo was reminded yet again that the Belgians' stated commitment to speedy trials for accused criminals meant little in real life. He'd been behind bars for nearly as long as he'd rented his office at the Diamond Center; only a jail like the Prison of Antwerp could make him long for the dingy little apartment on Charlottalei.

Since the so-called Man of Gold had been arrested, much had happened on the outside. His son Marco's wife had given birth to a baby girl whom Notarbartolo had seen only during his family's infrequent visits to the prison. His close friend Mimmo Falleti—Antonino Falleti's brother—had died of cancer.

Notarbartolo kept up with the news of his friends and family with an expensive telephone habit. Prisoners were allowed phone calls, but only if they paid exorbitant fees for them. Notarbartolo spent about €4,000 per year, a fortune considering that most prisoners were stone broke. He was never foolish enough to risk a call to Finotto, D'Onorio, or Tavano. So he could only imagine how they were spending their time, and their money, while he waited in the overcrowded prison for the trial to start.

On Thursday, January 13, 2005, the disagreement over which language to use in the summonses veered in a direction the defendants never expected: The appeals court upheld the lower court's order that the summonses be translated into Italian, but also declared that the trial would be held at the appellate level, not first at the Correctional Court level. Doing so meant that the appeals court would try the case directly, skipping the lower court level completely. In other words, the defendants had one less chance of appeal; it removed an entire layer of the process. There was nothing comparable in U.S. criminal law.

This move may have been unexpected, but it wasn't accidental; Prosecutor Ben Theunis said that his office decided to appeal the translation issue with an eye toward convincing the appeals court to take the case away from the trial court. It was a cagey attempt to exploit this unique feature of Belgian jurisprudence to deny an avenue of appeal to the defendants. And it paid off.

"It's a kind of strategic move," Theunis said years later. "We had this judgment [regarding the order to translate the summonses into Italian] and we decided we will go into appeal ourselves. Of course, we thought about the fact that the Court of Appeal could keep the case."

To ensure the court knew of its options, "there was a suggestion" from the prosecutors' office to the judge that the case stay at the appellate level, Theunis said. The defendants' lawyers argued against it, but in vain.

"Of course, from the prosecutors' point of view this was a good thing because the accused, they lost an appeal," Theunis admitted.

The Supreme Court in Belgium was now the only higher authority available to review the outcome of the case, and that court heard only appeals based on errors of law. The key issues at stake in this trial were not ones of law, but of fact: Were the defendants involved in the robbery and, in Notarbartolo's case, was he the ringleader? The Antwerp Court of Appeal was highly regarded; it was unlikely the judges would commit any errors of law.

This development meant that, for all practical intents, the verdict of this one court was final and non-reviewable. Notarbartolo and his fellow defendants had just one roll of the dice to find out if they would go to jail for five to ten years or go free.

◆ ◆ ◆

The trial moved from the Correctional Court to the Court of Appeal building at Britse Lei 35A, just a three-minute drive from the Prison of Antwerp. The industrial-looking court house, built in the 1960s, was clearly influenced by the architecture of the time.

Courtroom A, the first on the left when entering the building, was almost perfectly cube-shaped, with a high ceiling. Adorned with a few wooden pews facing a long bracket-shaped table for the judges and court staff, the echoey room was bare of decorations, save for a tiny no-frills institutional clock that was the only relief on a vast wall of brown bricks behind the judges' bench. The judges sat on bright orange kindergarten-style plastic chairs that were a few shades more intense than the orange carpeting on their dais. These clashed mightily with fluorescent green desk pads and the electric blue curtains. To complete the palate, one wall was painted mustard yellow and the main door bright red. Fluorescent tubes hummed overhead. Overall, the room looked more likely to host Alcoholics Anonymous meetings than criminal trials.

The press was allowed to take pictures and film in the lobby, but not in the courtroom itself. The only pictures they were able to capture of the Man of Gold during the trial were snapped as police escorted him to and from the courtroom. Notarbartolo looked bookish and mild-mannered in casual civilian clothes and eyeglasses.

Although six people were on trial, only three defendants showed that day: Antonino Falleti, Leonardo Notarbartolo, and Adriana Crudo. The charges against Zwiep had been dropped, but she came to court to support her husband. The members of the School of Turin still hiding out in Italy—Finotto, D'Onorio, and Tavano—had hired Belgian attorneys, although these lawyers did not fully participate in the court case. The lawyers for the three defendants present in court needed to aggressively defend their clients since they faced immediate detention should they be convicted. The lawyers for the men in Italy, on the other hand, had a different and less straightforward role to play.

Of course their clients wanted to be acquitted, but these lawyers needed to tailor their participation carefully, with an eye toward later arguments in an Italian court over matters of extradition, were the men ever to be arrested. A likely argument would be that a Belgian conviction should be ignored on the basis that they were not present at their trial. In anticipation of such a situation, their lawyers needed to make a difficult decision. They could vigorously defend their clients in court in the hopes of getting them acquitted, or they could carefully limit their involvement by simply observing the proceedings. They could then later argue that their clients did not have full representation at trial.

The presiding judge sat in the middle and asked the majority of the questions, while the two associate judges flanking him mostly listened. Despite the difference in titles, they were theoretically equals; after the evidence was presented and the arguments heard, they would deliberate the verdict behind closed doors. The majority decision would stand as the unanimous decision, since there were no dissenting opinions accompanying Belgian verdicts as there were in the United States. Any dissent about a decision would stay between the three of them.

The trial also differed from those in the United States in that neither party called witnesses to testify before the court. Instead, sworn statements were simply admitted into evidence as part of the case file.

On March 10, 2005, the defense lawyers were finally able to make their arguments in court. Notarbartolo's lawyer, Walter Damen, argued that his client was not the ringleader. Damen wisely did not try to argue Notarbartolo's innocence—the evidence was difficult to dispute—but instead focused on arguing that the real mastermind remained safely in Italy. As Damen had said a year before on *Primetime Live*, when asked about his client's innocence, "Obviously, he isn't the most innocent guy you're likely to meet. I do agree that there is a series of important elements that indicate that Notarbartolo knows something about what happened. But there's always a minimum and a maximum penalty. We are looking for the minimum."

If successful, this tactic would cut Notarbartolo's sentence from a mandatory ten years to only five if he were found guilty. Considering he'd already served more than two years awaiting trial, it was possible under this scenario that he could be released before the end of the year, taking into account good behavior as a factor in early release, which was common in Belgium. Notarbartolo had been careful to be a model prisoner.

"When that gang in fact operates from Italy, and the real boss, therefore, sits there, then my client is not the leader and so the maximum penalty should be five years," Damen argued before the judges.

The lawyer's argument was not without merit. Even the lead investigators—both in Italy and Belgium—had doubts that Notarbartolo was the "mastermind" who coordinated, organized, and financed every detail of the Diamond Center heist. An operation of that complexity required a lot of financial backing. Rent alone at the office and the apartment had cost about €30,000 over the course of the planning for the heist. Other expenses such as airfare, technical equipment, and machining and engineering costs were harder to calculate with certainty, but they added up to sizable bill over the more than two years of plotting and reconnaissance. Notarbartolo may have been the face of the School of Turin as its crafty inside man, but those investigating the case were relatively sure he wasn't the leader. Detectives in both countries agreed that whoever masterminded the Diamond Center heist had never been identified. That didn't mean, however, that they thought Notarbartolo should be shown any leniency—they would be happy to see him serve as long of a sentence as possible for all the charges against him.

At least one reporter, *La Stampa*'s Lodovico Poletto, thought it unlikely that Notarbartolo had the acumen to mastermind such a complex and delicate job. Despite the mythology surrounding Notarbartolo, thanks to the lionizing press coverage, Poletto continued to consider him just a skilled amateur swept up in the plans of greater men. He suspected Pancrazio Chiruzzi, "the Soloist with the Kalashnikov," might have been the brains.

After the heist hit the newspapers in 2003, Poletto tracked down Chiruzzi to discuss it with him, finding the career criminal full of admiration for the job but also willing to offer a little post-heist analysis regarding some minor details he would have done differently. Chiruzzi denied any involvement, and he was never implicated by police, but Poletto remained skeptical. "You can see the hand of Pancrazio behind all of this," he said.

No alternate masterminds were mentioned in court, however. Notarbartolo was unwilling to address the judges. If he had talked, his legendary charm might have been able to persuade the court that someone else was the leader, but that would violate the criminal code he operated under. From the time he was arrested all the way through his trial, Notarbartolo never said a word that implicated anyone else although his lawyer blamed an unnamed person back in Italy as being the mastermind.

Another theory floating about was that Notarbartolo had been intentionally set up to take the fall for the heist by whoever dumped the trash. The thinking was that there could only be one mastermind, so Notarbartolo was being offered as the sacrificial lamb to take the longest prison sentence off the table for the rest of them.

None of the investigators gave this theory much credence, because such a double cross relied on far too many variables. The garbage was actually quite well hidden in the Floordambos if you discounted the fact that the forest was scoured almost daily by an obsessive caretaker. For the theory to make any sense, the conspirators would have had to have known Gust Van Camp would find the garbage quickly. Plus, it relied on Notarbartolo's having the nerve to go through with his plan to badge back into the Diamond Center after the discovery of the garbage, and on his being intercepted by police. The garbage had also led investigators to four of the perpetrators, not just Notarbartolo. D'Onorio was most obviously implicated because his business card and work invoice were discovered. In fact, it had taken a fair amount of detective work to learn of Notarbartolo's involvement.

Yet another theory was that Notarbartolo had agreed to take the risk of being nabbed as the leader in order to protect the others. Insurance investigator

Denice Oliver was a proponent of that idea; she believed Notarbartolo knew enough about the habits of the Belgian police from his time of reconnaissance to consider the possibility of doing real time to be extremely low.

"The guy came back and he thought, 'Fat chance of anything because they never get any results anyway,'" she said. "It's renowned around the world that the Belgian police are useless, with all due respect to Patrick [Peys] and Agim [De Bruycker]."

Arrestees were rarely held for long periods in Belgium, which made such a calculated risk all the more reasonable. Typically, suspects were held for a maximum of six months unless evidence emerged of their involvement in new crimes or in an ongoing crime. This was why the court released Falleti on bail after six months of detention.

Even in cases in which the evidence of a suspect's guilt was overwhelming, as it was in this case, it was unusual for the courts to order the suspect detained until the start of the criminal proceedings. Since the heist was a one-time event, it seemed logical that a lawyer could have arranged for Notarbartolo's release. That had been the basis for Damen's nearly successful plea for bail in November 2004. The plea had been granted but then denied on appeal.

In Oliver's view, the judicial department took exception from the norm for Notarbartolo because the stolen goods hadn't been recovered; suspicion of possessing stolen goods could constitute his ongoing participation in a crime. "That guy came back thinking, 'What's three [to six] months? I'll be out and having a great life and [be] driving to Italy and seeing my wife and son and whatever,'" Oliver explained.

From the prosecutors' perspective, Notarbartolo was the ringleader because he was clearly involved on the deepest level. The prosecution team was determined to make someone pay for what had happened; it would have lowered their chances of getting the maximum penalty to admit any uncertainty they may have had regarding who organized the heist. In fact, the Italian investigation into the matter was ongoing, with detectives in Italy still trying to find out who was involved, even as the trial against the known suspects was underway.

Damen and the other defense attorneys unsuccessfully argued for a further delay pending the outcome of the Italian investigation. Damen was especially interested in what would become of inquiries by the Anti-Mafia

Brigade in Palermo, which had sent a unit of detectives to Belgium to question both Falleti and Notarbartolo about suspected ties to organized crime. Damen hoped the investigation could sow doubt about Notarbartolo's role as the ringleader.

Palermo, the capital of Sicily, is a well-known hub for drugs entering Europe from South America and Afghanistan, and investigators knew that Notarbartolo's family hailed from there. While Notarbartolo also had an uncle with Mob ties that the authorities asked him about, it was his cousin Benedetto Capizzi they were interested in. Anti-Mafia police had once photographed Notarbartolo while he attended the wedding of Capizzi's son in Palermo. Additionally, Notarbartolo made calls while in prison to Capizzi's wife.

Capizzi was the alleged head of the Villagrazia area of Palermo at the time and was later selected to be the boss of bosses for Cosa Nostra. In December 2008, police arrested Capizzi, along with almost a hundred other suspects, to prevent a bloodbath as another Mafia faction had its own ideas for who should be the new head of the entire Sicilian Mafia.

The anti-Mafia investigators theorized that the Mob had sponsored the heist to finance a drug operation but their investigation eventually went nowhere.

The judges decided not to wait for the Italians to finish their work, ruling that the results wouldn't change the materiality of the evidence against the defendants. After the trial, the defendants' Italian attorneys claimed that this was one of the ways in which their clients' rights had been violated: by rushing to court before the Italian investigation was complete.

On March 17, 2005, Damen tried another tactic: arguing that his client would not be able to get a fair trial as a result of investigators' cooperation with the media, namely *Primetime Live*. Millions of viewers in the United States had watched "The Great Diamond Heist." The decision by police officials to cooperate with the program sent shockwaves through the Belgian legal community, as the Belgian judicial system grants greater protection for the privacy interests of defendants, before or after conviction, than does the United States. In Belgium, there's little belief in the public's right to know about a pending legal case. Therefore, the *Primetime Live* show startled many people in that Peys and De Bruycker discussed actual evidence against the perpetrators. After an eternity of "no comments" to the media, they had appeared on TV to explain in detail how a high-profile crime had occurred and why they thought the defendants had done it.

In court, Damen argued that the case against his client should be thrown out as the police had violated Belgian laws regarding the confidentiality of an open investigation and prejudiced the case against Notarbartolo. Though the Court of Appeal strongly disapproved of the police participation with ABC, it ruled that the program would not affect the case. Since the case would be decided by judges and not a jury, the court didn't have to consider how the program might have influenced its members. The judges simply said they would base any decision solely on the case file and would ignore what was said on the program.

On March 24, 2005, it was Jan De Man's turn to argue Falleti's case. He told the judges that Falleti had an innocent explanation for everything that the prosecution believed tied him to the crime: his prepaid phone, his role in carrying the rug out of the apartment, and other such details. He may have done those things, De Man said, but he didn't know what he was doing; he hadn't known anything about the crime. De Man argued that the prosecutors needed to prove that Falleti "knowingly" participated in the criminal conspiracy. The court agreed and the charges against Falleti were altered to specify that in order to be found guilty, it would have to be proven that he knew he was helping cover up a crime.

On Thursday, May 19, 2005, after more than a month of hearings, the Court of Appeal rendered its decision. The court convicted four of the defendants, only one of whom was in the courtroom. Leonardo Notarbartolo was sentenced to ten years in jail and fined €1 million. If he did not pay the fine, then he faced an additional three months in jail. The other convictions were for the three defendants who were still safe in Italy.

It had seemed, briefly, that these three might get off on a technicality. In D'Onorio's case, an Italian court had ruled that his DNA evidence had been obtained from his home illegally. D'Onorio's lawyer, Patrick Kortleven, argued to the Belgian court that the DNA evidence against him was inadmissible for the same reason. The court agreed, but ultimately concluded that there was enough evidence against him without the DNA to support a conviction.

Likewise, Finotto's Italian lawyer, Monica Muci, later complained that the DNA evidence against her client shouldn't have been brought up in court at all because the laboratory testing had been done without a defense expert present. The method used to test the DNA had destroyed the sample, so Finotto's defense team didn't have a chance to perform an independent comparison. In the end, Muci claimed Finotto was railroaded. She was the same attorney who had convinced an Italian appeals court to overturn his conviction for the 1997 bank robbery attempt by arguing that Finotto was only casing the bank, not attempting to rob it.

Arguments about the DNA during the trial went nowhere, and Finotto, D'Onorio, and Tavano were each sentenced to five years in jail and fined €5,000.

In addition to the jail time, the court ordered all four convicted defendants to pay a total of more than €4.5 million to the diamond merchants they had robbed. In the Belgian system, civil plaintiffs could participate in a criminal proceeding to recover the value of items stolen from them. Seventy-five victims were reported altogether; not everyone who was robbed elected to be part of this case. Of these, thirty plaintiffs had only a single euro awarded to them to indicate that, while they were owed money, the amount of that money had yet to be determined.

Notarbartolo began serving his term immediately, while the court promptly issued arrest warrants for the other three.

When the three defendants in Italy heard that a court in Belgium had sentenced them to five years in jail each, they would have found the classic quote by Brendan Behan, the Irish writer and revolutionary, appropriate: "Court-martialled in my absence, sentenced to death in my absence. So I said, right, you can shoot me—in my absence."

◆ ◆ ◆

The court cleared Antonino Falleti and Adriana Crudo. The prosecutors had asked the court to sentence them to eight months and eighteen months in jail, respectively, as well as a fine. There was not enough proof that they had knowingly attempted to cover up the crime, even though they had been helping to clear out the apartment that had been used as local headquarters for the heist.

For Falleti, it was the end of a nightmare. He regretted the outcome for his friend, but the fact that he had been officially acquitted was too overwhelming to make him anything but ecstatic. Falleti, his wife, and his legal team went to a nearby café to celebrate with a few bottles of champagne. Jan De Man, the lawyer he'd found by yelling out of a cell window, clinked glasses and congratulated his client, but had a dire prediction for Notarbartolo. Typically, prisoners in Belgium only served a third of their sentence before they were considered for early release. De Man's opinion was that Notarbartolo was so publicly reviled that he'd do every day of his ten years, which, when counting time served, would see him released in 2013. Notarbartolo would be sixty years old.

For Notarbartolo, the only bright side of his conviction was that he wouldn't be returning to the Prison of Antwerp. After he was trotted past the media outside the courtroom so they could get good shots of the now-convicted master thief, Notarbartolo was sent to a long-term detention facility in Hasselt, an hour's drive southeast of Antwerp. The new €38.4-million facility had been opened just weeks before his conviction.

Hasselt was more like an assisted living complex than a prison. Visitors could be forgiven for thinking the building was a modern art museum. It was smartly designed in contemporary style with artistic touches on the external façade. While Notarbartolo still lived in a cell, his Hasselt quarters were at least modern and more spacious than those in the Prison of Antwerp.

The visitor's area resembled a mall food court, with paintwork on the floor tiles in the style of a Jackson Pollack, vending machines, and comfortable IKEA-esque tables and chairs. Within the prison, there was a small store where visitors could buy gifts for the inmates. Depending on the time of year, prisoners could receive Valentine's presents, Christmas gifts, and Easter baskets chosen from this little kiosk. Even the outfits were nicer: canvas boat shoes, khaki pants, and a light khaki jacket worn over a blue polo shirt.

Of course, as comfortable as it might have been, it was still a prison, and Notarbartolo would have taken stock of its security features, if only out of habit. Video cameras, both hidden and overt, covered every inch of the facility. Windows lacked bars but the high-impact security glass was laced with wire mesh. Solid steel doors controlled access to the different wings and cell blocks. Biometric locks screened personnel as they moved around the building. A twenty-foot-tall fence armed with razor-sharp wire on top surrounded the entire complex.

Five months later, in October 2005, the Supreme Court of Appeal rejected Notarbartolo's and Tavano's appeals. Since Notarbartolo's lawyer had introduced no written objections on issues of law during the trial, it had been clear from the start that his argument on procedures had no chance of success. But it was the only appeal available to his client, and, as such, needed to be attempted nonetheless.

Notarbartolo began counting the days.

◆ ◆ ◆

In Italy, the others should have been busy counting their lucky stars. The ruling of the court was taken seriously in that they immediately began legal proceedings to challenge their convictions, but it meant little as long as they lay low and contented themselves with staying in Italy, where they had the best odds of never being arrested or extradited to serve their sentences. They might have settled in to enjoy a quietly luxurious lifestyle had D'Onorio not decided to take a vacation only a few months after the verdict was delivered in order to check out a real estate investment. Although he was well aware that his freedom was in jeopardy outside Italy's borders, he boarded a plane in February 2006 and flew to the Cape Verde Islands off the coast of West Africa.

A former Portuguese colony, the Republic of Cape Verde was an archipelago nation made up of nine inhabited islands with a population of half a million. It was an up-and-coming tourist destination, where detectives believe D'Onorio traveled to scout out an investment in coastal land and perhaps even a hotel. On his return flight, he brought with him glossy brochures for property in Cape Verde. Patrick Peys believed he planned to hide at least a part of the School of Turin's ill-gotten gains there.

While changing planes at the Lisbon airport in Portugal, D'Onorio was arrested on the morning of February 23, 2006, a little more than three years after he'd played a key role in the Antwerp diamond heist. D'Onorio now found himself an unwilling guest of the Portuguese Republic, and the timing couldn't have been worse. While he was stuck in Portugal, his lawyers were arguing in the Belgian courts that his conviction should be overturned based, in part, on the argument that he hadn't had the opportunity to properly defend himself because he wasn't present in court. Finotto's attorneys were making the same appeal. D'Onorio was arrested as a fugitive on the basis of a European Arrest Warrant (EAW) that had been issued by Judge Dirk Verhaeghe, the examining judge back when the trial level criminal court handled the diamond heist case.

At the time, the EAW was a relatively new development, the result of an agreement by European Union Member States to streamline arrest and extradition policies. Portugal had already implemented changes to its extradition procedures about two and a half years before D'Onorio's trip.

D'Onorio fought hard in a Portuguese court against his extradition with a number of different arguments, from the very technical to "a violation of the principle of two levels of jurisdiction, because [he] was tried by the Court of Appeal in Antwerp." He also argued that he shouldn't be extradited to Belgium as he had not been present at the trial against him, but was instead tried in absentia.

This fight took time and, after ninety days, Portugal let D'Onorio out of detention, attempting to ensure he remained in Portugal by confiscating his passport—a move that, of course, didn't deter the Roman from beating a hasty retreat back to Latina. The lack of a passport posed little problem to him since the countries between Portugal and Italy effectively had no hard borders, and, therefore, very little control on who passed through them. By the time the Court of Appeal of Lisbon decided on July 11, 2006, to send D'Onorio to Belgium, it was too late. He was long gone.

On October 31, 2006, the Belgian Supreme Court ruled against D'Onorio's and Finotto's appeals. Their sentences of five years imprisonment stood.

By 2006, Italy was proving a less hospitable refuge for a man like D'Onorio, wanted in one country and on the lam from an extradition proceeding in another. Italy was still slow to change its legal regime to accommodate EAWs—it was the last EU Member State to do so—but it slowly became more cooperative about surrendering its own citizens to other countries. D'Onorio was proving to be an embarrassment to Italy thanks to his jaunt to Cape Verde, and Belgium exerted great pressure on the Roman courts to hand him over. The computer and alarms specialist fought against this in the Italian courts for seven months, but eventually lost this battle. The diamond detectives flew from Brussels to escort D'Onorio to his new accommodations, a prison in Merksplas, Belgium. Since he'd already been tried and convicted, there were no court appearances. He went straight to jail.

After finally succeeding in D'Onorio's extradition, the Antwerp prosecutor again requested that Italian police arrange for Finotto and Tavano to join him behind bars. This time, they were both arrested and held in Italy for possible extradition. Marco Martino, the commander of the Mobile Squadron, personally arrested Tavano in a shabby studio apartment near Fontanella's locksmith store. The infamous criminal who'd helped orchestrate the theft of hundreds of millions of dollars' worth of diamonds didn't even have a bed; Tavano slept on the couch.

By November 2007, all four of the convicted perpetrators were under arrest and in prison. Notarbartolo and D'Onorio were in Belgium, and Tavano and Finotto were in Italy, just beginning their own series of hearings fighting against extradition.

Chapter Thirteen

THE LOOT

A diamond is the hardest substance known to man, especially if he's trying to get it back.

—Proverb

A few months after the big heist, a procession that was simultaneously somber and hopeful made its way through the space-age glass doors of the HRD. The victims of the robbery were a diverse crowd, young and old, elegant and gruff. Some had rented safe deposit boxes at the Diamond Center in which they kept every item of value they owned, while others were representatives of multinational corporations covered by iron-clad insurance policies. Each person badged through the HRD's turnstiles with a visitor's pass and headed to a ground-floor conference room filled with police detectives and diamond industry representatives.

Numbered plastic bags containing the remnants of the heist covered long tables in the middle of the room. The bags were filled with the loot that had been left on the white tile floor of the Diamond Center's vault. After the items had been checked and tested for forensic evidence, the police had stored them in the vault of a local bank until they were ready to be returned to their rightful owners—a time that had finally come.

Quietly but thoroughly, each person went from bag to bag in the hope of finding something of theirs that the thieves had deemed not worth stealing.

Philip Claes, the HRD lawyer who had helped coordinate the return of the looted property, watched the process from a respectful distance. He was aware of how emotional it was for some of the victims, especially those who learned that nothing of theirs remained from the heist.

"For some of them, it was a personal drama," Claes recalled, "because not only their diamonds were in the safe but also the family jewels and some savings they'd made." It was cathartic, he said, for the victims to go through the process of examining the leftovers of the heist and to speak to the detectives about the case. "People came, they could talk about it. They could see that things were done to solve everything, that things were done to maybe give them some of their belongings back."

Many items defied easy identification—like loose pearls. Claes was touched to see that the victims who had pearls stolen didn't claim them unless they were certain of their ownership. None of them wanted to accidentally take anything that wasn't theirs.

Those who found items that had come from their safe deposit boxes told Claes or one of his assistants, who jotted down the bag number and the name of the claimant. "Some of them were very cool. 'Okay, this is mine. Great. Thank you very much,'" Claes recalled. "Others were really happy. If you see that the ring of your grandmother is there, it has an emotional value. Maybe it is worth nothing, but it has an emotional value. Then you really saw it on their faces that they were extremely happy that they had recovered it."

Other victims had less luck, circling the tables again and again that day, and returning throughout the week for another look. Some brought their spouses or friends on subsequent visits, hoping they might recognize something that they had missed.

Fay Vidal was among the lucky ones. Even though she had looked in vain through the debris on the floor the morning the heist was discovered, she decided to go to the HRD on the chance that she overlooked something.

"I still found a few things that I hadn't found in this enormous heap on the floor," she said. "I had a few stones in amethyst and turquoise that I bought once and never made anything out of it. And then someone comes up to me and says, 'Isn't this yours?' It was a little hanger in gold with a teeny-weeny little diamond on it, and on the back it was my daughter's name. She'd received that from her grandmother when she was small on her birthday. So [the thieves] couldn't do anything with that."

At the end of the week, the list of claimed items was tallied. Out of the multitude of things the School of Turin had left behind, only two—a gold bracelet and a watch—were claimed by more than one party. Mediators from the World Federation of Diamond Bourses settled those situations privately.

There were also many things that weren't claimed, mostly small loose diamonds, pearls, and other gems that were difficult to identify. Those were gathered up and held at the World Federation of Diamond Bourses for a year. When no other claimants stepped forward in that time, the items were sold and the money donated to a local charity. Even these dregs of the heist, the crumbs that the thieves discarded and were left unclaimed by their rightful owners, amounted to a small windfall. Aside from the School of Turin, the charity was the only beneficiary of the Diamond Center heist.

Claes said that while it was cathartic to see the perpetrators of the crime sentenced and eventually jailed, it wasn't what was most important to the victims. "The most important thing is, where are the other belongings?" he said. "Where are the diamonds?"

♦ ♦ ♦

The reported amount stolen came to at least 100,000 carats of rough and polished diamonds; thirty-three pounds of pure gold; cash in various currencies amounting to at least $1.5 million; more than two dozen premium men's and women's watches from designers such as Rolex, Venus, Omega, and Bulgari; and millions of dollars' worth of securities, rare coins, and jewelry. The stolen jewelry included hundreds of earrings, bracelets, pendants, chains, brooches, and tie clips. They were made of gold, platinum, and silver and contained a galaxy of precious stones, from pearls and emeralds to rubies and—of course—more diamonds.

Thirty safe deposit box owners reported their losses of cash and goods as "unspecified," meaning that the total haul was far bigger than the accounting listed in court records and on insurance claims. Although police estimate the thieves could have made off with as much as a half a billion dollars' worth of loot, insurance payouts only amounted to $21 million.

Investigators never settled on an official estimate of the take, although three days after the heist was discovered they announced that it was over €100 million ($108 million at the exchange rate at the time of the heist, $140 million at the time of this writing in July 2009). As the investigation proceeded, the estimate went up. During the trial, a prosecutor told the judges that he believed the amount stolen to be closer to €400 million. During an interview in 2008, when asked about the original figure of €100 million, Belgian detective Patrick Peys said, "I assure you it's more." He believed the take may have been as high as €400 million (which would have been $432 million at the time of the heist and $560 million at the time of this writing in 2009).

The list of items that were recovered beyond the confines of the vault was far smaller: a few hundred dollars found in Finotto's girlfriend's safe in France; the foreign currency from the garbage in the Floordambos; a pinch of emerald pointers recovered from the Floordambos and the fibers of the rug Falleti had been carrying; and small diamond shards found in the vacuum bag and on the floor of the Charlottalei apartment. Their combined worth wasn't much more than the face value of the cash.

Everything else vanished, including the cash and diamonds that had surfaced briefly during the Mobile Squadron's initial search of Notarbartolo's house in Trana. The last place detectives believe the bounty was all in one place was at the rendezvous site near Lake Iseo, but what happened to it when the School of Turin went their separate ways was anyone's guess. If the entire haul had been exchanged for cash to an unknown fence, mastermind, or financier, then not even the men who stole it would know its whereabouts now.

The most likely fate of the stolen goods was that they were divided into categories and disposed of separately. The euros taken during the heist could have been laundered through the School of Turin's legitimate businesses. The earrings, rings, pendants, and necklaces that were too distinct to risk selling could have been disassembled, the gemstones added to the pile of loose goods while the precious metals went into their own piles depending on whether they were silver, gold, or platinum. One diamond ring alone was valued at more than a million dollars, far too risky to chance selling in one piece.

The precious metals could be melted in a high-temperature furnace and then poured into casts of any shape and size so that they would be impossible to identify.

Gold mixed with other metals—such as copper or zinc—had to be smelted in order to purify it, a process that involved melting the metal and adding chemicals to separate the different components. Smelting required chemistry skills and was dangerous—drop an open container of molten gold at your feet and at best, you'll be burned to the bone—but it ensured the thieves would get full market value for the gold, and rendered it completely untraceable to the heist.

Items like the high-end watches would have been sold to a trusted jewelry fence. Trying to sell them at retail, such as at one of Notarbartolo's jewelry stores, would have been too risky to contemplate. And, although it would have been tempting for one of them to slip the gold Patek Philippe watch onto his arm, it would have been an equally bad idea to keep anything so distinctive for themselves. This Swiss timepiece alone could have cost between $20,000 to well over a million dollars, depending on the model. Despite the prices some of these watches commanded, they would earn only pennies on the dollar when sold to most fences. During the robbery, the thieves were careful to keep the watches in their original packaging material when it was available, which proved their authenticity and made them less suspect when sold again further down the line.

As for the diamonds, many of them would, in all likelihood, eventually make their way back to Antwerp. It was a painful irony for the heist victims to consider, but there was no way around the fact that the Diamond District was the obvious place to process and sell the diamonds, particularly the rough stones, since eight out of every ten rough diamonds found throughout the world go through Antwerp.

"Dealing in stolen diamonds is relatively easy, if you know where to go with those diamonds," explained Patrick Peys. "Unfortunately, we know that stolen diamonds can be sold. If you get it for a cheap price, and you are sure that they can't be identified, you get profit. And as always, there will be people in the diamond business that want to make an easy profit."

With billions of dollars' worth of diamonds coursing through the Diamond District's offices and factories every year, the chance that any but the most unique stones would be recognized was infinitesimal. The biggest problem faced by the School of Turin was the sheer quantity of diamonds to unload.

The smaller pieces of rough could have been exported to India or China for processing into gemstones, but the larger pieces of rough had to come back through Antwerp, according to Denice Oliver, the insurance investigator.

"The De Beers Sight had just come in (shortly before the heist) and they had a lot of the specials," Oliver explained. "The specials are the really big rocks and you have to figure out how you're going to cut them. The equipment to deal with the specials only exists in Antwerp. So a lot of the manufacturing today goes off to China, to India, because the labor is cheaper there. [But] the only place you have to process these goods is in Antwerp, the bigger goods. Once they have been processed, you can't recognize them anymore. One way or another, these goods are flooding back into the market."

As for the polished diamonds, they could be sold without any need to change their appearance, unless the thieves wanted to shave off a tiny bit so that they could be certified by one of the labs. If that were the case, it would then be impossible to identify a diamond as having been stolen; once it's been altered on the polishing wheel, it's a different diamond. But the School of Turin would hardly have had to bother; the authorities didn't circulate a list of stones that had been looted from the Diamond Center and, therefore, most merchants wouldn't have known what to look for, even if they were being careful not to buy stolen goods.

It's inevitable that honest dealers unknowingly helped traffic the School of Turin's loot from one merchant to the next, until a stolen diamond ended up in someone's engagement ring. There's even a chance that some ended up back in the Diamond Center's vault along the way, mixed into the stock of one of the diamond companies that moves thousands of stones a year. Such a stone could even end up in the same safe deposit box from which it was stolen in the first place.

◆ ◆ ◆

Notarbartolo, Finotto, Tavano, and D'Onorio had been caught, convicted, and incarcerated for pulling off the greatest heist of all time, but they managed to keep all the loot. Many would consider five or ten years in a Belgian prison to be a reasonable trade for a lifetime of riches.

During the course of the investigation, detectives in both Italy and Belgium scoured the men's assets and found that they were as disciplined in their expenditures as they were in robbing high-security vaults. As his sparse studio apartment attested, Tavano clearly didn't give in to the temptation to flaunt his share of the take with lavish expenses. Notarbartolo had been smart enough to put all of his assets in Crudo's name. Falleti noted that all Notarbartolo owned was a dog, and the dog died while he was in prison. The only clue as to what one of the thieves planned to do with the money was gleaned from D'Onorio's ill-fated trip to Cape Verde; apparently he at least considered investing some of his share of the loot in real estate.

Reluctant as they were to admit it, detectives in both Italy and Belgium had come to believe that their chances of recovering the stolen items were near zero. "We would give an arm to get them," Peys said. "But I can hardly imagine that there is some evidence somewhere . . . According to me, this case is finally closed."

Most of those who were robbed arrived at the conclusion that they wouldn't see their property again. "I think they gave up," Claes said of the robbery victims. "They don't have any illusion anymore. Maybe some of them still hope, deep in their hearts, that [the loot] might still show up. I'm really very curious what they did with it. And the people who have it now, what are they doing with it?"

The question of where the loot went would remain even after all the men were released from prison. Both the Mobile Squadron and the diamond detectives planned to keep a close eye on the convicted men's activities after their release.

"If Notarbartolo gets out of prison and starts a shop in diamonds or something like that, we will certainly try to investigate," Peys said. "But, I mean, Notarbartolo isn't an idiot. He knows quite well what we are going to do and what he can do and cannot do. But I can't imagine what he's going to do."

This was hardly idle curiosity. Many a successful thief—not to mention drug dealer, prostitute, and anyone else who made a living off of unreported cash—has wondered how to spend their ill-gotten gains without attracting the attention of the police. To see the danger criminals face in spending illegal cash wantonly, one need look no further than Al Capone, who was arrested and jailed for tax evasion because he couldn't prove a legitimate source of income for his lavish lifestyle.

Notarbartolo and the others also have to worry about the possibility of retribution. Avoiding the police was one thing, but the School of Turin also need to worry that their victims might take matters into their own hands.

Diamonds can pay for a lot of nefarious services and there are no shortages of shady characters on the fringes of the industry. It's hardly out of the question that a merchant who lost millions to the thieves will consider hiring a few former Mossad agents or African mercenaries to recover his losses outside of legal channels.

"A lot of those victims, they are angry," Peys said.

Notarbartolo and the others could follow the paths of thieves before them and relocate to a country that wouldn't question the source of their income. Since 9/11, however, the world has become a much smaller place for those wanting to hide funds from the authorities. Fewer countries than in the past turn a blind eye to wealthy foreigners who want to lie low. The countries that do pose a whole different set of concerns, primarily kidnapping and extortion.

It is hard to imagine Notarbartolo living anywhere but near Turin. For one thing, it will be safer than other options, as it's better to be well respected among local thieves, who look on him as an idol, than to risk becoming a target for less impressed gangs in foreign countries. Besides, Turin is home, even though much has changed since he's been in prison. For one thing, Crudo sold the house in Trana and moved to nearby Giaveno. And for another, Notarbartolo's manufacturing business in Valenza and the jewelry stores in Turin were either closed or sold to new owners. Even the smoky taverns, where the School of Turin's plots were formulated, are no longer smoky; while Notarbartolo was in prison, Italy passed a law banning smoking in public places, including the cafés.

He would have to start over to build a legitimate business, one that would satisfy the taxing districts and generate what looked like a legal income to keep the police at bay. Of course, it would have to be something wildly profitable, something that would allow him to enjoy the life of luxury he'd had to delay.

Sitting in prison in Hasselt, Notarbartolo had plenty of time to come up with just the right business plan: He would capitalize on his reputation as the most infamous thief in the world to partner with a major jewelry distributor. In preparation for this second act, the master thief spent his days behind bars sketching designs for his own line of jewelry.

He would call it "Diamonds by Leonardo."

EPILOGUE

Tess: *You're a thief and a liar.*
Danny: *I only lied about being a thief. But I don't do that anymore.*
Tess: *Steal?*
Danny: *Lie.*

—*Ocean's Eleven* (2001)

"I may be a thief and a liar. But I am going to tell you a true story."

—Leonardo Notarbartolo, quoted in *Wired*

The loot was gone, the crooks were in prison, and the case was closed, but for Gust Van Camp, the indignation remained. He had followed the investigation closely as it unfolded. At first, he had been excited that his discovery of the garbage had provided the detectives with the clues they needed to break the case open. Once the Belgian press suggested that the suspects had ties to the Mafia, however, he feared for his safety.

As the case wore on, any residual fear on Van Camp's part was replaced by profound resentment. It seemed to him that everyone involved had forgotten about him. He had hoped for a reward or at least some public recognition for the important role he'd played in helping detectives quickly identify the perpetrators. Instead, he hadn't even been given so much as a thank-you from anybody for helping bring the School of Turin to justice.

While the diamond detectives received the credit, all Van Camp got was a steady stream of reporters asking to be shown the thieves' dumpsite. After duly expressing his annoyance, he usually complied, always ending his guided tour with the same refrain: had he known at the time of his discovery how the authorities would have treated him, he wouldn't have called the police in the first place. Van Camp even took to asking visiting reporters to pass a message to the man he called "Mr. Bartolo." He wanted to apologize to the Italian for landing him in jail.

One day, Van Camp's bitterness got the best of him. If no one was coming to Vilvoorde to thank him, he was going to track someone down in Antwerp to demand it. Without bothering to change clothes from what he generally wore to patrol the forest, he drove to Antwerp with his wife and dog in tow.

Of all the different peoples and cultures to be found on the streets of the Diamond District, none stood out as much as Van Camp and his small entourage that day. He strode with purpose down Schupstraat in his rubber boots and faded camouflage T-shirt with his dog bounding happily at his heels. His only concession to city life was that he left his double-barreled shotgun at home.

When he reached 9–11 Schupstraat, Van Camp walked past the smokers loitering under the heavy awning and pushed through the plate glass doors into the Diamond Center. He told the security guard sitting in the enclosed glass booth that he wanted to speak to the manager, explaining in his heavily accented rural Flemish that he wanted to be thanked for solving the robbery that had happened there.

But when the guard informed Julie Boost about this unusual visitor, she was not in the thanking mood. The last person she wanted to talk to about the diamond heist was some rube in muddy clothes looking for gratitude. Rather than expressing her simple thanks in order to be done with him, Van Camp, his wife, and his dog were asked to leave the building.

Boost had good reason for refusing visitors with an interest in the heist: A number of victims had filed a lawsuit against the Diamond Center, alleging that its negligence had enabled the School of Turin to plunder their boxes in its vault. Anything she said could potentially be used as ammunition by the suit's plaintiffs or possibly further upset the tenants who had been robbed.

Boost, therefore, avoided talking about the crime—and that included saying "thank-you" to the man whose dedication to a clean forest led directly to the conviction of four of the perpetrators. And so, after a hearty argument with the security guards, Van Camp left the Diamond District more resentful than ever.

Patrick Peys was all too familiar with Van Camp's ire; he too had been pestered for an official thanks, but protocol prevented the police from acknowledging Van Camp's contribution to solving the crime. Belgium's strict rules forbidding the police from discussing cases extended to recognizing the citizens who helped solve them. Nevertheless, while he waited for the next big heist that would send him and his fellow detectives racing to the Diamond Square Mile, Peys took the time to address this final lingering detail of the great Diamond Center robbery. Turning to his computer, he spent some time creating an elaborate document marked by fancy fonts and official language.

It was a certificate of sorts, an expression of gratitude extended on behalf of the federal diamond detectives to August Van Camp, for meritorious service in the assistance of a criminal investigation. Peys didn't have the authority to express official gratitude on behalf of the government, but he suspected that Van Camp wouldn't mind, even if he knew the difference.

Peys was right; Van Camp was happy to be recognized at last for his role in solving the heist of the century.

But he still would have preferred a reward.

♦ ♦ ♦

Litigation aside, Boost had another reason for refusing to discuss the heist: the nagging questions of how the School of Turin knew the combination to the vault door and whether anyone on the Diamond Center's staff was involved.

Of those who knew the code at the time of the break in, Jacques Plompteux was the only one who had left the employ of the Diamond Center between the heist and autumn 2009. Boost still managed the building; Jorge Dias De Sousa was still the head caretaker; Grünberger was still Boost's boss. All—including Jacques—were thoroughly investigated, to no avail.

"The thing that . . . had never been resolved and that is still a question unanswered is: was there any cooperation from the inside?" Patrick Peys pondered while discussing the case in the fall of 2008. "That's actually a major question in this case, because you have [perpetrators] who are very specialized, but they do need a certain knowledge for that. Inside knowledge, you would say. I can assure you that that was investigated very thoroughly.

The simple fact is, if you don't find any evidence or major indications that there was some inside cooperation, then there wasn't. In this case, nobody was prosecuted and, in all honesty, I wouldn't know who to accuse or who to prosecute."

The only people who could say for certain whether one of the Diamond Center's staff had been involved in the heist were generally happy to leave the mystery unsolved. There was little reason for the School of Turin to reveal any of its secrets while four of the perpetrators were behind bars; after all, police believed there were others involved who had not been identified and who were therefore never brought to justice. The smartest move was to keep their secrets and do their time.

And yet, while still in prison, Notarbartolo couldn't resist the temptation to tell his story—for a price.

During a face-to-face meeting at the Hasselt prison in Belgium in September 2008 by one of these authors, Notarbartolo attempted to negotiate payment for the exclusive right to tell his story. There was already a six-figure offer on the table, he claimed, from a California-based movie production company called Underdog Inc. If the authors could either beat the price Underdog was offering or guarantee that a Hollywood studio would pay for his life rights in order to make a movie about the heist, he promised to tell "the greatest story." (Notarbartolo had made a similar offer to at least one other journalist in 2008, an American filmmaker producing a documentary about the heist.) The authors of this book declined to pay for an interview with Notarbartolo, citing a conflict of interest in making a financial arrangement with a source for his cooperation.

At times during the meeting, Notarbartolo—who had lost his modest paunch in prison and was lean and fit, sporting a thin white-whiskered soul patch that ran from his bottom lip to the tip of his chin—seemed desperate to make any sort of deal, no matter how specious. Unsuccessful in his effort to start a bidding war over his story, Notarbartolo offered to tell the authors his tale in exchange for a signed guarantee granting him a very small percentage of the eventual book's royalties. Under the terms he proposed, in which his take would only kick in after the authors had earned a completely unrealistic amount from sales, he would probably have never seen a dime. But Notarbartolo wasn't a stupid man; he probably didn't expect to earn much from the arrangement. What may have been even more valuable to him would have been a document he could show to authorities if anyone questioned his source of income once he was released from prison. An official contract signed by two American authors promising him a percentage of book sales would probably satisfy most inquiries about how he could afford certain luxuries in life.

Again, the authors declined to enter into any financial arrangement with Notarbartolo and the meeting ended amicably.

Soon after the prison meeting, the authors received word from Antonino Falleti and Jo-Ann Garbutt (Falleti's girlfriend after his divorce from Judith Zwiep) that Notarbartolo had signed a deal with *Wired* magazine reporter Joshua Davis that "satisfied his [Notarbartolo's] commercial needs," according to their e-mail. Davis is the author of a book titled *The Underdog*, and a company named "Underdog Inc." is registered with the California Secretary of State with a business address that's the same as Davis's home address in San Francisco. In the e-mail, Notarbartolo's friends asked the authors to discontinue contact with them and Notarbartolo; whatever the arrangement with Davis, it seemed to include an exclusivity provision.

In its April 2009 edition, *Wired* published Notarbartolo's largely uncontested account of the crime under the headline "The Untold Story of the World's Biggest Diamond Heist." The article did not include any information about how or whether Davis satisfied Notarbartolo's "commercial needs" in exchange for a series of interviews Notarbartolo granted Davis while in prison. But, in an online video interview with Davis that ran on *Wired*'s Web site as a supplement to the article, Davis credits his own journalistic doggedness in getting Notarbartolo to talk.

The article notes that Notarbartolo "refused to discuss his case" with any journalists other than Davis during the time he was incarcerated. However, while in jail, Notarbartolo himself placed calls to reporters in Belgium, Italy, and the United States. For example, he asked *ABC News* producer Simon Surowicz to fly from New York to Belgium in order to discuss his case. Notarbartolo also made contact with these authors through his friends in the Netherlands. During our meeting with Notarbartolo at the Hasselt prison, he made it clear that his story was available to whoever was willing to pay the most for it.

The climax of the *Wired* story was Notarbartolo's claim that the plot to rob the Diamond Center was really a conspiracy of Jewish diamantaires to rip off their insurance companies. Notarbartolo said that the safe deposit boxes the School of Turin broke into had been emptied in advance by diamantaires in on the plot. In Notarbartolo's version of events, the thieves themselves ended up getting scammed. It was a twist worthy of Hollywood.

In his telling, Notarbartolo had rented an office and a safe deposit box in the Diamond Center without any intention of robbing the place. It was only after he was an established tenant, he said, that he was approached in 2001 by a Jewish diamantaire (whom Notarbartolo refused to identify) about the feasibility of ripping off the Diamond Center's vault. For a fee paid by this man, Notarbartolo secretly photographed the vault, assessed the security, and concluded it was impossible to rob.

This mysterious financier disagreed and, just as in *Ocean's Eleven*, built a full-scale replica of the vault from Notarbartolo's photos. Once inside, *Wired* reported, "Notarbartolo felt like he had stepped into a movie." During this first visit inside the replica vault, the diamond dealer introduced Notarbartolo to three of his accomplices, all of whom happened to be Italian. The men were to rob the vault, then meet up with their backer at a rendezvous spot in Italy afterward.

In the context of the *Wired* article, Notarbartolo didn't name any of the men who were in on the plot, but referred to three of them as The Genius, The Monster, and Speedy. Considering the traits of the others arrested for the crime, these aliases clearly referred to D'Onorio, Finotto, and Tavano, respectively. To those familiar with the case, it was as if a fat man, a redhead, and a tall guy had been convicted of robbing the Diamond Center and Notarbartolo attempted to disguise their identities by calling them Chubby, Carrot Top, and Stretch.

There was another man involved whom Notarbartolo referred to as the King of Keys. Those familiar with the School of Turin knew that Aniello Fontanella's nickname was the Wizard with the Keys, and Giovanni Poliseri's were John the Tunisian and the King of Thieves. The character in Notarbartolo's tale was further described, in Davis's words, as an "older" man who "looked like somebody's grandfather," which was suggestive of Poliseri. Fontanella was in his mid-fifties at the time, the same general age as the rest of the School of Turin. Poliseri, on the other hand, was almost seventy at the time of the heist.

According to Notarbartolo's tale, the accomplices—who, with the exception of Speedy, Notarbartolo had supposedly never met before he was introduced to them in the replica vault—committed the robbery while he waited outside in a car all night. This contradicts evidence presented in court that showed Notarbartolo's phone was in use inside the Diamond Center on the night of the heist. Also, Notarbartolo claimed that "they worked in the dark" although the article did not explain why. But this detail is contradicted by the primary eyewitness: Jorge Dias De Sousa, the concierge who discovered the crime, reported to the diamond detectives that the lights were turned on in the vault and the foyer when he discovered the crime Monday morning. He confirmed that detail to the authors during a telephone interview.

Notarbartolo needed the vault to be dark for the crux of his tale to make any sense at all: he claimed that because of the darkness alleviated (solely when the thieves "turned on their flashlights only for split seconds—enough to position the drill over the next box" producing "muffled flashes"), they couldn't closely examine what they were stealing. The diamantaires kept their goods in "leather satchels," Notarbartolo said, so they stole those without bothering to look inside them. (The assertion that the vault was plunged into darkness the whole time also provides a reason for there to have been an expensive full-scale duplicate made of the vault, since the men would have needed to practice navigating it while blinded.)

Notarbartolo said it was only when he and the others opened the satchels back at the apartment, to find them empty, that they realized they'd been double-crossed by the Jewish diamantaire. Notarbartolo believed the diamantaire must have alerted his cohorts to empty their leather satchels of diamonds and then claim to have been robbed in order to collect an insurance payout, while still retaining their original goods.

Notarbartolo's scenario is unlikely at best. If, as he claimed, the School of Turin only made off with about 20 percent of the lowest estimated figure of what was stolen during the heist, this would mean that about fifty to sixty tenants had to be in on the plot. These tenants not only had to conspire together without anyone catching wind of it—or without getting cold feet or suffering a guilty conscience—but they had to be okay with exposing fellow tenants who weren't part of this criminal cabal to suffer huge losses. Heist victim Fay Vidal likened this suggestion to the conspiracy theory that Jews who worked in the World Trade Center stayed home on September 11, 2001, because they had foreknowledge of the terrorist attacks.

According to the story recounted to *Wired*, the mysterious financier never showed up at the appointed rendezvous back in Italy. As a result, Notarbartolo claimed, he and the others got off with "only" the $20 million in diamonds they'd gotten from those unlucky enough not to have been tipped off about the heist in advance, not the $100 million-plus reported in the press.

The story Notarbartolo told to *Wired* was remarkable, and it would have been even more so if it were true. However, mistakes, inconsistencies, and logical lapses throw the entire account into question. One contradiction is a scene at the beginning of the article that depicts a detective talking on his cell phone inside the vault, while part of Notarbartolo's tale depends upon the fact that there was no cell phone reception on the vault-level floor, let alone inside the vault itself. But other dubious assertions made the tale even less credible. For example, diamantaires don't usually keep their goods in leather satchels as Notarbartolo described. Diamonds are kept primarily in diamond papers and those packages are kept in whatever container is most handy at the moment, whether it's a $4,000 briefcase or a $1 piece of Tupperware. A simple glance at the crime scene photos—which depict dozens of bags, purses, and drawers scattered pell-mell on the floor—shows that diamantaires didn't care where they stored their diamonds as long as it was inside a safe deposit box. Moreover, if the thieves had taken a bunch of leather satchels, it's strange that these empty satchels were never found. None were recovered from the trash left in the Floordambos.

The chaos left on the floor, incidentally, also casts doubt on Notarbartolo's claim that the men worked in the dark and didn't bother opening their packages to discover there were no diamonds. Fay Vidal's own experience contradicts this part of Notarbartolo's story: when her box was looted, every item in a small package of trinkets was stolen with the exception of the one piece that could be traced back to her, a gold medallion engraved with the name of her daughter. Clearly, there was a selection process happening in the vault. "They did not take [that] because they couldn't do anything with it," Vidal said. "The rest of what was in the little bag they took. What they did was open everything and look inside and see what they wanted. What they wanted, what they could easily sell, they took."

In addition to numerous inconsistencies with known facts, there were also elaborately woven—and highly implausible—explanations for certain aspects of the crime that Notarbartolo seemed to have dreamed up purely with Hollywood in mind. For example, he told *Wired* that he rigged up a James Bond-style miniature video camera over the vault door to capture an image of the key stamp so the School of Turin's locksmiths could make a duplicate, as well as to record the combination as it was entered on the dial.

As detailed in an earlier chapter, the use of a video camera has never been ruled out, but Notarbartolo's explanation of how the thieves utilized a camera seems particularly far-fetched. The School of Turin's locksmiths would indeed have to be wizards to duplicate a three-dimensional double-bitted vault key based on a one-dimensional video still. In order to film the combination, the camera would have had to somehow overcome the considerable security precautions designed into the vault to prevent just that. Specifically, the dial was hooded so that the numbers could be viewed only through a small window covered by a magnifying lens, meaning they were only visible at a precise focal length. According to the article, Notarbartolo hid the camera "directly above [the concierge's] head." To see the numbers from that angle, the camera would have to have been capable of filming through the head of the concierge, which would have obscured the view as he bent over to view the numbers through the small window.

What made the claim about the video camera even more preposterous was the explanation of where its recording equipment was stored. "Nearby, in a storage room beside the vault, an ordinary-looking red fire extinguisher was strapped to the wall," the article read. "The extinguisher was fully functional, but a watertight compartment inside housed electronics that picked up and recorded the video signal."

In order to accomplish this, Notarbartolo would have not only had to rig a video camera over the door, while in full view of the foyer's CCTV surveillance camera, but he would also have had to sneak a "fully functional" fire extinguisher down to the vault level and place it in the adjacent storage room, which was locked, without anyone noticing. In order to watch the footage, he would have to sneak it out again. The fire extinguisher, incidentally, would have been clandestinely smuggled in and out of the same locked storage room that the thieves later had to break open with a crowbar.

Notarbartolo told *Wired* that when entering the building on the night of the heist, the thieves ignored the garage and instead used a ladder they'd stashed behind the Diamond Center to climb up to a second-story terrace on the back of the building. There, they used a full-sized "polyester shield" to approach and mask an infrared detector, then disabled a window alarm and crawled through the window in order to breach the building.

If this were true, it would mean the thieves either colluded with Jorge Dias De Sousa (the head concierge) or they were remarkably lucky not to encounter him, since the second story terrace on the back of the building is part of Jorge's private apartment. Jorge told police he'd returned from a night of visiting family while the heist was taking place. So, for Notarbartolo's story to be correct, Jorge would have had to return to his apartment and fail to notice a ladder leaning on the balcony, a polyester shield covering the IR detector, or the tampered window through which the thieves entered the building. He then would have had to have slept so soundly that he didn't hear three or four men burdened with a power inverter, an automotive battery, a bagful of drills and tools, a satchel of diamonds weighing at least forty pounds, another bag with more than thirty pounds of gold, and an untold volume of jingling gems and jewels as they nimbly—and apparently soundlessly— went out a window to Jorge's balcony and then escaped down a ladder.

This scenario also conveniently ignored that detectives found a homemade key amid the debris dumped in the Floordambos that only worked on one door: the door leading from the parking garage into the building via C Block.

Patrick Peys, after reading the *Wired* article, weighed the possibility that the infiltration of the Diamond Center could have happened as Notarbartolo said it did.

"What he says is theoretically possible," he began, going on to clarify, "I regard it the same as if he'd said 'we landed on the roof with a helicopter.' If you ask me if that's technically possible, I would say yes. Would they have done it? No. If you relate that part of his story to the rest of what he told, I would put it under the same name. And I name it bullshit."

Peys said "the biggest bullshit I've ever heard" was the claim of a double cross for the sake of running an insurance scam. "We know that very few victims were insured," he said. "Where is the scam?"

In fact, many of those who were robbed did not specify a loss on police reports—and therefore couldn't file an insurance claim—because they didn't know what was in their safe deposit boxes when the heist occurred.

Most in the Diamond District shared Peys's reaction, said the Antwerp World Diamond Centre's Philip Claes. When they heard about Notarbartolo's inside job conspiracy, people "laughed it off," he said.

"Everybody knew that it was nonsense, that it was just a story to get some media attention," Claes said. "But people were not very upset with it because everybody knows that it was so ridiculous. Some people were insulted, but generally people were thinking, 'Oh really, is that it? Poor guy.' Nobody is going to buy this. Everybody knows that it did not happen in this way."

Overall, Notarbartolo's story was a self-serving concoction in which he admitted guilt in only the most minimal way. Everything from the planning and the execution of the heist to the scale of the take and the mistakes that led to his capture was someone else's fault. As Peys said, "I really do understand his point of view because he wants to put the blame on everyone else."

◆ ◆ ◆

Notarbartolo's story only makes sense when one works backwards from what he would have wanted to accomplish with it. When he reached out to Davis and these authors in 2008, Notarbartolo may have known, or at least suspected, that he would qualify for early release in 2009. Belgian inmates rarely serve their entire sentences and Notarbartolo had already been imprisoned longer than the average convict, who, if he behaves well, can expect to be released after serving about a third of his sentence. Notarbartolo needed to spin his story into something that would make him money once he was released in early 2009.

Since he'd been convicted and incarcerated for the crime, it was pointless to claim he wasn't involved. But he needed to keep secret the involvement of anyone the police didn't already know and any elements of the heist that were not already documented. Based on his story, it was clear that he also didn't intend to take responsibility for any mistakes. In addition to blaming Tavano for the shoddy disposal of the trash, Notarbartolo said that his granddaughter had silenced his phone while playing with it. Therefore, he had no idea the Italian police raided his home in Trana while he was en route to Antwerp, otherwise he wouldn't have walked into the arms of the police by returning to the Diamond Center on the night he was arrested. However, this scenario ignores that Tonino Falleti successfully called Notarbartolo's cell phone that day for directions to the Charlottalei apartment.

Another important goal of the story was to minimize how much loot he'd gotten away with. The more money Notarbartolo was believed to have, the more of a target he would be both for the authorities and for other criminals looking to extort money from him.

Lastly—and perhaps most importantly to Notarbartolo—he needed to make the story exciting enough that Hollywood would be interested in it. Throwing in a double cross by a conniving diamantaire and a duplicate vault like in *Ocean's Eleven* would be just the trick. Despite his untold ill-gotten riches, he still had a desperate need for legitimate money so that he could openly spend it without attracting the attention of the authorities. The film world was just the ticket.

At least two of Notarbartolo's accomplices were upset that he implicated them in the crime by talking to *Wired*. Tavano sent a hand-written letter to the authors of this book from his Italian prison cell, in response to an inquiry seeking his comment about the portrayal of Speedy in *Wired*. He denied any involvement in the heist, and called Notarbartolo's version of events a "fairy tale" based on "lies" and "inventions."

Likewise, as for the evidence against him, D'Onorio claimed he was the victim of tragic coincidences. He said he met Notarbartolo at a security conference in Milan, at which point Notarbartolo asked him about installing a security camera system in his office at the Diamond Center. D'Onorio said he told Notarbartolo that he had a client in Brussels, so the side trip to Antwerp wouldn't be a problem. He visited the Diamond Center only to consult with Notarbartolo, he said. Regarding his DNA found on a piece of duct tape used to mask the security cameras in the vault, D'Onorio said he must have left a roll of tape in Notarbartolo's office during the consultation and that Notarbartolo later used the tape in the commission of the crime. In all, he said he was nothing more than a "scapegoat" because of his past troubles with Italian authorities.

D'Onorio was upset that he was identified as The Genius in the *Wired* article. D'Onorio benefited from early release and found himself back home in Latina by January 2009. Speaking with the authors by phone in late spring 2009, he said he was at first angry that Notarbartolo fingered him as The Genius. But that changed when he talked with Notarbartolo, who claimed that Davis, the reporter from *Wired*, was the one responsible for identifying him. D'Onorio claims that The Genius had never been found and is still on the loose.

Detectives and criminals weren't the only ones who were skeptical. A month after publishing Notarbartolo's account of the crime, *Wired* printed a letter to the editor that asked, "Who, exactly, is supposed to be fooled by this silly tale? You expect us to believe that . . . these same guys wouldn't realize that leather pouches supposedly full of diamonds are actually empty? It sounds like Notarbartolo used his time in jail to dream up the script for an *Ocean's Eleven* prequel. He must be hoping that George Clooney will play him."

The magazine printed a response that read, "*Wired* doesn't make this stuff up; we even employ a sizable crew of researchers to keep things truthy [*sic*]. Still, some of you found Joshua Davis' article hard to believe."

Among the ways *Wired* keeps its articles "truthy," according to Articles Editor Mark Robinson, is to verify quotes with sources. Robinson said the magazine's researchers verified with Notarbartolo that Davis had properly transcribed what Notarbartolo told him. And acknowledging the possibility that Notarbartolo was himself less than honest, Robinson points to the very end of the story, where Davis wonders if he was lied to.

"It's true that significant parts of the article do rely on Notarbartolo's version of events," Robinson wrote in an e-mail to the authors. "But as the article itself repeatedly reminds readers, Notarbartolo could have been lying." He later added, "Notarbartolo's claims were checked when it was possible to check them."

However, the article contains no quotes or statements casting doubt on Notarbartolo's claims from Peys, De Bruycker, or Denice Oliver (all of whom were quoted on other matters). The article also lacks other sources that could have raised legitimate questions as to the veracity of his tale. Anyone in the diamond business could have cast doubt on Notarbartolo's

Jewish conspiracy theory, if only they had been asked if it was common to keep diamonds in leather satchels. One doesn't have to be a storied crook (or a crook at all) to find it outlandish that a gang like the School of Turin would have spent so much time and effort to rob the Diamond Center without taking a few seconds to verify they were stealing diamonds and not empty bags.

Peys and De Bruycker were surprised by what they read in *Wired*. In an e-mail, Peys wrote, "From what we read, most of what [Notarbartolo] is stating is absolutely wrong."

De Bruycker said the diamond detectives have been trying to distance themselves from the article since it was published. "We participated in that thing, but we certainly take—how can I say?—distance from the theories that Joshua Davis makes about the interviews he did with Notarbartolo," De Bruycker said. "Certain theories that he makes in his article are things that don't come from us. That's his account."

On March 8, 2009, Notarbartolo was released from prison. Four days later, *Wired* posted its article online, before the magazine hit newsstands. A week later, Notarbartolo got the deal he'd been angling for: *Variety* reported on March 16 that film producer J. J. Abrams had bought the movie rights to Davis's article as part of Abrams's film deal with Paramount Pictures. Part of the deal Davis had arranged with Notarbartolo, according to *Hollywood Reporter*, was for Davis to obtain Notarbartolo's "life rights," which could be sold to a film studio, in exchange for telling his story.

Davis was named as an executive producer on the future film.

◆ ◆ ◆

By the summer of 2009, all of the men convicted in the "heist of the century" had benefitted from early release programs in the countries where they were held and were again free men. D'Onorio was released in January, Notarbartolo in March, and Finotto and Tavano in July. The last two had served their sentences in Italy, thanks to the work of their defense attorneys who successfully argued against their extradition to Belgium.

Notarbartolo served the most time of them all—just over six years. It was hardly a steep price to pay, considering that none of the diamonds had been recovered and it was assumed the men would return to their homes to enjoy a life of quiet luxury financed by the spoils of the diamond heist.

That may well have been the case had the Italian police not been so unwilling to let the case rest. On the afternoon of July 14, 2009, the police stopped and searched Notarbartolo's car in Milan. He was driving a brand new gray BMW 120 D five-door hatchback. It was a flashy car for a man newly released from prison, but, as with all of his other family property, the car was registered in his wife's name.

According to press reports, police claimed Notarbartolo was stopped because he was acting "suspicious." With him were a sixty-three-year-old man whom the police hadn't identified and that man's twenty-three-year-old son. All that was known at the time of this writing was that the older man was well known to the investigators in the Mobile Squadron and he was not one of the men convicted in the heist.

Of more interest to police than Notarbartolo's traveling companions was what authorities found stuffed between the sports car's seats: approximately a kilogram of rough and polished diamonds dispersed among twenty-one bags and one envelope. Notarbartolo claimed he bought the diamonds in London and that there were not gem quality diamonds, but cheap industrial diamonds. A few days later, he produced a receipt for their purchase showing that the diamonds had been bought on June 3, 2008 (while he was in prison), for €10,450 from a company called Profile Business Service Limited of London. Italian police believed the receipt was a fake.

The diamonds were confiscated and, once again, the Italian and Belgian police focused their attention on Leonardo Notarbartolo. Italian police e-mailed photos of the diamonds to the Belgian detectives. From the pictures, De Bruycker could see they were a mixture of rough and polished stones, but without analyzing them in a lab, it was impossible to tell whether they were connected to the heist. He immediately began making arrangements to fly to Italy to retrieve the diamonds for testing in Belgium, which required permission from the Italian courts. The detectives were elated at the prospect that the goods might be part of the loot that they had given up hope of recovering.

"We are, of course, very excited. Can you imagine?" De Bruycker said a few days after he'd received the news. "Of course, our task is to see if these diamonds originated from the theft in 2003."

The excitement soon turned to frustration, however. While it would take only a few hours for experts to compare the confiscated goods to the inventory of stolen stones, Italian bureaucracy soon proved as hard to cut through as the diamonds themselves. The detectives waited months for the Italians to permit them to take possession of the stones. As summer turned to autumn, still the diamonds remained unanalyzed. "It's too long, but it's not in our hands, it's not in our power. We're waiting for the permission to come," said Detective Kris De Bot in late September.

Even if the diamonds proved to be from the heist, Notarbartolo would be unlikely to face new charges unless the detectives could build a separate case against him.

"Leo cannot be condemned anymore for the same thing," De Bruycker said. "He was convicted for the theft, so [even if he were] to sell these diamonds, you cannot convict him anymore. Of course, we can confiscate [the diamonds] and maybe—maybe—there are possibilities for a new investigation in Italy on money laundering, but those are things that we have to discuss with the colleagues and the magistrates in Italy.

"You can't convict the thief for stealing something and then convict him again for selling it," De Bruycker said.

It's a different story for the two men who were in the car with Notarbartolo when the diamonds were discovered. Since they were not among those convicted of the heist, investigators might bring charges against them if they can show they received, trafficked, or dealt in any way with the stolen diamonds.

Of course, there was also the possibility that Notarbartolo was telling the truth, that these were low-value industrial diamonds having nothing to do with the Diamond Center heist. Once the diamond detectives have the stones, it will be easy for them to get an expert determination as to whether they are cheap industrials worth around €10,000 (as Notarbartolo claimed) or valuable stones worth a small fortune.

No matter how this situation played out, no one in the Diamond District expected it to lead to a full recovery of the stolen goods.

"Maybe it's the beginning of the recovery of some or all of the diamonds, but people here are very realistic," said Philip Claes of the AWDC. "They took so many things with them that people realize that it's almost impossible to recover everything."

Indeed, Claes said that rather than being hopeful that the discovery would lead to a positive conclusion, the general mood among the people in the Diamond District was one of anger. "The feeling here is that they got out very early," Claes said. "They've done their time and that's it. Now they can start spending money if they do it in a cautious way . . . That's frustrating. When you know what they took with them, they earned their money very fast.

"Maybe you can ask yourself, 'Is it all worthwhile?' when they are released so early," he said.

That may be a question the diamond detectives ponder after seeing the thieves they worked so hard to catch released from prison after just a handful of years, but for Notarbartolo, Finotto, Tavano, and D'Onorio, the answer is clear. The risk, the difficulty, and even their capture and incarceration for the largest diamond heist in history seems to have been well worth the price they paid.

They have the rest of their lives—and a fortune in stolen diamonds—to make up for lost time.

JOINT ACKNOWLEDGMENTS

This book has been a long time in the making and was reliant on the generous help of numerous people in several countries.

Our list of thanks must start with our literary agents, Scott Hoffman of Folio Literary Management and Ayesha Pande of Collins Literary Agency. Their hard work and dedication early in the process made this book possible. Everyone at the Union Square Press imprint of Sterling Publishing showed amazing dedication and support for the book at every step of the way. Editor Iris Blasi is deserving of special thanks for championing this book and working tirelessly to make it shine. Without her help, this would have been a lesser work. Thanks as well to production editor Mary Hern, copyeditor Jessie Leaman, designer Gavin Motnyk, and publicist Caroline Mann. Also, we'd like to thank Philip Turner for seeing the value in our project early on.

For help with understanding various Italian legal issues, we would like to thank Ciro Grandi of the University of Ferrara and Franco Impalà. Special thanks go to Valentina Zuccherino for help with Italian law and translation, but also with our research while in Turin.

We would like to thank several journalists, but none more so than Simon Surowicz, formerly of ABC's *Primetime Live*. Without his initial work on this story, it's safe to say that later reporters would have had a far more difficult, if not impossible, time locating sources and information. We would also like to thank Michael Freilich of *Joods Actueel*, filmmaker Todd Moss, Lodovico Poletto of *La Stampa*, and Jean-Charles Verwaest of *Het Nieuwsblad*.

Special thanks go to the members of diamond squad of the Belgian Federal Police of Antwerp and the Squadra Mobile of the Italian State Police in Turin. Also to Peter Kerkhof, Crime Scene Officer, Belgian Federal Police, Antwerp Forensics Lab.

In Antwerp, we would like to thank Lucien Cornelissens, the director of the Antwerpsche Diamantkring, for a tour of his bourse in February 2006; the staff of the Antwerp World Diamond Centre, especially Karin De Mulder for a tour of the Beurs voor Diamanthandel; and Jennie Baeten for a tour of the HRD laboratory. In addition, Philip Claes, Chief Officer of Corporate Affairs for the AWDC, was extremely helpful.

In Amsterdam, Barry Wels, Annet Crouwel, and Paul Crouwel shared their expertise in lock picking and safe cracking. Pieter De Vlaam, Manager of Testing and Certification of LIPS/Gunnebo, helped immensely with vault issues and LIPS history. Paul De Vos provided invaluable information about the Diamond Center's vault and was more than hospitable with his time. Thanks for the waffles and the wine, Paul.

For help with Antwerp and its rich diamond related history, thanks go to Vera Verschooren of Stad Antwerpen/Toerisme Antwerpen; Marteen Gillis and the Antwerp Diamond Museum; and the Stadsarchief of Stad Antwerpen.

Others who contributed valuable help include Johanna Bergman Lodin for research in Sierra Leone; Michael Maggiano and Jennifer Dawn Rogers for advice from Hollywood; Jo-Ann Garbutt; Antonino Falleti for tours of Turin and for introducing the authors to Punt e Mes and limoncello; Christophe Olsen for showing the authors around his Antwerp apartment, Leonardo Notarbartolo's former heist headquarters; Fay Vidal; Tyler Moore; Christoffer Jerkeby; Ben Theunis; David P. McGuinn of Safe Deposit Specialists; Dr. Emmanuel Fritsch, professor at the University of Nantes; Denice Oliver of Oliver Insurance Services; Lieve Peeters of Infinity Diamonds; David Horowitz of IDH Diamonds; Retired Brig. Gen. Carter W. Clark of Gemesis Corp.; August Van Camp for telling his tale yet again (thanks for the pumpkins, Gust); Stef Leunens of KBC Group NV; Carl Alberto Bettini, Antonia Bonito, Elisa Galuppi, Angela Pizzolla, and Monica Quarra for translation from Italian; Elke Van Rompuy and Leendert Trouw for translation from Flemish/Dutch; Bettina Wirbladh for translation from Portuguese; August Evans for translation from French.

Special thanks to Xennie Doolhof for her willingness to accompany the authors throughout Belgium providing translation services, and to researcher Julia Symmes Cobb for organizing and making sense of three years' worth of documents.

Thanks to our friends Johan Åkesson and Jakob Sönnerstedt for accommodations in Antwerp, as well as their willingness to teach the authors all about Belgian beer. In Turin, thanks go to Elisa Dal Bosco and the rest of the helpful staff of the Town House 70.

There are many others who assisted in valuable ways, but who preferred to remain anonymous. We thank them for their contributions.

Greg Campbell: I would like to thank Leonardo Notarbartolo for the gracious meeting while behind bars in Hasselt prison, and Julie Boost for not calling the police when I tested the CCTV surveillance in the Diamond Center by going to the vault level without permission. I cannot possibly thank my family enough for their love and support. My wife, Rebecca Campbell, and my son, Turner Campbell, kept me sane and grounded through many long weeks. I promise to take you guys next time I go to Italy. Thanks too to my parents for a lifetime of love and support, as well as to my close friends Chris Hondros and Joel Dyer for their advice and their enduring friendship. A special thanks is due the staff at the Bean Cycle in Fort Collins. Finally, I'd like to reiterate my thanks to my agent, Ayesha Pande, for pushing me to new heights and believing in my work. A writer couldn't ask for a better combination of coach, guru, and therapist, and I'm in her debt.

Scott Andrew Selby: I'd like to thank my family: my brother Todd; my parents Richard and Rikki; Maria Olga Garcia and her son Christopher; and my cousins Marc (and Vicky) Goldstone, Mitchell Goldstone, and Carl Berman.

My agent, Scott Hoffman of Folio Literary Agency, worked tirelessly to put together this book deal, and I will be forever grateful to him.

I'm indebted to the Raoul Wallenberg Center at Lund University, where I wrote my masters thesis on blood diamonds and man-made diamonds. I'd especially like to thank my thesis advisor, Professor Mpazi Sinjela.

I've been fortunate enough to have some amazing teachers over the years that I would like thank James Cerillo of Northfield Mount Hermon; Kathleen Moran of UC Berkeley; Stephen Sugarman of Boalt School of Law (UCB); and Daniel Meltzer, Frank Michelman, and Charles Nesson of Harvard Law.

I'd also like to thank my friends who've helped at some point with this project or with other projects of mine. These include Nicolette Amette, Phyllis Asher, Åsa Borgas, Mara Cates, Laura Dawson, Cori Dulmage, Janet Dreyer, Kristina Edman, Valgerður Eggertsdóttir, August Evans, Catherine Culvahouse Fox, Anna Gilbert, Heather Gordon, Grétar Halldór Gunnarsson, Jane Hait, Ashley Harder, Christina Holder, Kerstin Jonusas, Mandy Jonusas, David Kairis, Kate Klonick, Kate Lacey, Katherine Lampert,

Rachel McCullough-Sanden, Gabriel Meister, Annie O'Hare, Jessica Pilot, Annabel Raw, William Salzmann, Jeremy Sirota, Alfred "Dave" Steiner, Amber Sterling, Sara Turner, Miako Ushio, Nader Vossoughian, Evan Webb, and Abigail Wick.

Finally, thanks to the cafés where I've worked on this project over the years. In New York City: Blackbird Parlour, Café Gitane, El Beit, McNally Jackson Café, Marlow, Mud, Teany, Think Coffee, and Verb. In Orange County, California: Neighborhood Cup. In Malmö (Sweden): Glassfabriken and Café Simpan.

APPENDIX

Leonardo Notarbartolo

Ferdinando Finotto

Elio D'Ornio

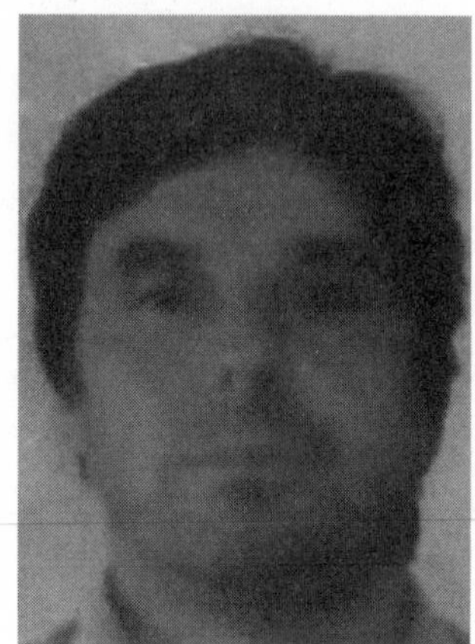

Pietro Tavano

The four members of The School of Turin who were convicted, jailed, and released for pulling off the heist of the century: **Leonardo Notarbartolo**, the charming inside man who for more than two years played the part of a mild-mannered Italian diamantaire; **Ferdinando Finotto**, the well-rounded master criminal whose failed 1997 bank robbery provided a template for the 2003 Diamond Center heist; **Elio D'Onorio**, the alarms specialist who most likely discovered the ingenious solutions to defeating the Diamond Center's most daunting security measures; and **Pietro Tavano**, Notarbartolo's longtime trusted friend who was later blamed for sending them all to prison.

Spett.le Damoro... ...
Via ...hupstraat 9/11
Anversa Belgio.
P.I. 07937530017 5°P.

COMMESSA DI LAVORO

n° 3	Telecamere B/N 220 VAC 0.13 Lux	306,00	
n° 3	Obiettivi 3.5-8 mm F1.4 DC IRIS	...50,00	
n° 3	Custodie complet... di staffa ... ...nonizzate	155,00	915,00
n° 2	Videocompressori 4 ingressi una uscita	813,00	..750,00
n° 1	Monitor 9 pollici B/N 800 linee	312,00	312,00
n° 1	Videoregistratore time lapse Sony	1625,00	1625,00
		Totale	5693,00
	Totale scontato del	20%	4554,40
n° 3	Contatti magnetici con doppio bilanciamento magnetico	158,00	474,00
		Sc. 30%	331,80
	Montaggio e collaudo del materiale sopraelencato, con l'esclusione dei cavi di cablaggio e il passaggio degli stessi fino al punto dell'installazione		1500,00
	Totale IVA esclusa		€ 6.386,20

Il prezzo è completo di montaggio e collaudo nel luogo sopra indicato

Distinti Saluti.

This tattered invoice from Elio D'Onorio, which gives an estimate on the cost of installing a video surveillance system at Leonardo Notarbartolo's front company, was pieced together by detectives after it was found with the heist garbage in the Floordambos. It was one of many clues that led to the identification of those who robbed the Diamond Center.

HISTORIC HEISTS

Putting together a list of the ten biggest heists turned out to be a much more complicated task than one would expect. The first issue that came up was deciding what constitutes a "heist."

We omitted any cases in which a government took money from its own bank, as happened before the fall of Nazi Germany or Iraq. The same rationale applies to corruption by a government leader such as former Philippines President Ferdinand Marcos and his wife Imelda. We also took out art heists, since values for stolen famous works do not reflect the actual market value of the stolen goods. For example, if someone stole the *Mona Lisa,* it could be valued at an astronomical figure, but no one would buy it for anything near what it's worth. Its real value would be what it could fetch on the black market, which would be very little, or in reward or in ransom.

The next issue was the amount stolen. Although news reports used specific figures for the amounts believed to have been taken, numerous problems often exist with such numbers. As we've seen with the Antwerp diamond heist, the amounts given are generally estimates and sometimes it's hard to put an exact number on the losses, such as with a safe deposit box job. Even when a single business, such as Harry Winston, was hit, the question arises whether the amount cited was the wholesale value or the retail value and how much the thieves could expect to make fencing such goods.

Another problem pertains to currency exchanges. For instance, the estimate given by police at the time of the Antwerp diamond heist was more than €100 million. A prosecutor later alleged it was closer to €400 million. We used the exchange values at the time of the heist, but that lowers the dollar amount of the Antwerp diamond heist versus the Harry Winston heist as the value of the euro against the dollar went up in the meantime, making the two amounts look much closer in dollars than they do in euros.

The Graff Diamonds heist happened after this chart had first been drawn up, knocking the Brink's-Mat heist from the "World's Ten Biggest Heists." Brink's-Mat was the theft of three tons of gold worth $37.5 million at the time. It took place on November 26, 1983, in London.

World's Ten Biggest Heists:

HAUL (Dollars)	TARGET	LOCATION	STOLE	DATE
1. $108–432 million	Diamond Center	Antwerp, BE	Diamonds	February 15–16, 2003
2. $105 million	Harry Winston	Paris, FR	Diamonds	December 4, 2008
3. $99 million	Armored Car at Airport	Amsterdam, NE	Diamonds	February 25, 2005
4. $92 million	Securitas Cash Depot	Tonbridge, UK	Cash	February 22, 2006
5. $70 million	Central Bank	Fortaleza, BR	Cash	August 6-8, 2005
6. $65 million	Knightsbridge Safe Deposit Centre	London, UK	Cash and Gems	July 12, 1987
7. $65 million	Graff Diamonds	London, UK	Diamonds	August 6, 2009
8. $50 million	Northern Bank	Belfast, N. Ir	Cash	December 20, 2004
9. $50 million	British Bank of the Middle East	Beirut, Lebanon	Cash	January 22, 1976
10. $45 million	Carlton Hotel	Cannes, FR	Diamonds	August 11, 1994

World's Five Biggest Jewel Heists:

HAUL (Dollars)	TARGET	LOCATION	STOLE	DATE
1. $108–432 million	Diamond Center	Antwerp, BE	Diamonds	February 15–16, 2003
2. $105 million	Harry Winston	Paris, FR	Diamonds	December 4, 2008
3. $99 million	Armored Car at Airport	Amsterdam, NE	Diamonds	February 25, 2005
4. $65 million	Knightsbridge Safe Deposit Centre	London, UK	Cash and Gems	July 12, 1987
5. $45 million	Carlton Hotel	Cannes, FR	Diamonds	August 11, 1994

Sources for amounts of heists:

1. Diamond Center: Three days after the heist was discovered, authorities released an estimate of at least €100 million. Given that it was a safe deposit robbery, an exact figure for the amount stolen was impossible to obtain. As the investigation proceeded, the estimate went up. During the trial, a prosecutor told the judges that he believed the amount stolen to be closer to €400 million. The exchange rate at the time of the heist, February 15, 2003, was 1 euro to 1.08 dollars. Some American news reports forgot to convert the figure at all, giving an erroneous number of $100 million. The euro has since gone up in value so if it were converted at the same time as, say, the 2008 Harry Winston heist, it would produce a much higher dollar figure. For instance, at the time of this writing, July 4, 2009, 1 euro was worth about 1.40 dollars, which would put the value of this heist at $140 million to $560 million. If this chart were in euros, it would be clearer that the Antwerp diamond heist was much bigger than the runner-up with €100–400 million versus €80 million for Harry Winston.

2. Harry Winston: News sources vary by a few million dollars on the amount; the euro amount given is 80 million. Doreen Carvajal, "The Heist at Harry's," *New York Times*, December 12, 2008.

3. Armored car at airport: This one is a near tie with the Securitas job at €75 million or £52 million. "Dutch Seek Clues to Jewel Heist," *BBC News*, February 26, 2005. Converting euros on the heist date at $1.3194 to the euro equals about $99 million. "Thieves Pull Big Diamond Heist in Holland," *MSNBC*, February 25, 2005. Oddly, in a UK version of this list, 3 and 4 would be reversed; as based on pounds, Securitas would be a bigger heist than this one.

4. Securitas Cash Depot: It was £53 million in pounds sterling of which £21 million has been recovered. Chris Summers, "What Happened to the Securitas Cash?" *BBC News*, January 28, 2008. In dollars, the total taken was $92 million. Sean Alfano, "3 Suspects Charged In $92M Heist," Associated Press, March 2, 2006.

5. Central Bank: One of the leaders of this heist was later kidnapped and despite payment of a large ransom, he was executed. "Suspect in Major Brazil Robbery Is Found Dead," Associated Press, October 22, 2005.

6. Knightsbridge Safe Deposit Centre: Estimates are always tricky with safe deposit boxes. Estimates went up from $32 million to $47 million ("Estimate of Big London Heist Rises," Associated Press, August 14, 1987) to $65 million ("Tariq Panja, "Photos of UK's Largest Cash Robbery," Associated Press, August 1, 2007).

7. Graff Diamonds: The same place was robbed for $37.8 million in 2003 and for $16.4 million in 2007. The most recent heist was captured on a cell phone video camera. Miguel Marquez and Ammu Kannampilly, "Record-Breaking Jewel Heist, Captured on Camera," *ABC News*, August 12, 2009.

8. Northern Bank: The robbers, believed to be IRA related, stole £26.5 million. However, $31 million worth of that was in new notes printed by the target bank, which promptly recalled all its new notes. This left around $19 million in currency that was not subject to this recall. Glenn Frankel, "Police Pin Bank Heist On IRA," *Washington Post*, January 8, 2005.

9. British Bank of the Middle East: Tied with the Northern Bank job, this heist is put just below it in the chart as estimates for it range from $20 million to $50 million. However, that is in 1976 dollars, so it would be worth much more today. This robbery, widely attributed to the PLO, occurred during the Lebanese civil war so there was no need for stealth and clever tricks, just military might. "British Bank of the Middle East—1976—Top 10 Heists," *Time*, December 8, 2008.

10. Carlton Hotel: Judy Ausuebel, "A Look at Some Major Jewel Heists," Associated Press, December 5, 2008.

SELECTED BIBLIOGRAPHY

Campbell, Greg. *Blood Diamonds: Tracing the Deadly Path of the World's Most Precious Stones*. New York: Basic Books, 2004.

Epstein, Edward Jay. *The Rise and Fall of Diamonds: The Shattering of a Brilliant Illusion*. New York: Simon & Schuster, 1982.

Farah, Douglas. *Blood from Stones: The Secret Financial Network of Terror.* New York: Broadway Books, 2004.

Fleming, Ian. *The Diamond Smugglers.* New York: Pan Books, 1960.

Harlow, George E. *The Nature of Diamonds.* Cambridge, UK: Cambridge University Press, 1997.

Hart, Matthew. *Diamond: The History of a Cold-Blooded Love Affair*. New York: Plume, 2002.

Hazen, Robert M. *The Diamond Makers.* Cambridge, UK: Cambridge University Press, rev. ed., 1999.

Kanfer, Stefan. *The Last Empire: De Beers, Diamonds, and the World.* New York: Farrar, Straus, and Giroux, 1995.

Meredith, Martin. *Diamonds, Gold, and War: The British, the Boers, and the Making of South Africa*. New York: PublicAffairs, 2008.

O'Donoghue, Michael, ed. *Gems, Sixth Edition.* Oxford: Butterworth-Heinemann, 2006.

Paterson, Vicky. *Diamonds.* London: Natural History Museum, 2005.

Roberts, Janine. *Glitter & Greed: The Secret World of the Diamond Cartel.* New York: The Disinformation Company Ltd., 2003.

Zoellner, Tom. *The Heartless Stone: A Journey through the World of Diamonds, Deceit, and Desire*. New York: Picador, 2007.

NOTES

("Interview with author" covers interviews that were conducted by Greg Campbell and/or Scott Andrew Selby.)

Epigraph

viii *"better to have old second-hand diamonds than none at all"*: Mark Twain, *Following the Equator: A Journey Around the World* chap. xxxiv, epigraph from Pudd'nhead Wilson's New Calendar. (Hartford, CT: The American Publishing Company, 1897).

Prologue

xiii *Ali Baba expected to find . . . he went:* Edward Forster, trans., "The History of Ali Baba, and of the Forty Robbers, Killed by One Slave," *The Arabian Nights*, 4th ed., (London: William Miller, 1815), 4:231.

xv *They had robbed:* We are using *rob* and *robbery* in the colloquial sense throughout this book to include theft and burglary. A legal definition of *robbery* requires two things that were absent in the Antwerp Diamond Heist: 1) that the property be taken from the person/immediate presence of someone, and 2) that this be done by force or fear. As for *burglary*, a traditional definition applies only to theft from a dwelling at night; statutes have expanded this definition to include other buildings at any time. The Diamond Center satisfies the old-fashioned definition's requirement that it be at night, but although the concierges lived in the building, the parts of the building the thieves trespassed through were not used for living quarters.

Chapter One: The Trojan Horse

1 *Money isn't everything. There's also diamonds*: Evan Esar, *20,000 Quips & Quotes*, (New York: Barnes & Noble, Inc., 1968), 218.

2 *some 200,000 carats . . . million*: Philip Claes. Quoted in *Mega Heist* (executive producer/head writer Todd Moss), which aired December 16, 2008, on the Investigation Discovery Channel.

6 *the Hoge Raad voor Diamant:* The name and structure of this organization has changed over the years. The HRD (aka the Diamond High Council) was founded in 1973 and disbanded in 2007. It was replaced with the Antwerp World Diamond Centre (AWDC), which took over representation for the Belgian diamond sector. The AWDC in turn became the primary shareholder in HRD Antwerp NV (also known as HRD Antwerp or just the HRD), which handles the commercial activities of the former HRD. These include five divisions: the Diamond Lab, formerly HRD Certificates; the Precious Stones Lab; Education, formerly the HRD Institute of Gemmology; HRD Research; and HRD Equipment, formerly Comdiam. "Official Launch of AWDC and HRD Antwerp NV Announced at Press Conference in Antwerp," press release, HRD/AWDC, Antwerp, Belgium, May 30, 2007.

8 *"Tight as a nun's ass"*: Philip Carlo, *The Ice Man: Confessions of a Mafia Contract Killer*, hardcover ed. (New York: St. Martin's Press, 2006), 313.

9 *in a small and dingy one-bedroom apartment:* The description of Notarbartolo's apartment on Charlottalei is based on a visit by the authors on September 25, 2008. It had a new tenant then, but the furniture was the same as it belonged to the landlord (the apartment came furnished).

13 *None of the gold was recovered:* Denice Oliver, interview with author, in her office, Antwerp, September 29, 2008.

Chapter Two: The School of Turin

21 *"This is the city of Turin . . . twentieth century"*: *The Italian Job*, directed by Peter Collinson, written by Troy Kennedy-Martin (1969).

24 *as high as $200,000:* Marlise Simons, "Milan and the Mafia: Who Has a Line on Whom?" *New York Times*, July 1, 1991.

25 *making* il pizzo *tax deductible:* Ibid.

26 *the AutoVox Melody stereo:* Massimo Numa, "Chi E' Il Ladro Considerato la Mente del Colpo Milionario," *La Stampa* (Turin), February 28, 2003.

26 *Wooden Head:* Jo-Ann Garbutt, "A Chronicle of Criminal Coincidences," unpublished manuscript, August 2008.

29 *using scientific methods . . . they track:* For instance, in 1985, the FBI developed a computerized system of tracking unsolved murder cases in the United States with the hope of comparing them with other homicides. Detectives enter specific information about a victim, a crime scene, even the weather, and the database (known as Vi-CAP) matches them to similarities in other crimes. That way, homicide investigators can look for patterns or connections that wouldn't have been otherwise obvious, in the hope that they will lead to a suspect.

30 *delivering paper for a local company:* Numa, "Chi E' Il Ladro Considerato la Mente Del Colpo Milionario."

30 *within the booklet was a set of rules:* This booklet was for a special category of criminals, similar to parole; they had to carry it around always, like an ID. In case they were stopped by the police, they had to show it to them. It's not used anymore. Rules in it included: find a job within a month, find your residence and let us know within a month where you live, never leave your residence without notice to the public authorities, live honestly, obey the laws, never give rise to suspicion, do not habitually associate with people who have received sentences or who are under security or safety measures, do not come home after 11:00 p.m., do not leave your house before 6:00 a.m. unless you have a documented emergency, do not detain or carry weapons, do not habitually attend wine bars, and do not attend any public meetings. Authors viewed Notarbartolo's red book in Turin, Italy, January 2009. The rules are paraphrased from a rough translation provided by Antonia Bonito, an interpreter for the Turin police.

31 *But in September 1990 . . . once the police arrived:* Numa, "Chi E' Il Ladro Considerato La Mente Del Colpo Milionario."

36 *open an account at KBC bank:* The heist attempt was at the bank's old location on Pelikaanstraat. KBC left this location in 2007 and later sold the building. Stef Leunens, press officer, KBC, confirmed details of this heist attempt, e-mail to author, December 16, 2008.

Chapter Three: Probing Missions

39 *"Maybe I am . . . its field":* Valerio Viccei, *Live by the Gun, Die by the Gun: The Beautiful Women, the Diamonds, the Ferraris—My Whole True Story at Last* (London: Blake Publishing, 2004), 323.

40 *the stark white foyer:* The author recreated this on October 1, 2008, by taking the elevator down to the vault level and walking up to the day gate, then taking the elevator back to the lobby and exiting the building.

41 *a copy of the building's blueprints:* The original blueprints could also be viewed by members of the public for free at the Antwerp City Archives, but since the blueprints were copied for him by the building's staff, Notarbartolo didn't need to go through the trouble. At the archives, patrons could take all the notes they wanted, and with Notarbartolo's talents for drawing he could have taken his time and reproduced the whole plan. While photographing was forbidden, it would not be hard to secretly snap photos of the plans. The authors examined the building's blueprints, including the vault floor, at the archives (Stadsarchief, Stad Antwerpen) on September 26, 2008.

42 *Her boss, Marcel Grünberger:* Marcel Grünberger's father, Samuel Grünberger, founded their diamond company. He also purchased the Diamond Center in the late 1960s; the two properties at 9 Schupstraat and 11 Schupstraat had already been combined into a single property (9–11 Schupstraat) forty years prior. Samuel Grünberger hired the architect Leon Fox to completely rebuild the property. The permit for this work was approved in April 1969, and the building was completed

by 1972. Blueprints and other documents at the Antwerp City Archives, Stadsarchief, Stad Antwerpen, on September 26, 2008. For this reason, the Diamond Center is also often referred to as the Grunberger Building.

Marcel Grünberger was born in Antwerp on April 28, 1936, according to a legal document filed with the Commercial Court of Antwerp on May 29, 2006, for the "Foundation Marcel Grünberger." He eventually took over the building and diamond business from his father. "Grunberger Precision-Cut Small Brilliant Diamonds," available online at http://www.grunbergerdiamonds.com/about/about-Flash.html (accessed October 2, 2009).

42 *focus on his diamond-trading business:* The family's diamond company, Grunberger Diamonds, had an office in the Diamond Center as well as one in Great Neck, New York, run by Marcel's son David. Marcel's other son, Simon, also a New Yorker, was listed as the treasurer of the Foundation Marcel Grünberger, which was formed in 2006. From a legal document filed with the Commercial Court of Antwerp on May 29, 2006, for the "Foundation Marcel Grünberger."

They had two other offices run by nonfamily members, in Vietnam and China. Vietnam was where they did the cutting, with 850 cutters as of 2005. They first used Thailand but moved to Vietnam as labor there was cheaper. Their focus was on small brilliant diamonds. Robert Weldon, "Tiny Treasures," *Professional Jeweler Magazine* (Philadelphia), March 2005.

42 *nosy superintendent:* Boost began her career in the Diamond Center at Grunberger Diamonds. There she worked as Marcel Grünberger's head administrator. She also came to handle matters related to the building itself and eventually took over as manager of the building. Her duties included dealing with tenants, such as Notarbartolo, as well as handling the hiring and firing of the building's staff. In addition to her boyfriend being on the payroll as concierge, her mother worked for Grünberger in the building. Fay Vidal, interview with author, Antwerp, September 28, 2008.

43 *The others were Boost and Grünberger:* Marcel Grünberger told the police after the heist that while he had at one time known the combination to the vault, he no longer remembered it. In that case, there would be three people left who knew the combination.

43 *while keeping the important part safely in his pocket:* This also provided additional security in that, if the key were used as intended, one would need to obtain two parts of the key from two different locations.

45 *they relied purely on technology for the building's security:* Jean-Charles Verwaest, *De Diamantroof van de Eeuw* (Antwerp: Standard Publishing, 2006), 159.

45 *what the video monitors showed him:* Ibid., 160.

46 *the Beurs voor Diamanthandel . . . What a visitor noticed:* Author's visit to the trading hall of the Beurs voor Diamanthandel (with an HRD guide) on September 29, 2008. The discussion of membership in the diamond bourses comes from this visit as well as a visit two and a half years prior by the author to the Antwerpsche Diamantkring bourse (with Lucien Cornelissens, the director of the bourse), February 2006.

46 *unfolded into the shape of a paper box:* These white tissue packets, known as diamond papers, were folded up and used to hold loose diamonds with a trader writing information about the stone on the paper's flap. Traditionally, these have three pieces of paper: an inner layer of very thin and smooth bluish glassine, a middle layer of white glassine, and an outside layer of bond paper. Another high-value substance that is often traded in glassine is heroin. Lincoln Anderson and David Spett, "Fatal Heroin Overdoses Claim Two Lives in One Week," *The Villager* (New York), July 26, 2006.

46 *ten single-carat brilliant-cut diamonds . . . $200,000 at retail:* This figure is based on a one-carat ideal-cut, D-color, and IF-clarity diamond for sale on bluenile.com for $20,077. (Stock number LD01477526, viewed on

July 9, 2009). A one-carat diamond with a signature ideal cut, a D color, and FL clarity would cost significantly more. Certain fancy diamonds, such as red, would be much more expensive.

47 *also his extended family's:* The importance of family members vouching was one of the main reasons for the prominence of religious Jews in the diamond trade and, later, for the rise of Jains from India. Both groups share key characteristics linked to success in the global diamond trade—they are members of a religious minority accustomed to having to depend on each other and in which large families with extended relations exist with members spread around the world.

Although competitive at times, Jews and Jains work closely together in Antwerp and without animosity. The Jains rose to prominence in recent decades with their access to the cheap labor available in India, specifically Surat, making it possible to profitably polish small stones that previously had little value. Dan Bilesky, "Indians Unseat Antwerp's Jews As the Biggest Diamond Traders," *Wall Street Journal*, May 27, 2003.

48 *to be settled in civil court:* Iris Kockelbergh, Eddy Vleeschdrager, and Jan Walgrave, *The Brilliant Story of Antwerp Diamonds* (Antwerp: Ortelius Books, 1992), 231.

49 *"I remember times when there was absolutely no security"*: Fay Vidal, interview with author, Antwerp, September 28, 2008.

49 *"You'd put . . . worth of diamonds"*: Ibid.

50 *member of another bourse. The World Federation of Diamond Bourses:* All four bourses in Antwerp are members of the World Federation of Diamond Bourses (WFDB). A member of a WFDB-affiliated bourse can trade in any other member bourse in the world.

51 *diamonds were paid for . . . usually American dollars*: This reliance on cash described here relates to the time period leading up to and

including when the Diamond Center heist took place. In 2004, the Belgian Anti-Money Laundering Law was amended to effectively end the use of cash in Belgium's diamond business. It stated that merchants could not settle in cash a sale of goods at a price for more than €15,000. As the Antwerp diamond trade runs on amounts much higher than this, the legal use of cash for diamantaires effectively ended. Cash has still had its place since then though, to keep on hand in case of emergencies, for minuscule transactions, and for transactions that have been, for whatever reason, not aboveboard. See, e.g., "Belgium: Report on the Observance of Standards and Codes," IMF Country Report No. 06/72, February 2006.

52 *in its private offices, which was expensive:* In addition, such alterations would be at the tenant's own expense; the landlord would not give any credit for such changes. This then tied tenants down to their rented offices because if they moved out of the building, they gave up all the money they had sunk into security, which could be very substantial. This reality may have created a perverse incentive for the Diamond Center's owner to allow its security to lapse to the degree that many of the tenants were forced to protect their own offices rather than put their faith in the protections offered by the building. The building benefited by the tenants' being locked into the place.

53 *a smash-and-grab in 2003:* The visiting exhibit was "Art Deco Diamond Jewelry 1920–39." Eight and a half months after the Diamond Center heist, these two robbers bought tickets and entered as normal visitors. Once inside, they used sledgehammers to bash open the display cases and take off with the goods within a matter of minutes. In 2004, police made arrests based on DNA evidence left behind at the scene. Paul Geitner, "Belgian Authorities Catch Two Suspects in Last Year's Diamond Museum Heist," Associated Press, August 16, 2004.

54 *When you stepped off the elevators:* The description of IDH Diamonds' office in the Diamond Center is based on a visit by author on October 1, 2008.

55 *"Belgium is great for beer, but not for anything else"*: Antonino Falleti, interview with author, Turin, September 19, 2008.

56 *Notarbartolo's house was nearly hidden:* The description of Notarbartolo's former house in Trana is based on a visit there by authors on September 18, 2008.

59 Sans armes, sans haine, et sans violence, . . . *"Without guns, without hatred, and without violence"*: Rene L. Maurice and Ken Follett, *Under the Streets of Nice: The Bank Heist of the Century* (New York: Knightsbridge Publishing, 1990), 21.

Chapter Four: Where the Diamonds Are

61 *"What do I know about diamonds? Don't they come from Antwerp?"*: This line is spoken by the character Turkish, played by Jason Statham. *Snatch*, written and directed by Guy Ritchie, (2000).

62 *as insurance investigator Denice Oliver tells the story:* Denice Oliver, interview with author, in her office, Antwerp, September, 29, 2008.

62 *with an Israeli named Amos Aviv:* A second Israeli and a Brazilian were also working with Aviv. "Part of Diamond Heist Returned," *The Victoria Advocate* (Victoria, Texas), February 4, 1995. The second Israeli was Alberto Shabao and the Brazilian was Baruch Torenheim.

62 *10.3 pounds of diamonds worth $4.7 million:* "Diamonds Returned from Antwerp Heist," *Akron Beacon Journal* (Ohio), February 5, 1995.

62 *the equivalent of half a million dollars:* Ibid.

63 *names of the accomplices from him:* This would not have happened in the United States where clergy members, including rabbis, generally have a privilege so their congregants can freely confess to them without fear that their religious advisor will be forced to reveal this confession to the police. This is known as the "clergy-penitent privilege" or the "clergy

testimonial privilege." Also note that the Belgian authorities appear to have pressured this rabbi into violating Jewish law, which holds that a rabbi in a situation such as this one should hand over the stolen goods but keep the confidence of those who have confessed to him as doing so does not place anyone else in danger. *See, e.g., Magen Avraham, Orach Chaim,* 156:2 and *Babylonian Talmud, Tractate Yoma,* 4b.

63 *"The rabbi was about to get his nails pulled out"*: Denice Oliver, interview with author, in her office, Antwerp, September, 29, 2008.

63 *diamonds are used to pay spies:* For example, Robert Hanssen, the FBI agent, was paid in part with diamonds by the Russians to give them information. "It was a further part of the conspiracy that defendant HANSSEN would and did ask the KGB/SVR for additional payment in the form of diamonds, and that the KGB/SVR would and did pay him in diamonds on several occasions." *USA v. Robert Philip Hanssen* Indictment, Count 1(b)19 (E.D. Va.), May 16, 2001.

64 *they were a threat to the reputation of the whole industry*: Members of the Antwerp diamond community were not just worried about the reputation of the diamond industry as a whole, but also of Antwerp's reputation as a safe, good place to deal diamonds. At the beginning of the twenty-first century, Antwerp was feeling its reputation as the center of the diamond world slip, as new markets such as Mumbai and Dubai courted diamond companies with lavish perks. Dubai even offered a fifty-year moratorium on taxes. "Antwerp's Pre-Eminence Threatened," *The Financial Express* (Delhi, India), April 3, 2005.

64 *Industry titan De Beers:* "De Beers" is often used in this book to refer to all of the De Beers Group's subsidiaries, affiliated companies, and prior incarnations. As such, this term sometimes encompasses De Beers Consolidated Mines, De Beers Mining Company Ltd., the Diamond Trading Company, the Central Selling Organization, De Beers Société Anonyme (DBsa), Namdeb, Element Six, Forevermark, Debswana, Diamdel, and the entire "Family of Companies."

64 *funding wars in Africa:* De Beers stopped buying diamonds from the open market in 1999. De Beers, *Report to Stakeholders 2005/6*, 47. Confirmed by Lynette Gould, Media Relations Manager, De Beers Group, e-mail to author, May 1, 2009.

64 *certified by the company to be conflict free:* Before this, De Beers sold diamonds not only from mines that it controlled, but also diamonds from mining companies that it had distribution deals with and diamonds that it bought on the open market through its Outside Buying Office. After this, it likely had conflict diamonds still in its stockpiles, but as the term had not yet been defined and agreed upon by international authorities at the time they were purchased, De Beers could claim with a straight face that the diamonds in its stockpile were conflict free no matter if they had blood on them. De Beers's managing director Gary Ralfe admitted the day before he retired that "I look back and think it is awful that we were buying diamonds that might have fueled conflict in the 1990s. It didn't seem wrong at the time but with hindsight it probably was wrong." Rebecca Bream and Nicol Degli Innocenti, "Diamond Profits Are Not Forever," *Financial Times* (London), February 27, 2006.

64 Washington Post *investigation in late 2001:* Douglas Farah, "Al Qaeda Cash Tied to Diamond Trade: Sale of Gems From Sierra Leone Rebels Raised Millions, Sources Say," *Washington Post*, November 2, 2001, A01. *See also* Douglas Farah, *Blood from Stones: The Secret Financial Network of Terror* (New York: Broadway Books, 2004).

66 *"Some of them wish we'd all drop dead":* Patrick Peys, interview with author, in his office, Antwerp, September 26, 2008.

66 *you cannot trace a diamond backward:* There are a few exceptions to this rule: if a thief does not have access to a polisher, then the diamond could be traced if it has a laser inscription or if a retail customer has used a service like Gemprint, which is a noninvasive diamond identification and registration system. Gemprint uses "low-powered laser to capture

the unique sparkle pattern of each diamond and registers this image in its database," according to their Web site. The problem would be that in either case someone would have to look it up and this would likely happen only if the police happened upon suspicious stones.

Another exception would be a highly unusual stone such as a large, fancy diamond with a rare color. A bit of polishing could do the trick with any but the most famous stone. A famous stone could require the thief to break it up into parts. For example, the Hope Diamond turned out to have been cut from the stolen French Blue.

66 *the hardest substance found in nature:* "In nature" is the key phrase here. Aggregated diamond nanorods, which are man-made, are harder. As this book was going to press, research came out that two natural substances, wurtzite BN and lonsdaleit, appear to be harder than diamonds as well. However, these substances are just simulations, as both are too rare in nature for this research to be tested at this time. Zicheng Pan et al., "Harder than Diamond: Superior Indentation Strength of Wurtzite BN and Lonsdaleite," *Physical Review Letters* (February 6, 2009), 102(5).

66 *almost a billion . . . 4.25 billion years:* "About Diamonds—The De Beers Group," available online at http://www.debeersgroup.com/en/About-diamonds/ (accessed October 2, 2009).

66 *Other carbon materials aren't nearly as strong:* In 1812, Friedrich Mohs came up with a scale of relative mineral hardness, so any minerals could be compared. If one mineral can scratch another, then it is higher on the scale. While one form of carbon, graphite, scores near the bottom of this scale, another form, diamond, scores a ten for most hard. Jessica Elzea Kogel, *Industrial Minerals & Rocks: Commodities, Markets, and Uses, 7th Edition,* (Littleton, Colorado: Society for Mining, Metallurgy, and Exploration, 2006), 508, 1175.

66 *be broken by another diamond:* Diamonds can still easily shatter or burn. They are not indestructible, just impossible to scratch or polish with any

natural material other than another diamond. It's important to remember that hardness is not the same as toughness; this is why diamond polishers can cleave a diamond but if they drop one, it could break into pieces.

67 *For thousands of years . . . source of diamonds:* Borneo also had a small number of diamonds, but there is no evidence that any of these stones ever reached Europe. George E. Harlow, ed., "Following the History of Diamonds," *The Nature of Diamonds* (Cambridge: Cambridge University Press, 1997), 139.

67 *geological debris of kimberlite:* The rest of the chapter talks primarily in terms of kimberlite pipes, as the vast majority of gem-quality diamonds originate from kimberlite. Lamproite pipes containing diamonds deemed worth mining commercially are found only at the Argyle Mine in Western Australia. The Crater of Diamonds State Park in Arkansas also has a lamproite source.

67 *not all kimberlite contains diamonds:* Around one out of two hundred kimberlite pipes contain gem-quality diamonds. Scientists have learned ways to determine which kimberlite pipes likely contain diamonds without having to mine the pipes, by focusing on certain indicator minerals that are known to accompany diamondiferous kimberlite pipes. *See, e.g.,* Matthew Hart, *Diamond: The History of a Cold-Blooded Love Affair* (New York: Plume, 2002).

67 *as far down as men can dig:* Diamonds contained beneath the surface in their original pipes are known as primary sources. The elements eroded away the above-surface parts of the ancient volcano so that what once was a mighty volcano could now be a flat field with its diamond pipes covered by surface dirt.

68 *80 percent of all diamonds pulled out of the ground: Microsoft Encarta Online Encyclopedia,* s.v. "Diamond, VI: Industrial Uses," available online at http://encarta.msn.com/encyclopedia_761557986_2/Diamond.html (accessed on July 29, 2009).

68 *a diamond-mining boom there:* In 1866, a fifteen-year-old Boer shepherd found a pretty yellow rock along the banks of the Orange River, and thought it would make a nice gift for his younger sister. The little girl didn't own it long; while she was playing with it in the street, it caught the eye of a passerby who thought it might be a diamond. The children's mother gave it to him and learned only later that it was a spectacular 21.25-carat yellow diamond; it was appropriately called the Eureka.

The stone, however, was dismissed as an oddity. Some even proposed that it had been carried from far away by ostriches. No one suspected that the South African soil was practically exploding with diamonds. A second find of nearly 9 carats generated some interest and prompted the discovery of other, smaller stones.

Three years later, they found a whopper, an 83.5-carat diamond the size of a lump of coal that was dubbed the Star of South Africa. That discovery opened the floodgates, as prospectors from around the world stampeded to stake their claims along the Orange and Vaal river valleys.

68 *the foundation of De Beers Mining Company:* Rhodes cofounded this with the lesser-known Charles Rudd. The name "De Beers" came from the farmers Johannes Nicholaas De Beer and Diederik Arnoldus De Beer, who used to own the land that was ground zero for the diamond rush. They sold their property early on for £6,300. Although they no longer had ownership of the land, one of the two main mines dug out of the property was named after them. The De Beers Company in turn took its name from this mine—these two Afrikaners had nothing to with the business itself. In 1888, De Beers Consolidated Mines Limited was formed when Rhodes and his main competitor, Barney Barnato, merged their interests. *See, e.g.* Martin Meredith, Diamonds, *Gold, and War: The British, the Boers, and the Making of South Africa*, (New York: PublicAffairs, 2008), and Stefan Kanfer, *The Last Empire: De Beers, Diamonds, and the World*, (New York: Farrar, Straus, and Giroux, 1995).

69 *almost three metric tons of diamonds:* This open-pit mine, known as "the Big Hole," had 2,722 kilograms of diamonds recovered by miners

using only picks and shovels, starting in 1871 with individual claims and ending in 1914 under the united control of De Beers. Twenty two and a half million metric tons of dirt and rocks were excavated in the process. "Welcome to the Big Hole, Kimberly," available online at http://www.thebighole.co.za/VisitorsCentre.htm (accessed October 2, 2009).

69 *from $14 to $3.75 by 1885:* Interestingly, as noted in the same article, "this fall in price is not only due to overproduction. It is estimated that 10 to 15 percent of the fall is due to the sale of stolen diamonds." "Diamonds in South Africa," *Manufacturer and Builder: A Practical Journal of Industrial Progress* no. 9 (September 1, 1885), 17:204.

69 *increase the price of diamonds by 50 percent:* Hart, *Diamond: The History of a Cold-Blooded Love Affair*, 46.

70 *most successful monopolies in the history of human commerce:* The history of De Beers can be broken down into four main periods. The first one was a true monopoly when the company controlled all of South Africa's production, and thus the vast majority of world diamond production. In its second stage it was a monopsony (single buyer) combined with a cartel structure. De Beers no longer controlled all of the world's major diamond mines; instead it set up exclusive deals with those who did. Such outsiders sold their rough to the Central Selling Office, which in turn carefully controlled the supply of stones to the cartel of major diamond polishers and traders who made up its Sightholders. The third stage involved a shift from deals with private companies to the equivalent of treaties with nations. For example, when the Soviet Union discovered diamonds in Eastern Siberia, the CSO had an agreement with them in place within a year of the start of their mining operations. The fourth stage began with the hiring of outside management consultants for the first time in the company's history. De Beers retained Bain & Co. to help them adjust to the new realities the company faced coming into the twenty-first century. De Beers is still a major player in the world diamond market and is making adjustments to its business practices—away from a "custodial" role to one of "preferred supplier."

As De Beers increasingly lost control of the world's diamond supply, it came to realize that its old ways of doing business no longer worked. Large quantities of diamonds now come out of areas beyond their direct control such as Australia, Canada, Siberia, and countries in Africa no longer beholden to them. Its own mines now produce only 40 percent of the world's rough diamonds by value, although through distribution deals the DTC "currently sorts and values about two-thirds of the world's annual supply of rough diamonds by value" according to their official Web site.

Even without outright agreements, other diamond producers may understand that their interests now dovetail with De Beers—to maintain a stable, high price for diamonds. As such, they would be foolish to flood the markets and watch their own product's value fall. It helps that only five diamond-mining companies control between 85 and 90 percent of the market, making this an oligopoly. These are Alrosa, BHP Billiton, De Beers, the Lev Leviev Group, and the Rio Tinto Group. Even with all the changes in the industry, the DTC still managed to raise prices twice in 2005—altogether increasing them 9.5 percent over the year before. "DTC Reports Sales of $6.54 Billion in 2005," *Israel Diamonds Magazine* (Ramat Gan, Israel), April 1, 2006.

70 *"I am [the] chairman . . . in the business"*: De Beers Chairman Nicky Oppenheimer's Speech at the Harvard Business School Global Alumni Conference, Capetown, South Africa, March 1999. De Beers later issued a disclaimer to accompany copies of this speech stating that it was "an off-the-record speech prepared for a closed audience of HBS alumni. Speaking as a private citizen, Mr. Oppenheimer made his opening remarks intentionally dramatic and provocative, as suitable for a keynote address. This speech should in no way be construed as an official statement of the De Beers Group." Debora L. Spar, "Forever: De Beers and U.S. Antitrust Law," *Managing International Trade and Investment*, (London: Imperial College Press, 2003), 220.

70 *market-driven supply-and-demand model:* After World War II, the U.S. Justice Department took a strong interest in De Beers's activities and their potential violations of our antitrust laws. The Justice Department

filed criminal indictments against De Beers in 1945, 1957, 1974, and 1994 for price-fixing and anti-competitive practices.

As a result, De Beers's executives avoided travel to the United States and did their business there indirectly. The company was careful to avoid having assets in the United States for the government to go after. These cases did not go anywhere until De Beers decided to change its business strategy. The issue was not whether the company was in violation of our antitrust laws—it clearly was—the problem was whether they were subject to the jurisdiction of the courts here. This came down to the question of whether De Beers did business in the United States as the legal system then understood it. Because of the company's careful dealings, it did not.

When De Beers came to understand that its custodial role, as it euphemistically referred to its control of the diamond market, had come to an end and it needed to change its business tactics, the growing strength of European antitrust enforcement may have had something to do with this. While De Beers was beyond the reach of U.S. law enforcement, it was vulnerable to the EC Competition Commissioner, Mario Monti, with his increasing aggressive enforcement of competition law. Reportedly, when the De Beers managing director entered the commissioner's office, Mr. Monti told him that "it was very wise of you to come and see me; it would have been a matter of a few months and we would have come to you!" Chaim Even-Zohar, "An Industry Facing Uncertainties," *IDEX Magazine*, no. 195, July 1, 2006.

In June 2004, the company pled guilty in the United States to the criminal price-fixing of industrial diamonds and paid a $10 million fine. In December of 2006, De Beers settled a major class-action lawsuit that had been filed against it on behalf of U.S. consumers, jewelry makers, and retailers who bought diamonds from the start of 1994 to the settlement date. The complaint alleged that the company had artificially boosted the price of diamonds through false advertising and restraint of trade though control of the supply of rough diamonds. The settlement did not come cheap, though: the price tag added up to $250 million—roughly twice the low-ball estimate of what the School of Turin had stolen from Antwerp three years before. De Beers also agreed to follow U.S. federal and state antitrust laws.

De Beers keeps settling cases. In 2006, it settled two more class action suits for an additional $45 million. Combined with an earlier settlement for an industrial diamonds case for $26 million and the $5 million it claimed for settlement costs, De Beers has recently spent $325 million to settle cases. As Andy Bone, De Beers's spokesperson, said in reference to the company's desire to negotiate settlements to its outstanding default judgments, "It is part of our general strategy to put all of these things behind us." Rob Bates, "De Beers Settles Some Suits, Still Has Others," *Jewelers Circular Keystone*, February 1, 2006.

Antitrust problems continued to plague the company though. In July 2005, a group of Antwerp diamond dealers, Belgium's Polished Diamond Dealers Association (BVGD), alleged that De Beers was still engaged in anti-competitive actions. They filed their complaint with the European Commission Competition Authority. Rosie Murray-West, "Diamond Dealers Attack De Beers' Supply Strategy," the Daily Telegraph (London), July 18, 2005.

The commission ruled against De Beers in an unrelated case, ordering De Beers to eventually stop buying rough diamonds from Alrosa, which controlled the Russian production of diamonds and was the biggest producer of diamonds after De Beers itself with a quarter of the world's output . This ruling though was overturned on appeal. Mike Gordon, "EU Diamond Ruling Rejected," *Wall Street Journal*, July 12, 2007.

70 *Oppenheimer's descendants still run De Beers:* De Beers went private in 2001 with ownership of De Beers Société Anonyme (DBsa), the holding company for the De Beers Group, divided into 45 percent for Anglo American, 40 percent for the Oppenheimers, and 15 percent for the government of the Republic of Botswana. "The Family of Companies—The De Beers Group," available online at http://www.debeersgroup.com/en/Inside-De-Beers/Family-of-Companies/ (accessed October 2, 2009). However, the Oppenheimers still own a significant number of shares in Anglo American, which was founded by Ernest Oppenheimer in 1917. Antony Sguazzin, "Oppenheimers Sell a Third of Stake in Anglo American," *Bloomberg*, November 10, 2006.

71 *rough diamonds in a vault in London:* This stockpile allowed De Beers to control the flow of diamonds of different kinds into the marketplace to prevent a collapse of prices. But more than that, by retaining a huge stockpile of rough diamonds, De Beers could potentially destroy any large mining companies that threatened its interests. Like a nuclear option, these diamonds sat in a vault and could be unleashed by De Beers to flood the market and depress diamond prices. De Beers could ride out this storm while its competitors would go out of business. This could even be done in a targeted strike, as only certain stones that resembled what a given mine produced could be released, thereby depressing the prices for that mine's output.

Rhodes actually used his stockpile early on to depress diamond prices and the shares of diamond mining companies. He then was able to gain control of Barnato's Kimberley Central Diamond Mining Company and through it, the Kimberley Central Mine.

De Beers sold its stockpile when it decided to give up its role as "market custodian." It was valued at $5.2 billion dollars in 1999; since then, De Beers has aimed to sell its diamonds on an intake only basis. Instead of stockpiling, it now cuts down on production. With diamond prices having fallen as much as 40 percent at the time of this writing, De Beers cut its first-quarter 2009 production by 91 percent to try to limit supply. Carli Lourens, "De Beers Diamond Production Plunges 91%, Anglo Says," *Bloomberg*, April 30, 2009.

71 *between one hundred and two hundred:* The DTC has drastically reduced the number of Sightholders in recent years: around 120 in 2003 went down to 84 in 2004. For 2008–2011, there are 79 Sightholders (including the four who only have access to the Botswana/Namibia Sights). Rob Bates, "De Beers Trims Sightholder List," *Jewelers Circular Keystone*, February 1, 2008.

It used to be that there was only one location for a Sight—London—but now there are additional Sights in Kimberley (South Africa), Gaborone (Botswana), and Windhoek (Namibia). The DTC divides its Sightholders into six categories: DTC UK Sightholders, DTC SA Sightholders, DTC Botswana Sightholders, Namibia DTC

Sightholders, DTC Canada Sightholders, and DTC Industrial Diamonds Sightholders. "Directory of Diamond Trading Company Sightholders," available online at http://www.dtcsightholderdirectory.com/Sightholder/Welcome.aspx (accessed October 2, 2009).

74 *$500 million to $700 million:* Philip Claes, interview with author, via telephone, April 10, 2009.

74 *Internal flaws usually dictate this:* The shape of the rough stone is another major factor, as a polisher wants to minimize how many carats he loses while retaining the largest polished diamonds possible. With a fancy stone, he would be even more loath to lose carats in cutting and polishing. How many gems are cut out of a rough stone and their shape can be a high-risk decision, especially for large, valuable stones. Dealers with such stones know that Antwerp is the leading place in the world for handling this.

75 *even for professionals:* Cubic zirconia is a cheap imitation of diamond; more expensive imitations, such as moissanite, are even harder to tell apart from a diamond. Man-made diamonds are impossible for a dealer to detect without machinery, as they are in fact diamonds, just ones with a different history and internal structure.

75 *a diamond's weight:* Technically this is a unit of mass. The full name of this measurement is the metric carat, which was set a century ago at 200 milligrams. Each carat is made up of 100 points, so for diamonds below a carat, the trade refers to how many points a stone has. One point then is 2 milligrams, and such small stones are called pointers; thus a 0.70-carat diamond would be a 70 pointer. Reaching a full carat is an important distinction; the difference between a one-carat diamond and a 97 pointer is much bigger than that between a one-carat diamond and a 1.03-carat one.

This measure was once based on the carob seed, not because carob seeds were standard in weight but because it was easy to remove outliers and thus roughly standardize the weight of these seeds. *See* Turnbull et al., "Seed Size Variability: From Carob to Carats," *Biology Letters*, (September 22, 2006): 2(3):397–400.

75 *in terms of value:* Fancy stones have a description of their color instead of the values used for white diamonds. While a yellowish hue is bad for a white diamond, a dark yellow color is valuable, as that makes it a fancy canary diamond. Different scales exist for fancy stones; there is not a single uniform standard as there is for white diamonds.

76 *judge a loose, polished diamond:* Certificates used by diamond traders, such as those of the HRD, do not state a monetary value or financial estimate of any sort. Instead, traders can use their own knowledge of the marketplace or consult the *Rapaport Diamond Report*. These certificates differ from the so-called "Appraisal Reports" or "Identification Reports" that some retailers provide to perspective clients. Think twice before trusting any document that places a monetary value on a stone someone is trying to sell to you. These often contain inflated values to create the illusion of a bargain. Plus, to add insult to injury, if you insure a diamond based on such a report, you will pay premiums based on this figure, but when it comes time to pay out on the stone, insurance companies will often cite a much lower number as the replacement value. Besides the inflated values, the actual grading done by labs used in appraisal reports may not be all that reliable, as *Dateline* NBC found out in a 2005 investigation called "Diamonds: Is There Such a Thing as 'A Deal'?"

76 *requested the certificate in the first place:* This person's name is not on the certificate nor available even if a member of the public calls up the HRD. Only law enforcement can request this name from the HRD, and then it may likely quickly lead to a dead end, as tracing the diamond's path takes a lot of luck in terms of each subsequent buyer recording the certificate number and who he in turn sells it to. Plus each buyer has to be willing to share that information with the police, who are not all that popular in the diamond world.

Chapter Five: The Plan

78 *"Obviously crime pays, or there'd be no crime"*: G. Gordon Liddy. Quoted in Ted Goodman, *The Forbes Book of Business Quotations: 10,000 Thoughts on the Business of Life*, (New York: Black Dog & Leventhal Publishers, 2007), 143.

82 *the garage doors operated. . . . electronics retailer:* Barry Wels, interview with author, Amsterdam, September 21, 2008.

84 *kill the power to the entire city:* "The pinch," as they call it, could not exist in the size and power they depict. It even violates a fundamental principle of physics. Ben Stein, "The Con-Artist Physics of *Ocean's Eleven*: Hit Movie Plays Fast and Loose with Nature's Laws," Inside Science News Service, January 8, 2002.

86 *"torch and drill resistant layers"*: Pieter De Vlaam, Manager of Testing and Certification of LIPS/Gunnebo, e-mail to author, May 2, 2009.

86 *Drilling even a small hole would take days:* More modern doors are equipped with a clever anti-drilling countermeasure; between the lock and the outer surface of the door is a glass plate. The glass is laced with wires connected to heavy steel tension rods called relockers. They're best described by imagining several pinball plungers that are drawn back and hooked into place, eternally waiting to be released so they can slam into the machine to set the pinball in motion. If a drill shatters the glass, it would release the wires and these rods would fire into their receiving holes and further bar the vault door. Not even the right combination would open the door then. The Diamond Center's LIPS door was too old for this better-mousetrap technology though. Paul De Vos, interview with author, in his home, Heist-op-den-Berg (Belgium), October 3, 2008.

86 *the vault was equipped with seismic alarms:* Patrick Peys and Jean-Charles Verwaest. Quoted in *Mega Heist*.

88 *the person who knew the vault door the best:* The material about Paul De Vos in this section comes from an interview with author, in his home, Heist-op-den-Berg (Belgium), October 3, 2008, as well as from numerous phone calls in April and May 2009.

Chapter Six: Safeguards

92 *Always keep in . . . the lock completely:* Mark McCloud, Gonzalez de Santos, *The Visual Guide to Lockpicking,* 3rd ed. (Champaign, IL: Standard Publications, 2007), 9.

92 *his involvement in a string of robberies:* "Otto Miliardi con 3 Soli Colpi," *Corriere della Sera* (Milan), September 26, 1992. The conversion rate around the time of this article was roughly 1,300 Italian lire to one U.S. dollar.

97 *The concierges kept the two pieces attached together in the lock box*: Patrick Peys, interview with author, in his office, Antwerp, September 23, 2008.

99 *only explanation for this security lapse . . . the outside*: "If the door contact was not installed with the vault door, it would have been much easier and less expensive to place the sensor on the outside. Putting this sensor inside would have required a penetration in a thick concrete or steel vault wall to run the security monitoring wire. Security sensors inside are usually wired and installed when the vaults are built." David P. McGuinn, Safe Deposit Specialists, via e-mail, May 16, 2009.

Chapter Seven: My Stolen Valentine

104 *No pressure, no diamonds:* This proverb is commonly attributed to Thomas Carlyle or to Mary Case, but it appears to be a proverb that was not created by either Carlyle or Case.

104 *Elio D'Onorio strode toward the Diamond Center*: The description of D'Onorio's activities in the Diamond Center on February 10, 2003, is based primarily on the following: The police deduced this from the

fact that (1) the CCTV videotape of that day was stolen as well as on the night of the heist, indicating that one of the thieves had been inside that day; (2) they found the work order (with D'Onorio's business card), leading them to believe it was D'Onorio who snuck in on that day; and (3) the work done to the magnetic alarm was time consuming, leading them to believe that that was the point of recon, to fix the magnetic alarm and place a video camera. Patrick Peys, interviews with author, in his office, Antwerp, September 23 and 26, 2008.

105 *the stairwell door into the vault foyer:* One person contacted for this book believed that the stairwell door on the vault level had a doorknob only on the foyer side, not on the stairwell side, in order to prevent people from using the stairs to get to the vault. Others couldn't recall if this was the case; the stairs weren't regularly used to get to the vault level. The authors could not independently determine whether the door could be opened from the stairwell at that time. If it's true that there was no doorknob on the stairwell side, it would not have been difficult for Notarbartolo to use tape to secure the latch so that the door could simply be pushed open from the stairwell side. Because the door was beyond the range of the video camera on that level, he would simply have needed to wait until there were no other tenants in the vault before making the modification. In investigators' minds, there is no question that the thieves used the stairs and not the elevator.

105 *dutifully recording the dark foyer:* This was another security flaw. The lights were off on the vault floor after hours, so even if someone was watching the monitors or video, unless the thieves turned on the lights before covering over the CCTV cameras he or she would see nothing but darkness.

107 *used heavy-duty double-sided tape:* The tape was still there along with the shortened bolts when the police examined the magnets after the heist was discovered.

109 *he went to the vault twice daily:* Since the video was stolen for that

Monday police don't know if Notarbartolo went to the vault that day, but they do have him on video going there twice a day that Tuesday, Wednesday, and Thursday. On Friday, he went three times. From the Court of Appeal of Antwerp judgment in this case on May 19, 2005.

109 *he removed an aerosol bottle . . . and sprayed the lens:* Police are split on their theories about this; a minority of them believe Notarbartolo wouldn't risk the spray being discovered and that the School of Turin waited until the heist was underway to mask the motion detector. Most of the police officers we spoke with believe that the more likely explanation is that he sprayed the lens before the heist.

110 *the early winter start to Friday prayers:* The Jewish Sabbath begins on Friday night, whenever the sun sets on that particular day. In winter, this takes place earlier in the day, meaning that the Diamond District empties out earlier on a Friday in winter than on one during the summer. On Friday, February 14, 2003, sunset was a few minutes before 6:00 p.m., although different groups calculate nightfall slightly differently. Candle-lighting time is generally eighteen minutes before sunset. That Friday, religious Jews lit candles at 5:37 p.m. according to Chabad's Web site. Various Jewish groups had candle-lighting times that varied from this by a small amount.

112 *through the tight aisles:* The description of the Brico in Mechelen is based on a visit by authors on October 3, 2008.

113 *the hand of a dead man was an invaluably lucky talisman*: The thought was that candles held in the hand of a dead man couldn't be seen. Havelock Ellis, *The Criminal*, 3rd ed. (London: Walter Scott, 1901), 184.

113–114 *a study of two hundred Italian murderers:* Ibid. at 185–187.

114 *known to snort cocaine:* Turin reporter Lodovico Poletto, who had covered crime for *La Stampa* newspaper since the late 1980s, said that using cocaine was a common practice among the city's thieves. It gave

them the illusion of invincibility. He was quick to add that there is no evidence this was the case with the men who robbed the Diamond Center in 2003. Lodovico Poletto, interview with author, in the *La Stampa* office, Turin, January 16, 2009.

According to Antonino Falleti, Notarbartolo was notoriously antidrug, and it's hard to imagine that he would tolerate the risk that his accomplices be caught and arrested with drugs after meticulously planning a heist like the one at the Diamond Center. Antonino Falleti, interviews with author, various locations in Turin, September 2008.

114 *they destroyed the phones:* An example of how disciplined thieves were about their phones can be found in a highway robbery that took place on the motorway between Turin and the Brenner Pass in 2005. About a dozen thieves assaulted two vans transporting cash from Italy to Austria. Investigators identified eleven telephones and corresponding numbers used by the thieves that were only used to call each other. Police put the numbers—both the phone numbers and the cell phones' unique serial numbers that were transmitted with each call—on an international watch list. For two years, there was nothing. But then one of the phones began making calls in Morocco. Investigators tracked down the phone's owner, and found a common merchant, not an elusive cell of Italian thieves. The merchant explained that he had bought the phone used in the market from a vendor who sold them by the tens of dozens. The criminal who used it as part of the heist probably donated it to a charity similar to the Salvation Army or Goodwill. As for the others, they may well have been thrown in a lake. Interview with confidential source, a member of Italian law enforcement with knowledge of this case, September 2008.

Chapter Eight: The Heist of the Century

115 *"Smash-and-grab job . . . than that": Ocean's Eleven,* directed by Steven Soderbergh, screenplay (based on the 1960 story) by Ted Griffin (2001).

115 *they couldn't identify:* Based on their later investigation, they came to believe that as many as eight or more people were involved in the overall

operation. Patrick Peys, interview with author, in his office, Antwerp, September 23, 2008.

115 *Pietro Tavano drove the thieves to the Diamond Center:* "The analysis of the phone calls shows Tavano was a phone user during the four crucial times of the theft and that he was in Belgium. It is also proved he left the Charlottalei apartment on February 15, 2003, at 11:47 p.m. to go to the Diamond District. That he undoubtedly provided for the transport to the Diamond Center, considering that his phone call to Notarbartolo was intercepted in Charlottalei on February 16, 2003, at 33 minutes past midnight, he was repeatedly in contact with Notarbartolo." From the Court of Appeal of Antwerp judgment in this case on May 19, 2005.

116 *three-quarters of a mile:* The drive from the apartment to the side entrance of the Diamond Center was shorter than the drive back owing to one-way streets. The drive there was a little over a half a mile, but the drive back was a bit under three-quarters of a mile. It was about a three-minute drive either way.

117 *to meet his brother-in-law for drinks on the plaza: According* to what he later told police, Jacques Plompteux left the Diamond Center through the garage at some point late on Saturday night to sneak off with his brother-in-law to have some beers at the Café Joseph on the plaza around the corner. He came and went through the C Block door for the same reason as the thieves: using his badge would have left a computerized trail, showing the building's management that he'd left his post.

117 *At 12:14 a.m.:* The exact times used in this chapter come from police reconstructions of mobile phone traffic/locations as reported in the Court of Appeal of Antwerp judgment in this case on May 19, 2005.

119 *"In my opinion there is no way that a camera":* Paul De Vos, interview with author, via telephone, April 26, 2009.

119 *suggested by insurance investigator Denice Oliver*: Denice Oliver, interview with author, in her office, Antwerp, September, 29, 2008.

120 *"the auto-scramble function is rarely used"*: Pieter De Vlaam, Manager of Testing and Certification of LIPS/Gunnebo, e-mail to author, January 31, 2009.

120 *another eureka moment when watching any hidden video*: According to this theory, after Notarbartolo rented a safe deposit box in the Diamond Center and got a feel for the security there, he planted a small video camera out of view of the CCTV cameras. It was aimed at the vault door, not in an attempt to read the actual combination but to record the concierges' actions when opening and closing the vault door. From this, the School of Turin could have learned that that the concierges did not enter the code to the combination, but kept that portion of the vault door unlocked. Notarbartolo would not have placed the camera there in the hopes of seeing something like this, but just to learn more about their procedures and to see if either concierge used a cheat sheet of any kind. The human element tends to be the weak link with a security setup such as this, and so it is the easiest thing to check first. According to police, one concierge had a cheat sheet, and it would have been easy for the thieves to steal it from him, copy it, and put it back. If the combination was not being used, then all the thieves had to do was plant a camera again before the heist to make sure that nothing had changed. This meant one less lock the School of Turin had to get around and it explains how they got around the combination lock without inside help or drilling, something that lock experts such as Paul De Vos still find to be the greatest mystery at the heart of this entire affair. Paul De Vos, interview with author, in his home, Heist-op-den-Berg (Belgium), October 3, 2008.

123 *"tampered with"*: Patrick Peys, interview with author, in his office, Antwerp, September 23, 2008.

123 *"We asked everybody . . . with any detector"*: Ibid.

125 *As they forced open each new box, the loot began to pile up:* The contents of the various described boxes come from the Court of Appeal of Antwerp judgment in this case on May 19, 2005.

127 *The thieves stole every carat:* While there were a few big diamond companies in the Diamond Center, most of the tenants were small businesses. Bigger companies preferred the more secure buildings in the area, or tended to keep their goods under their own security measures in their offices.

127 *brown cognacs to yellow canaries:* The more intense the color, the more value it adds to a stone. For instance, an intense green diamond would be worth much more than a comparable stone with a green hue to it. The stone with the green hue though would still be worth more than a comparable white diamond. While brown and yellow are the two most common colors, and as such are generally worth less than comparable white diamonds, diamonds come in a wide range of colors such as red, orange, green, blue, purple, black, gray, brown, and pink. More than three hundred different colors have been labeled thus far by the industry.

These colors are the result of imperfections in the stone itself—a perfect diamond is by definition colorless. The causes of such colors vary—blue is the result of boron contaminants; yellow, often nitrogen contaminants; red, structural defects; and green, radiation in Earth's crust. *See, e.g.*, Emmanuel Fritsch, "The Nature of Color in Diamonds," *The Nature of Diamonds* (edited by George Harlow).

127 *in their blister packs . . . proved authenticity:* In addition, it would have taken time to remove them all from blister packs. And this information helps establish the value of each diamond, so having it made things easier when the time came to split up the goods.

128 *the pulling tool wouldn't have worked at all:* Of course then Notarbartolo's own box would have been upgraded so he and his fellow thieves would have known about this problem. While their device would

no longer have been an option, perhaps they would have come up with some other solution to this barrier and still robbed the place.

129 *brooch depicting a bird in its nest made of gold and diamonds:* Such a piece would have been risky to sell as is. The safest course of action would be for the thieves, or whoever bought it off them, to remove the jewels and melt down the gold. This would result in a loss of value, as the whole was worth more than the sum of its parts, but it would no longer be recognizable. The tragedy of this is when treasured pieces of art, especially of historical importance, are destroyed in order to make their constituent parts unrecognizable.

130 *had been thoroughly cleaned:* As they knew going into the job that they would have to leave equipment behind, they should have brought with them something to destroy any trace of evidence that could have remained on their tools or been left during their time in the vault. For example, the thieves in a 2008 bank vault heist sprayed the vault with a fire extinguisher and plugged a sink to flood the place. David P. McGuinn, Safe Deposit, available online at http://www.sdspec.com/PDF/SDBM.pdf (accessed October 2, 2009).

130 *tapes that had recorded the happenings of February 10:* The tapes were organized and clearly labeled by date, so this was not as hard as it would have been if the Diamond Center had used another method for marking the tapes such as sequentially numbering them.

131 *outdated Belgian francs:* Although Belgian francs had stopped being legal tender about a year before the heist, they could still be exchanged at the Belgian National Bank for euros. The exchange rate was set in January 1, 1999, with one Belgian franc valued at €0.024789. There is no time limit for this exchange for banknotes in Belgium so although traders could no longer use this money for diamond transactions, there was no rush for them to exchange them for euros. Coins, though, became worthless at the start of 2005. "Opinion of the European Central Bank at the Request of the Nationale Bank van België," the European Central Bank, June 26, 2001.

132 *four or five hundredths of a carat:* They were four or five points, which means 0.04 or 0.05 carats. Stones so small would not be polished in Antwerp but in a country with very low labor costs such as India, Thailand, or Sri Lanka. Stones like that are worth about a dollar a carat, so 4 or 5 cents a stone. Lieve Peeters, the expert used by the court regarding these stones, interview with author, via telephone, February 1, 2008.

132 *"Even though this . . . small coins"*: Patrick Peys, interview with author, in his office, Antwerp, September 23, 2008.

Chapter Nine: One Man's Trash Is Another Man's Treasure

135 *"They always call it 'the crime of the century,' but it never is"*: Lodovico Poletto, interview with author, in the *La Stampa* office, Turin, January 16, 2009.

135 *"The lights were on . . . everything on the floor"*: Jorge Dias De Sousa, interview with author, via telephone, April 24, 2009.

136 *"People were making gestures . . . how it was possible"*: Philip Claes, interview with author, in his office at the AWDC, September 22, 2008.

137 *"Apparently, he had memory problems . . . like a headless chicken down there"*: Denice Oliver, interview with author, in her office, Antwerp, September 29, 2008.

137 *"Our dear Jorge . . . from the inspector"*: Fay Vidal, interview with author, Antwerp, September 28, 2008.

137 *"Not me . . . I don't know that"*: Jorge Dias De Sousa, interview with author, via telephone, April 24, 2009. Note that the other concierge, Jacques Plompteux, quit working at the Diamond Center shortly after the heist and couldn't be located by the authors.

138 *following his boss's orders to keep his mouth shut:* Denice Oliver, interview with author, in her office, Antwerp, September 29, 2008.

138 *they could tell from a glance that it was a professional job*: Patrick Peys, interview with author, in his office, Antwerp, September 26, 2008.

138 *Two forensic technicians:* The description of forensic collection in this chapter comes from author's April–June, 2009, e-mail correspondence with Peter Kerkhof, who was one of these technicians. He was a federal police officer, specialized in forensic investigations; in Belgium he is a member of the Technical and Scientific Police; in the United States, he could be called a crime scene investigator. The second forensic technician in the vault that day was his colleague Gerlinde Vermeiren.

139 *"We spoke about it . . . So we didn't"*: Patrick Peys, interview with author, in his office, Antwerp, September 23, 2008.

139 *"I can assure you . . . bar of gold"*: Ibid.

139 *"The landing was full of people . . . opened or not"*: Fay Vidal, interview with author, Antwerp, September 28, 2008.

139 *"decimated, destroyed"*: Ibid.

140 *"The floor was littered . . . floor as well"*: Ibid.

140 *"Everything in that building was just so lax"*: Denice Oliver, interview with author, in her office, Antwerp, September 29, 2008.

140 *De Vos explained that . . . he always averted his eyes:* The description of De Vos's activities the day the heist was discovered come from his own narration of these events to authors. De Vos was present when the combination was reset, as it had been his job to come in and reset the combination whenever a manager or concierge left the job. That way, only the owner, manager, and two concierges ever knew the code, and former employees did not. Paul De Vos, interview with author, in his home, Heist-op-den-Berg (Belgium), October 3, 2008.

141 *Once, he discovered a pile of dozens of old tires . . . a victim of foul play:* The description of Van Camp's activities surrounding his discovery of the trash in the Floordambos comes from his own narration of these events to the authors. The authors accompanied him on a guided tour of the dumpsite on October 3, 2008.

142 *turned on to a wooded road where a tongue of dirt emerged between the trees on the right and led into the cornfield:* At the time of the heist and its aftermath there was no gate between the dirt path and the paved road. There was only the gate inside the property between the cornfield and the woods. A locked gate was later installed here to protect the property. Ibid.

142 *decided to take a stroll into the forest:* Van Camp's cousin was with him that day, but he left before Van Camp contacted the police. August Van Camp's wife, Annie Lauwers, interview with author, via telephone, April 28, 2009.

144 *His wife, however, tells a slightly different story:* August Van Camp's wife, Annie Lauwers, interview with author, at her house, Vilvoorde (Belgium), October 3, 2008.

145 *"On every highway . . . collect it":* Patrick Peys, interview with author, in his office, Antwerp, September 23, 2008.

145 *Doing so would have risked drawing unwanted attention:* Peys explained that if the thieves set the garbage on fire "then police might cross the highway and ask 'what's burning.' Seen afterward they made an enormous mistake, but again it's partly coincidence and partly because there are no other options just to throw it away and get away. You could take it to Italy if you would have the nerves and, in Italy, I would imagine when you are at home you would know where to get rid of it . . . or even burn it in a quiet place where you wouldn't see anybody. They likely didn't have the nerve." Ibid.

145 *"We're talking about . . . by people"*: Ibid.

146 *"It was the day after . . . I assure you"*: Ibid.

146 *The bags contained . . . emerald pointers*: Ibid. Also, Peter Kerkhof, e-mail to author, April 20, 2009.

147 *more than €100 million to more than €400 million:* Belgian authorities announced the more-than-€100-million figure three days after the heist was discovered. Some American journalists forgot to convert this number into dollars, leading to them reporting a figure of $100 million. The €400-million figure is what the police believe and what one of the prosecutors told the court during the criminal case. Philip Claes also placed the amount stolen at €400 million in *Mega Heist.*

147 *"It was no good . . . trust anymore"*: Philip Claes, interview with author, in his office at the AWDC, September 22, 2008.

148 *"My colleagues started . . . to find"*: Patrick Peys, interview with author, in his office, Antwerp, September 23, 2008.

149 *"We saw that . . . hadn't been opened"*: Ibid.

150 *suspicion away from the staff*: The staff was eventually cleared of any involvement, although they would never live down many people's suspicions. Such suspicions lingered given that it was never known for sure how the thieves got past the combination lock on the sturdy LIPS vault door.

150 *empty of anything worthwhile:* One published account of the heist noted that there was a packet of diamond papers, a small black Samsonite case, and a yellow notepad in Notarbartolo's safe deposit box. Jean-Charles Verwaest, *De Diamantroof van de Eeuw*, 179.

151 *it would be very difficult to extradite:* At the time of the heist, the thieves were relatively safe from extradition as long as they stayed in Italy. All four known thieves were Italian citizens. Article 26 of the Italian Constitution did allow for extradition of citizens under certain circumstances. This was also set forth in article 697 et seq. of the Code of Criminal Procedure. However, as a practical matter, it would have been hard for Belgium to extradite them from Italy. The law later changed to make extradition easier with Italy's implementing the European Arrest Warrant (EAW) in 2005. This had to do with extradition between Italy and other European Union member states such as Belgium.

Chapter Ten: Been Caught Stealing

152 *"If you want to steal . . . be caught":* Keith B. Richburg, "Mobutu: a Rich Man in Poor Standing; As He Teeters in Zaire, Questions Mount Over His Wealth," *The Washington Post,* October 3, 1991. Mobutu was president of Zaire at the time of this quote, which is from a May 1976 statement he delivered to a conference of his ruling party. A fascinating book on the blatant kleptocracy that Mobutu ruled over is *In the Footsteps of Mr. Kurtz: Living on the Brink of Disaster in Mobutu's Congo* by Michela Wrong.

152 *they believe it was a villa:* Patrick Peys, interview with author, in his office, Antwerp, September 23, 2008.

154 *didn't even put Notarbartolo in the same league:* Lodovico Poletto, interview with author, in the *La Stampa* office, Turin, January 16, 2009.

154 *"He was a man with a dream":* Ibid.

155 *the caravan of police cars wound through:* Much of the information regarding the search of Notarbartolo's house in Trana is based on a series of interviews, both in person and via e-mail, with a confidential source, a member of Italian law enforcement who was present at both searches of this property.

155 *brothers opened the door without a fight:* Interview with confidential source, a member of Italian law enforcement with knowledge of this case, via e-mail, May 15, 2009. The source was present at both searches of Notarbartolo's house in Trana and was 100 percent certain that the door was not knocked down on either occasion. Instead, the police were let in.

158 *He'd made the trip from Haarlem in the Netherlands to Antwerp with time to spare:* The description of Falleti's activities the day he and Notarbartolo were arrested comes from his own narration of these events to the authors in a series of in-person interviews in Italy, the Netherlands, and Belgium in September 2008. Also of assistance in describing Falleti's point of view that day was "A Chronicle of Criminal Coincidences," an unpublished manuscript, dated August 2008, by Jo-Ann Garbutt, with whom Falleti cooperated to tell the story of his involvement in the case. Garbutt was Falleti's girlfriend after his divorce from Judith Zwiep. The diamond detectives also discussed what they knew of his activities that day and the Court of Appeal of Antwerp judgment in this case on May 19, 2005, contained some relevant details.

159 "*ridiculous*": Philip Claes, interview with author, in his office at the AWDC, September 22, 2008.

162 "*It doesn't happen . . . the permission*": Patrick Peys, interview with author, in his office, Antwerp, September 23, 2008.

162 "*The interview with . . . go first*": Kris De Bot, interview with author, via telephone, April 24, 2009.

163 "*We needed guys . . . it stops*": Patrick Peys, interview with author, in his office, Antwerp, September 23, 2008.

163 "*I'm not always . . . stalling him*": Ibid.

164 "*ten seconds*": Kris De Bot, interview with author, via telephone, April 24, 2009.

164 *"Notarbartolo, because he's . . . burned his last bridge"*: Patrick Peys, interview with author, in his office, Antwerp, September 23, 2008.

165 *took the elevator to the -1 parking level:* While Notarbartolo had intended to be in and out before closing time, Boost's delay combined with the police questioning resulted in his still being in the building after closing time. Normally the front entrance would be locked and the gate pulled down sharp at 7:00 p.m., so Vidal had no way of knowing that had been delayed, and she headed to the only exit normally open at that time, the garage. Fay Vidal, interview with author, Antwerp, September 28, 2008.

165 *"That's not one . . . leave that building"*: Fay Vidal, interview with author, Antwerp, September 28, 2008.

165 *"I see a man standing . . . 'What do you want?' "*: Ibid.

165 *"absolutely nobody"*: Ibid.

166 *He drank a shot of grappa:* Also, the police found a shot glass and grappa bottle in the sink at the apartment, both with Falleti's fingerprints on them. Garbutt, "A Chronicle of Criminal Coincidences."

167 *"He was very confused . . . looking for him"*: Kris De Bot, interview with author, via telephone, April 24, 2009.

168 *"He was very afraid . . . the authorities"*: Ibid.

169 *While his sister was getting the warrant:* Interestingly enough, Kris De Bot didn't know until later that it was his sister who was getting the warrant for him. Earlier that same day, during his drive with Notarbartolo from the apartment to the police office, he'd seen his dad. "My father was driving his car, but he didn't see me. It's unbelievable. It can't be true, it's a joke, but it really happened." Ibid.

170 *"The time was very short . . . the car downstairs"*: Ibid.

170 *The handwritten search warrant . . . at 8:58 p.m.*: Patrick Peys, interview with author, in his office, Antwerp, September 23, 2008.

Chapter Eleven: Checkmate

171 *"Whether we fall . . . own dust"*: *The Duchess of Malfi*, act 5, scene 5. These are the final words of Duke Ferdinand before he dies. It is not known for certain if this play was written in 1613 or 1614.

171 *Notarbartolo continued playing the part*: The description of Peys's interrogation of Notarbartolo comes from Peys's own narration of this event to authors over the course of two interviews in his office in September 2008 as well as in follow-up phone calls and e-mails.

171–172 *"I first treated him . . . [the heist]"*: Patrick Peys, interview with author, in his office, Antwerp, September 23, 2008.

172 *"He [said he] had . . . perfectly empty"*: Ibid.

172 *Notarbartolo didn't have the keys . . . found those in his apartment*: Ibid.

173 *this was no alibi at all*: It would have been much harder for Notarbartolo to manufacture an alibi in Antwerp than it would have been for him back in Turin. In Antwerp, Notarbartolo lacked the friends, family, criminal connections, and various local ties that could have enabled him to create a decent alibi.

173 *"As a policeman . . . with the right guy"*: Patrick Peys, interview with author, in his office, Antwerp, September 23, 2008.

173 *"Look, what do you think . . . Who is he"*: Ibid.

173 *"He didn't move . . . so unreal"*: Ibid.

173– 174 *"We were absolutely . . . I didn't know"*: Ibid.

174 *"He said very politely . . . case with us"*: Ibid.

174 *Investigators had more luck talking to Falleti*: The descriptions of Falleti's interrogations by the police and time in prison come from his own series of in-person interviews with authors in Italy, the Netherlands, and Belgium in September 2008. Also of assistance was "A Chronicle of Criminal Coincidences" by Jo-Ann Garbutt. Falleti confirmed the accuracy of Garbutt's account to the authors. Additionally, court documents detailed the results of his interrogations, and the Belgian police confirmed details of their interactions with Mr. Falleti.

174 *inspection back at the forensics lab*: The crime scene officers took the rug back to the Antwerp forensics lab, where they used a "vacuum cleaner . . . [the kind] you can buy at any mall; the filters used, however, are produced by the National Institute for Criminalistics in Brussels . . . The vacuum cleaner uses no bag but instead filters, which are put on top of the flexible hose, just behind the nozzle. These filters collect all kinds of small particles. Immediately after using one of those filters, they are sealed with a top layer, packed in paper bags, labeled, confiscated, and sent to Brussels (National Institute)." Peter Kerkhof, e-mail to author, April 20, 2009.

175 *"very small 'glass fragments' . . . possible emeralds"*: Peter Kerkhof, e-mail to author, June 25, 2009.

175 *"Everything went so fast . . . everything downstairs"*: Jean-Charles Verwaest and MVDB, "DNA-Onderzoek in Diamantroof," *Het Nieuwsblad* (Belgium), March 1, 2003.

176 *Falleti said he had been at a friend's birthday party . . . home that night*: Falleti's later explanation for this discrepancy was that his wife had forgotten about his going to the birthday party as she had not gone with him but had instead stayed home that night. Garbutt, "A Chronicle of Criminal Coincidences."

176 *Falleti later described the subterranean holding cell:* Ibid.

177 *She said she was afraid . . . removed from the apartment*: From the Court of Appeal of Antwerp judgment in this case on May 19, 2005.

177 *As viewed from the street:* Visit to the Prison of Antwerp by authors, October 3, 2008.

178 *Notarbartolo did catch Falleti's eye . . . an apologetic shrug:* Garbutt, "A Chronicle of Criminal Coincidences."

179 *"being held on suspicion of being co-authors in the theft"*: Andrew Osborn, "Four Held For Record Antwerp Gem Theft," *The Guardian* (London), February 26, 2003.

180 *a brilliant-cut . . . weighing 0.70476 carats:* The HRD issued its grading report for this stone on February 18, 2002.

180 *They were like disciplined soldiers . . . to the consequences:* As it turned out, there were no consequences. Years later, police in both countries were able to laugh at the brothers' unshakable composure in the face of potentially dire repercussions. Italy is not like the United States, where most police interrogators control their anger and avoid punching out their suspects if only for fear of a police brutality accusation. Italians are famously hot blooded, and that goes for the police as well, who sometimes don't restrain themselves. One investigator told the authors that Marco Notarbartolo "wasn't beaten" for violating the binding order to safeguard the safe contents, as if to demonstrate that interrogators were exceedingly patient with him. Perhaps they could tell from his stoicism that it would have been a waste of energy. In the end, Marco Notarbartolo wasn't even charged for failing to abide by the order. Interview with confidential source, a member of Italian law enforcement with knowledge of this case, September 2008.

181 *From the wiretap inside . . . 1997 bank job in Antwerp:* Giorgio Ballario, "Il Furto Del Secolo Al Diamond Center," *La Stampa* (Turin), March 29, 2003.

181 *Both men denied their involvement . . . their innocence*: In the order to arrest Fontanella and Spurgo, the Attorney General wrote: "Fontanella and others are enthusiastic and dedicated to the daily planning of crimes against property . . . the business [Personal Chiavi] serves only as a place of meeting to plan crimes." Information sheet provided by a source in Italian law enforcement.

181 *he had been in jail . . . Turinese jewelry store:* Giorgio Ballario, "Giovanni Spurgo con Altri Due Complici Era Inserito nell'Elenco dei Sospetti del 'Colpo del Secolo' di Anversa," *La Stampa* (Turin), May 10, 2003.

181 *Giovanni Poliseri . . . a cream or a gel*: Also, Poliseri and Scelza were believed to own a house in Germany; Belgian detectives would discover through cell phone records that some of the thieves involved in the diamond heist returned to Italy though Germany. Both Poliseri and Scelza denied so much as knowing Notarbartolo. Massimo Numa, "I Due Rapinatori Arrestati l'Altro Giorno in Una Gioielleria Belga Erano nella Lista dei Sospettati per il Colpo al Diamond Centre," *La Stampa* (Turin), May 7, 2003.

181 *But just two months later . . . outside of Antwerp:* Ibid.

182 *Falleti later laughed about . . . overlooked it entirely:* Antonino Falleti, interviews with author, various locations in Turin, September 2008.

183 *Detectives kept him under surveillance . . . for DNA analysis:* Information obtained from an Italian law enforcement official with close knowledge of the case who requested anonymity. September 2008.

184 *cagily pocketing the butts . . . wouldn't leave DNA behind:* Ibid.

184 *There were seven "entities," . . . closed network:* Peys used the term *entities* to differentiate from *people* because he said there could have been as many as eight perpetrators involved in the heist. Patrick Peys, interview with author, in his office, Antwerp, September 23, 2008.

185 *Using this triangulation technique . . . until 4:44 a.m.:* From the Court of Appeal of Antwerp judgment in this case on May 19, 2005.

185 *The calls were placed to Tavano's prepaid cell . . . Charlottalei apartment:* Ibid.

185 *Whoever left Belgium from Brussels . . . for his getaway:* If one or more people did fly somewhere other than to Italy from Brussels, it was not any of the suspects whose names the detectives did have. They ran those and found no hits for them anywhere. Patrick Peys, interview with author, in his office, Antwerp, September 23, 2008.

186 A *gem expert in Valenza:* This expert was Dr. Carlo Cumo. From the Court of Appeal of Antwerp judgment in this case on May 19, 2005.

186 A *gemologist in Antwerp . . . the heist trash:* Lieve Peeters of Infinity Diamonds identified these as small cheap emeralds in a marquise shape. The diamond detectives gave her a green stone found in the apartment and one found at the Floordambos dumpsite and asked her for a written report on these two stones. To the untrained eye, they could have appeared to be small green diamonds. Lieve Peeters, interview with author, via telephone, February 1, 2009.

187 *at the time of the robbery . . . busy at his job:* The birthday party that Falleti had told police he went to, and his wife had not mentioned, was not his alibi but an accounting of where he was the night after the heist.

187 *The nature of the heist . . . heard minor criminal matters:* We have used the French names here as the system is based on a French one. Names of government institutions such as the courts in Belgium tend to exist in

sets of two, one in Flemish and one in French. The courts in Antwerp used Flemish though, and so people there would have referred to them by their Flemish names, not the French ones used here.

188 De Standaard *newspaper reporter . . . address its flaws:* Jean-Charles Verwaest, *De Diamantroof van de Eeuw*, 232.

188 *the time Notarbartolo punched an inmate:* Garbutt, "A Chronicle of Criminal Coincidences."

188–189 *Notarbartolo apologized for the mess he'd gotten his friend into:* Ibid.

189 DNA *tests showed no connection:* The Belgian police had also sent Falleti's and Zwiep's DNA to British police to test against evidence from a jewel heist there. The results were negative. Patrick Peys, interview with author, in his office, Antwerp, September 23, 2008.

190 *"This uncertainty is killing us . . . by pure coincidence":* Jan Heuvelmans, "Parket-generaal Wil Plots Geen Verwijzing Meer voor Zwiep," PagiA (a small press bureau for legal news in Antwerp), November 15, 2004.

Chapter Twelve: The Trial

192 *"Any time you . . . a million dollar job": The Killing*, directed by Stanley Kubrick, written by Stanley Kubrick, Jim Thompson, and Lionel White (1956).

192 *"the Man of Gold":* Giorgio Ballario, "Il Furto del Secolo al Diamond Center," *La Stampa* (Turin), March 29, 2003.

192 *another called the decision . . . "beginners":* Maria Maggiore and Lodovico Poletto, "Nel 2001 Notarbartolo Aveva Preso in Affitto i Locali Dentro il Palazzo dei Diamanti di Anversa," *La Stampa* (Turin), February 28, 2003.

192 *A third wrote . . . Merry Men:* Massimo Numa, "I Due Rapinatori Arrestati l'Altro Giorno in Una Gioielleria Belga Erano nella Lista dei Sospettati per il Colpo al Diamond Centre," *La Stampa* (Turin), May 7, 2003.

192 *belonging to the Mafia:* Jean-Charles Verwaest, "Recordbuit van 100 Miljoen Euro Bij Diamantroof," *De Standaard* (Antwerp), February 28, 2003.

192 *describing Notarbartolo not only . . . a drug dealer: De Standaard* newspaper's characterization of Notarbartolo as Mafioso was refuted by Notarbartolo's lawyers and also, strangely enough, by *La Stampa*. Almost as if to set the record straight and defend Turin's honor, the Italian paper wrote in response to Belgian press accounts that the School of Turin was nonviolent and not involved in organized crime. But in fact, Notarbartolo has relatives in the Sicilian Mafia. Mafia involvement in the heist, while not considered likely by investigators, has never been entirely ruled out. Jean-Charles Verwaest, "Italiaanse Maffia Bereidde Kraak Twee Jaar Lang Voor," *De Standaard* (Antwerp), February 28, 2003.

193 *"Nobody left Antwerp . . . a great job"*: Philip Claes, interview with author, in his office at the AWDC, September 22, 2008.

193 *"kicked out of many buildings":* Simon Surowicz, interview with author, via telephone, April 23, 2009. The description of Surowicz's activities in this section comes from multiple telephone and e-mail interviews between him and the author in 2009.

193 *they were directly ordered by their supervisors:* Patrick Peys, interview with author, in his office, Antwerp, September 26, 2008.

194 *"I went to the place . . . I know of":* Simon Surowicz, interview with author, via telephone, April 23, 2009.

194 *The hour-long show aired almost exactly a year after the heist: Primetime Live*, "The Great Diamond Heist," ABC, February 12, 2004.

194 *compared the perpetrators to . . .* Ocean's Eleven: Correspondent Jay Schadler made the comparison to *Ocean's Eleven* three different times during the program. Ibid.

195 *after he'd been imprisoned for nearly six months:* The timing was not a coincidence; in Belgium, six months is the limit that the government can imprison someone without a certain amount of evidence.

195 *mid-September 2004 when . . . to continue the case:* "Zes van Zeven Verdachten Antwerpse Diamantroof Naar Rechtbank," *Gazet van Antwerpen* (Antwerp), September 21, 2004.

195 *"absolutely no reason . . . these proceedings"*: "Parket Succesol in Beroep Tegen Voorlopige Vrijlating Notarbartolo," *Gazet van Antwerpen* (Antwerp), November 16, 2004.

197 *There was nothing comparable in U.S. criminal law:* A court of final instance, such as the Supreme Court of the United States for federal cases, exists for a possibility of a further appeal, although the chances of a case being heard may be slim. Criminal cases are heard at a trial level first, then can go to a court of appeals, and a court of final instance may or may not agree to hear a final appeal. However, there are very unusual circumstances in which civil cases could be heard for the first instance at a non-trial court level. For example, under section 2 of Article 3 of the Constitution, the U.S. Supreme Court has original jurisdiction for cases involving diplomats and states. It is extremely unusual that the Court avails itself of this power and holds an actual trial.

197 *"It's a kind of strategic . . . keep the case"*: Ben Theunis, interview with author, via telephone, May 4, 2009.

198 *"there was a suggestion"*: Ibid.

198 *"Of course . . . lost an appeal"*: Ibid.

199 *although these lawyers did not fully participate in the court case:* Finotto hired Belgian lawyers Stanislas Le Paige and Pierre Monville; Tavano hired Belgian lawyer Philippe Carsau; and D'Onorio hired Belgian lawyer Patrick Kortleven. These attorneys participated in varying degrees during the trial and in fact didn't even come to court some days. That meant there were times when some defendants were not represented in the proceedings at all.

199 *their lawyers needed to make the difficult decision:* This is similar to what happens in the United States when one is sued and wants to argue that the court in question has no jurisdiction. For example, if a defendant is sued in California over a business dispute that has occurred primarily in Colorado, she could hire a lawyer to argue that the California court lacks jurisdiction in the case, or she could default, just having a lawyer listen to the case but not do anything. In this case, when the plaintiff comes after her in Colorado, she can challenge the original jurisdiction of the California case, but if she loses then, she has to accept the default judgment. We don't have this with criminal cases, as courts need to have custody of the defendant in criminal cases in the United States.

199 *Any dissent about a decision . . . the three of them:* Jean-Charles Verwaest, interview with author, in the courtroom where the appellate level trial was held, Antwerp, September 30, 2008.

200 *"Obviously, he isn't the most innocent . . . for the minimum"*: *Primetime Live*, "The Great Diamond Heist," ABC, February 12, 2004.

200 *"When that gang in fact . . . be five years"*: Jan Heuvelmans, "Parket-Generaal Wil Plots Geen Verwijzing Meer voor Zwiep."

201 *"the Soloist with the Kalashnikov"*: Lodovico Poletto, "Libero e Ricco il Solista del Kalashnikov," *La Stampa* (Turin), April 15, 2008.

201 *"You can see the hand of Pancrazio behind all of this"*: Lodovico Poletto, interview with author, in the *La Stampa* office, Turin, January 16, 2009.

202 *"The guy came back . . . and Agim"*: Denice Oliver, interview with author, in her office, Antwerp, September 29, 2008.

202 *"That guy came back . . . and whatever"*: Ibid.

203 *While Notarbartolo also had an uncle with Mob ties:* Garbutt, "A Chronicle of Criminal Coincidences."

203 *Notarbartolo while he . . . son in Palermo:* Antonino Falleti, interview with author, Turin, September 20, 2008. Also, Garbutt, "A Chronicle of Criminal Coincidences." In the latter account, Notarbartolo claimed he recognized one of the anti-Mafia investigators as the man who took his photo at the wedding in Palermo.

203 *Notarbartolo made calls while in prison to Capizzi's wife:* Garbutt, "A Chronicle of Criminal Coincidences."

203 *Capizzi was the alleged head . . . entire Sicilian Mafia:* Peter Popham, "Mafia Chiefs Seized as They Select Godfather," *The Independent* (London), December 17, 2008.

203 *the Belgian judicial system . . . the United States:* This means that the Belgian public may not get as much information about criminal cases as the American public typically would. Generally, court actions are public record in the United States in the interests of ensuring the transparency of the justice system, unless there's a specific court order sealing them, and even those can be challenged by the public. Not so in Belgium. As a matter of course, information about criminal cases is kept secret. Even lawyers do not have routine access to files, documents, and transcripts of a case once the legal process has concluded, even if they were involved in it.

204 *they would base any decision . . . the program:* Of course, as much as one tries to do so, it is ultimately impossible to completely disregard something like this. A case in the States has a famous quote about this issue: "It is not an easy task to unring a bell, nor to remove from the mind an impression once firmly imprinted there." *State v. Rader*, 62 Or. 37, 40, 124 P. 195, 196 (1912).

205 *"Court-martialled in . . . my absence":* Brendan Behan, *The Hostage*, (London: Methuen & Co, 1958), act 1. This version is from Brendan Behan, *The Complete Plays: The Hostage, The Quare Fellow, Richard's Cork Leg* (New York: Grove Press, 1994), 161.

206 *went to a nearby café to celebrate:* Antonino Falleti, interview with author, Hasselt, Belgium, September 22, 2008.

206 *The visitor's area resembled:* The description of Hasselt Prison is based on a visit there by authors on September 22, 2008.

207 *the Supreme Court of Appeal rejected Notarbartolo's and Tavano's appeals:* Hof van Cassatie on appeal from Hof van Beroep te Antwerpen, file P.05.0907.N, unpublished opinion, October 4, 2005.

207 *the only appeal available to his client:* There also was the European Court of Human Rights, but that was a long shot at best and not a real appeal, just a forum in which to argue that Belgium had violated his human rights.

207 *glossy brochures for property in Cape Verde*: These were found when he was searched in conjunction with his arrest at the Lisbon airport. Patrick Peys, interview with author, in his office, Antwerp, September 23, 2008.

208 *the EAW was a relatively new development:* The Council of the European Union adopted the Council Framework Decision of June 13, 2002, on the European arrest warrant and the surrender procedures between Member States. Framework Decision No. 2002/584/JHA.

As the Portuguese court responsible for deciding whether to extradite D'Onorio explained about the EAW: "Its effectiveness depends on the trust between the EU Member States as to their legal recognition and acceptance and the decisions of their courts. Its aim, agreed by all EU states, is to ensure that criminals cannot escape justice anywhere in the EU." Tribunal da Relação de Lisboa (the Court of Appeal of Lisbon), Case extraditing Elio D'Onorio, Procedure: 2134/2006–5, July 11, 2006.

208 *about two and a half years before:* "In Portugal, Law No. 65/2003, of 23.8, approved the legal regime of the European arrest warrant." Ibid. This law was dated August 23, 2003.

208 *"a violation of the principle . . . Appeal in Antwerp":* D'Onorio argued that this violated "the requirement of a fair trial under the provisions of Article 6 of the European Convention on Human Rights." Ibid.

208 *the Belgian Supreme Court ruled:* Hof van Cassatie on appeal from Hof van Beroep te Antwerpen, file P.06.0614.N, number RC06AV5_1, October 31, 2006. D'Onorio's lawyer for this final appeal was Daniel Vedovatto of Brussels, and Finotto's was Pierre Monville of Brussels.

208 *against D'Onorio's and Finotto's appeals:* While he had been in custody in Portugal, D'Onorio not only fought his extradition from that country, but also he had a lawyer in Belgium working on overturning his conviction there. He and Finotto had instructed their lawyers to not actively participate during the original case, and the May 19, 2005, judgment at the Court of Appeal against them was a default judgment. After losing their case, these two decided to fight their conviction and succeeded in getting a new trial. This time, their lawyers fully represented them and argued on their behalf in court but to no avail. They lost again on March 16, 2006, at the Antwerp Court of Appeal. The court had made a point of noting that they did not consider the DNA evidence to which both men's attorneys objected. Even without the DNA, the evidence was ruled to be sufficient on its own to form the basis of the decision. It was this March 16, 2006, Antwerp Court

of Appeal decision that the Belgian Supreme Court upheld. Hof van Cassatie on appeal from Hof van Beroep te Antwerpen, file P.06.0614.N, number RC06AV5_1, October 31, 2006.

209 *but eventually lost this battle:* The Italian case extraditing D'Onorio to Belgium was La Corte Suprema di Cassazione, Sezione Feriale Penale, Sentenza N. 00013/2007, August 21, 2007. On appeal from the Corte Appello di Roma's decision dated June 26, 2007.

Chapter Thirteen: The Loot

210 A *diamond is the hardest . . . get it back*: Evan Esar, *20,000 Quips & Quotes*, 218.

211 *"For some of them . . . their belongings back"*: Philip Claes, interview with author, in his office at the AWDC, September 22, 2008.

211 *"Some of them . . . recovered it"*: Ibid.

211 *"I still found a . . . anything with that"*: Fay Vidal, interview with author, Antwerp, September 28, 2008.

212 *There were also many things that weren't claimed:* There were a number of reasons items from the floor of the vault never made it back to their original owners. For one, not every heist victim came to the HRD that week to look. Also, some items were simply impossible to identify, so some owners might not have wanted to risk receiving something that actually belonged to someone else. But another possibility is that the items left behind had been obtained illegally in the first place, or they had been smuggled into Belgium to avoid taxes. The fear of facing penalties for tax evasion might have been stronger for some heist victims than the desire to get their goods back. Patrick Peys said it's not unusual that heists and robberies sometimes result in the recovery of goods that no one wants to admit having had in the first place. Patrick Peys, interview with author, in his office, Antwerp, September 23, 2008.

212 *"The most important thing is . . . the diamonds"*: Philip Claes, interview with author, in his office at the AWDC, September 22, 2008.

212 *The reported amount stolen came to . . . and on insurance claims:* From the Court of Appeal of Antwerp judgment in this case on May 19, 2005.

213 *$140 million at the time of writing in July 2009:* The July 2009 rate was about 1.40 euros to the dollar.

213 *"I assure you it's more"*: Patrick Peys, interview with author, in his office, Antwerp, September 23, 2008.

214 *rendered it completely untraceable to the heist:* If gold were mixed with copper, for example, the copper would be extracted using a high-temperature liquid that would bond to the copper but not the gold. Liquefied glass works well. Borax is often added to the mixture to thin the liquid for ease of pouring. Once cooled back into a solid state, the purified gold would have to be smashed out of the copper-infused glass that would form on its surface. Do-it-yourself smelters would probably leave some impurities in the gold.

214 *sold to most fences:* Thieves generally take stolen goods to a fence to sell instead of trying to offload them on their own. In return, they get ten to thirty cents on the dollar on average, as stolen goods sell for much less than legitimate goods and the fence takes a large cut of the profits. For thirty cents on the dollar, *see, e.g.*, Tom Van Riper, "Holiday Thieving Season," *Forbes*, November 15, 2006.

"Rarely do thieves get more than 10 percent of the value of stolen property," said FBI Special Agent Bob Wittman. Eric Noe, "Finding Buyers for Stolen Art," *ABC News*, November 11, 2004. Note that these figures are just for goods in general, they are not specific to diamonds. A famous group of American cat burglars known as "the Dinnerset Gang" received ten cents on the dollar for the diamonds and other gems they stole. *See* Chandra Niles Folsom, "On a Hot Tin Roof," *Fairfield County Weekly*, March 6, 2008.

214 *since eight out of every ten rough diamonds:* "Antwerp World Diamond Center: Strong City, Strong Stone," available online at http://hrd.mia.be/index.php?id=20 (accessed July 5, 2009).

214 *"Dealing in stolen diamonds . . . easy profit":* Patrick Peys, interview with author, in his office, Antwerp, September 23, 2008.

214 *billions of dollars' worth . . . every year:* In 2008, the Diamond District recorded $45 billion in turnover, or the value of transactions among the diamantaires. It's important to note that this isn't the export value. Philip Claes, interview with author, in his office at the AWDC, September 22, 2008.

214 *could have been exported to India:* Rough is polished in Surat, India, if it is too small to be profitably polished in Antwerp, because of the cheap labor available in the subcontinent. Indian polishers earn about 20 rupees (the equivalent of 43.5 cents) for each diamond they work on. This is a big business; out of every eleven rough diamonds, nine are worked on in Surat. The Indian polishing sector has been criticized in the past for using child labor, a practice that hasn't been entirely eradicated—children, it seems, are adept at polishing especially small stones because of their tiny fingers. *See, e.g.*, Aravind Adiga, "Uncommon Brilliance: How Did India Come to Dominate the Vastly Lucrative Global Market for Cutting and Polishing Diamonds?" *Time Asia Edition*, April 12, 2004. But *see* Ranjana Ghosh, "The Hidden Factory: Child Labour in India," *The South Asian*, March 7, 2005.

215 *"The De Beers Sight . . . into the market":* Denice Oliver, interview with author, in her office, Antwerp, September 29, 2008.

215–216 *the temptation to flaunt his share of the take:* Such temptation is an easy way for a thief to get caught. Picture Richard Pryor in *Superman III* when he shows up at work driving a new red Ferrari after having just having robbed his employer in an otherwise untraceable manner.

216 *all Notarbartolo owned was a dog:* Antonino Falleti, interview with author, Turin, September 19, 2008.

216 *"We would give an arm . . . finally closed":* Patrick Peys, interview with author, in his office, Antwerp, September 26, 2008.

216 *"I think they gave up . . . doing with it":* Philip Claes, interview with author, in his office at the AWDC, September 22, 2008.

216 *"If Notarbartolo gets. . . . going to do":* Patrick Peys, interview with author, in his office, Antwerp, September 26, 2008.

217 *"A lot of those victims, they are angry":* Ibid.

217 *The countries that do pose a whole different set of concerns:* For example, South American countries became known for their tolerance of fugitives, but also for their violent criminal organizations. Ronnie Biggs, a British thief who enjoyed a disproportionate amount of fame for a relatively minor role in the Great Train Robbery of 1963, lived openly in Brazil for more than twenty years because the Brazilian government refused to honor Great Britain's extradition request. However, he was kidnapped by bandits and smuggled to Barbados, where his captors attempted to ransom him to Scotland Yard. Peter Muello, "Great Train Robber on the Lam in Brazil Finds British Lion on Trail," Associated Press, October 5, 1997.

217 *Sitting in prison. . . . "Diamonds by Leonardo":* Antonino Falleti, interview with author, Turin, September 17, 2008.

Epilogue

218 *"You're a thief and a liar. . . . Lie": Ocean's Eleven* (2001).

218 *"I may be . . . true story":* Joshua Davis, "The Untold Story of the World's Biggest Diamond Heist," *Wired* magazine (San Francisco), April 2009.

219 *victims had filed a lawsuit:* The suit was still in litigation as of early 2009.

219 *Boost, therefore, . . . the crime:* Interestingly, Boost didn't seem to be against calling the diamond detectives with possible new leads in the case from time to time, such as when she noticed a tenant wearing a fancy new watch or some other high-priced item. In the wake of the heist, Boost was as suspicious of her tenants as they were of her.

219 *Van Camp left . . . than ever:* Gust Van Camp used the heist and his discovery of evidence in his ongoing campaign to clean up the Floordambos. According to a Belgian newspaper article from the early summer of 2008, Van Camp hoped to interest the authorities in draining a polluted canal in the forest by suggesting that the School of Turin had submerged the still-unfound loot from the heist at the bottom of it. Paul Demeyer, "Ruim Deze Beek en de Diamanten Komen Boven," *Nieuwsblad*, May 31, 2008.

220–221 *"The thing that . . . to prosecute":* Patrick Peys, interview with author, in his office, Antwerp, September 26, 2008.

221 *"the greatest story":* Leonardo Notarbartolo, interview with author while in prison, Hasselt, Belgium, September 22, 2008.

221 *Notarbartolo had made a similar offer . . . about the heist:* Todd Moss, a documentary filmmaker whose work appears on American cable networks, told the authors that "money was definitely the sticking point" in trying to negotiate an interview with Notarbartolo while he was still in jail. Through an intermediary, Moss offered him a token $300, which was politely rejected. Todd Moss, interview with author, via telephone, September 16, 2009.

222 *the authors received word . . . according to their e-mail:* The December 27, 2008, e-mail reads in part: "Leo was disappointed that no deal was forthcoming during the time following your visit to him, but he has since managed to finalize an exclusive signed deal with Joshua [Davis] that

satisfied his commercial needs. He has therefore told us he wanted to cut all ties with other journalists." The e-mail was from Falleti's e-mail address, but was signed by both him and Garbutt. Garbutt often helped Falleti compose messages and communicate with the authors because of her better mastery of English.

222 *registered with the California Secretary of State . . . Davis's home address in San Francisco:* Garbutt sent the authors an e-mail on October 8, 2008, with "the information about the company that is trying to make a deal with Leo. They are called underdog.inc." This e-mail included a Santa Monica address which turned out to be a Premier Business Centers location, a company that offers virtual office space and storefronts for small businesses. Incorporation information found at the California Secretary of State's Web site, last accessed on September 16, 2009.

222 *Notarbartolo's friends . . . and Notarbartolo:* Antonino Falleti, e-mail to author, March 13, 2009.

222 *an online video interview:* The video was embedded in the article online; *See* http://www.wired.com/video/trash-foils-diamond-heist/15404460001.

222 *Davis credits his own . . . to talk*: In a series of e-mail exchanges the week of July 23, 2009, *Wired* Articles Editor Mark Robinson said there was no financial arrangement between Davis and Notarbartolo, no promise of a movie deal, and no exchange of money aside from a small reimbursement by Davis to Notarbartolo for the cost of making some phone calls from prison. Robinson had no firsthand knowledge of Davis's discussions with Notarbartolo and referred the authors to Davis for details about the agreement. Davis did not reply to requests for comment. Also, Robinson said Notarbartolo agreed to be interviewed by Davis because he speaks French and because Davis had pursued the story for a long time. However, Antonino Falleti told the authors that Notarbartolo agreed to talk to Davis for a different reason. In an e-mail sent on December 27, 2008, Faletti wrote: "Leo was disappointed that

no deal was forthcoming [from the authors of this book] during the time following your visit to him, but he has since managed to finalize an exclusive signed deal with Joshua [Davis] that satisfied his commercial needs."

222 *"refused to discuss his case"*: The article states that Notarbartolo "has refused to discuss his case with journalists, preferring to remain silent for the past six years. Until now." Joshua Davis, "The Untold Story of the World's Biggest Diamond Heist."

222 *reporters in Belgium, Italy, and the United States*: In Belgium: Jean-Charles Verwaest, interview with author, Antwerp, September 30, 2008. In Italy: Lodovico Poletto, interview with author, in the *La Stampa* office, Turin, January 16, 2009. In the United States: Simon Surowicz, interview with author, via telephone, April 29, 2009.

222 ABC News *producer Simon Surowicz*: Surowicz was the producer of the *Primetime Live* episode on the Antwerp Diamond Heist. Simon Surowicz, interview with author, via telephone, April 29, 2009.

222 *made contact with these authors*: Author Scott Selby initially corresponded with Notarbartolo in March 2006 while Notarbartolo was in prison. Two years later, on March 22, 2008, Notarbartolo's friends contacted the authors on Notarbartolo's behalf and arranged for the authors to meet Notarbartolo in prison.

223 *"Notarbartolo felt like he had stepped into a movie"*: Joshua Davis, "The Untold Story of the World's Biggest Diamond Heist."

224 *"they worked in the dark"*: Ibid. The article did not say why the thieves worked in the dark, the reason given just being an explanation for how they were supposedly able to do this ("[s]ince they had memorized the layout of the vault in the replica").

224 *reported to the diamond detectives*: Patrick Peys, interview with author,

in his office, Antwerp, September 23, 2008. Detail later confirmed on April 24, 2009, in an interview between Jorge Dias De Sousa and author via telephone.

224 *"turned on . . . next box"*; *"muffled flashes"*; *"leather satchels"*: Joshua Davis, "The Untold Story of the World's Biggest Diamond Heist."

225 *Heist victim Fay . . . terrorist attacks:* Fay Vidal, interview with author, via telephone, July 20, 2009.

225–226 *"They did not . . . they took"*: Ibid.

226 *numerous inconsistencies with known facts:* Among the inconsistencies: In the *Wired* article, the thieves couldn't use cell phones in the vault due to a lack of reception, but earlier in the article, one of the diamond detectives was able to call Securilink from his cell phone while "standing inside the vault" with no problem; *Wired* claimed only one bag of garbage was disposed in the Floordambos, when in fact detectives collected four bags of garbage; in *Wired*, the Delhaize receipt was found in Notarbartolo's apartment when in real life it was found in the household garbage bag left with the heist trash in the Floordambos; in *Wired*, the thieves bypassed the vault's sensors by tinkering with wires above the ceiling slats (in the dark, no less), but those wires were not part of the vault's security system; *Wired* also claimed that Italian police broke down the door to the villa in Trana during their first search for supposed illegal weapons, but an officer who was involved in the search told the authors Marco Notarbartolo opened the door for investigators without complaint.

226 *locksmiths would indeed . . . video still:* Professional safecrackers have allowed that this isn't impossible—but the image would have had to be perfect and crystal clear. A smart thief fabricating a key like this would have made several to account for possible variances in the depth of the grooves cut into the bit. Barry Wels, e-mail to author, July 11, 2009.

226 *"directly above [the concierge's] head"*: Joshua Davis, "The Untold Story of the World's Biggest Diamond Heist."

226 *"Nearby, in a storage room . . . video signal"*: Ibid.

226 *"fully functional"*: Ibid.

227 *"What he says is . . . bullshit"*: Patrick Peys, interview with author, via telephone, April 23, 2009.

227 *"the biggest bullshit I've ever heard"*: Ibid.

228 *"We know that . . . the scam"*: Ibid.

228 *"laughed it off . . . in this way"*: Philip Claes, interview with author, via telephone, September 29, 2009.

228 *"I really do . . . on everyone else"*: Patrick Peys, interview with author, via telephone, April 23, 2009.

229 *Falleti successfully called Notarbartolo's cell phone:* Garbutt, "A Chronicle of Criminal Coincidences." Falleti's account predates Notarbartolo's discussion with Davis, and there was no reason at that time for Falleti to lie about his phone conversations with Notarbartolo that day.

229 *"fairy tale"* . . . *"inventions"*: Pietro Tavano, letter to author, April 20, 2009.

230 *D'Onorio claims . . . on the loose:* Elio D'Onorio, interview with author, via telephone, June 11, 2009.

230 *"Who, exactly, is . . . hard to believe"*: "Rants," *Wired* magazine (San Francisco), June 2009, but published online on May 22, 2009. The letter to the editor was attributed to Dave Millman of San Jose, California.

230 *"It's true that . . . been lying"*: Mark Robinson, Articles Editor, *Wired* magazine, e-mail to author, July 29, 2009.

230 *"Notarbartolo's claims . . . check them"*: Ibid., July 30, 2009.

231 *"From what we read . . . absolutely wrong"*: Patrick Peys, e-mail to author, March 29, 2009.

231 *"We participated in . . . his account"*: Agim De Bruycker, interview with author, via telephone, July 17, 2009.

231 Variety *reported on March 16*: Dave McNary and Tatiana Siegel, "JJ Abrams Producing Heist Film; Paramount Pic Based on Wired Article," *Variety*, March 16, 2009.

231 *film producer J. J. Abrams*: Abrams was the Hollywood powerhouse behind such hits as *Felicity*, *Alias*, *Lost*, *Fringe*, *Mission Impossible III*, *Cloverfield*, and *Star Trek* (2009). Abrams was also *Wired*'s guest editor for the magazine's May 2009 issue.

231 *according to* Hollywood Reporter: Jay A. Fernandez and Borys Kit, "Paramount Sets 'Diamond' with J. J. Abrams," *Hollywood Reporter*, March 17, 2009.

231 *Davis to obtain . . . in exchange for telling his story*: According to *Wired*'s Articles Editor Mark Robinson, the magazine reviewed its policies about reporters discussing the possibility of movie deals with their sources after the authors of this book raised questions about Davis's interaction with Notarbartolo. Robinson said in a July 30, 2009, e-mail, "It has sparked some internal discussion here at *Wired* and caused us to think hard about the potential for the appearance of conflict of interest. Going forward, we have decided that writers will not be allowed to make agreements about possible movie deals until after stories are closed." He clarified in a later e-mail that he does not believe there was a conflict of interest in this case. Mark Robinson, e-mails to author, July 29–31, 2009.

231 *an executive producer on the future film:* IMDb Pro, "Untitled J.J. Abrams Diamond Heist Project," Full Credits, available online at http://pro.imdb.com/title/tt1399110/fullcredits (accessed on June 30, 2009).

231 *successfully argued . . . extradition to Belgium:* The Italian case refusing to extradite Finotto to Belgium, instead having him serve his sentence in Italy, was La Corte Suprema di Cassazione, Sezione Penale, Sentenza N. 465, February 12, 2008. This case was on appeal from the Corte Appello di Torino's decision dated December 28, 2007. The Italian case refusing to extradite Tavano to Belgium, instead having him serve his sentence in Italy, was La Corte Suprema di Cassazione, Sezione Sezione Penale, Sentenza N. 464, February 12, 2008. This case was on appeal from the Corte Appello di Torino's decision dated December 28, 2007.

232 *On the afternoon . . . wife's name:* Details about this stop and confiscation of the diamonds found come from interviews with a confidential source, a member of Italian law enforcement with knowledge of this case, via e-mails, July and August 2009.

232 *a brand new . . . hatchback:* The sticker price in Italy was €30,900. Manfred Poschenrieder, Corporate Communications and Policy, BMW, via e-mail, July 20, 2009.

232 *"We are, of course . . . theft in 2003":* Agim De Bruycker, interview with author, via telephone, July 17, 2009.

233 *"It's too long . . . permission to come":* Kris De Bot, interview with author, via telephone, September 22, 2009.

233 *"Leo cannot be condemned . . . selling it":* Agim De Bruycker, interview with author, via telephone, July 17, 2009.

233 *"Maybe it's the beginning . . . recover everything":* Philip Claes, interview with author, via telephone, September 29, 2009.

234 *"The feeling here . . . released so early"*: Ibid.

234 *and a fortune in stolen diamonds*: Joshua Davis told a Belgian newspaper reporter that Notarbartolo claimed that there is no fortune to enjoy, that instead he and his associates had the "20 million euros" in loot (this being the figure that Notarbartolo told Davis) stolen from them by unnamed parties when they had it in an apartment in Milan. Douglas De Coninck, "Dader Kraak van de Eeuw Vrij," *De Morgen* (Brussels, Belgium), March 13, 2009.

INDEX

ABOUT THE AUTHORS

Scott Andrew Selby is a graduate of UC Berkeley and Harvard Law School. He also has a master's degree in Human Rights and Intellectual Property Law from Sweden's Lund University, where he wrote his thesis on diamonds. He is licensed to practice law in California and New York.

Greg Campbell is an award-winning journalist and the author of *Blood Diamonds: Tracing the Deadly Path of the World's Most Precious Stones* and *The Road to Kosovo: A Balkan Diary*. *Blood Diamonds* was used as the primary resource for the Academy Award–nominated film *Blood Diamond*. His work has appeared in the *Economist*, the *Wall Street Journal Magazine*, the *Christian Science Monitor*, and the *San Francisco Chronicle*. He lives with his family in Fort Collins, Colorado.

Visit **www.FlawlessBook.com** for more information about the Antwerp Diamond Heist, photos from research trips to key locations in Belgium and Italy, news updates about the case, and more.